Fascism
and the
Working Class
in Austria, 1918–1934

In the 1920s one in seven Austrians was a member of the socialist Free Trade Union, and one in ten was a member of the Social Democratic Party. The Austrian labour movement was one of the strongest in Europe between the wars with Vienna as the citadel of socialist economics. However, during the early 1930s the Communist and Social Democratic Parties and the Free Trade Unions were outlawed and parliamentary democracy was replaced by fascism. Why was the strong and well-organised Austrian working class unable to defend itself against its destruction? This study examines the reasons for the failure of the Austrian labour movement. Whereas other scholars generally concentrate on Vienna, the author suggests that one has to look outside the capital for an explanation. She shows that it was in the provinces, in Upper Styria in particular, that the labour movement was first broken to give way to working-class fascism.

This was due, she maintains, to employers' tactics, especially the undermining of labour legislation, and to inappropriate policies of the socialist leadership. As a result the Social Democratic Party was deprived of vital support and was fatally weakened in its fight against the growing threat of Austrian fascism.

Jill Lewis is Lecturer in Social History, University College of Swansea.

Fascism
and the
Working Class
in Austria, 1918–1934

The Failure of Labour in the First Republic

Jill Lewis

BERG

New York / Oxford

Distributed exclusively in the US and Canada by
St Martin's Press, New York

First published in 1991 by
Berg Publishers Limited
Editorial Offices:
165 Taber Avenue, Providence R.I. 02906, USA
150 Cowley Road, Oxford, Oxford, OX4 1JJ, UK

© Berg Publishers 1991

Library of Congress Cataloging-in-Publication Data
Lewis, Jill.
  Fascism and the working class in Austria, 1918–1934 : the
failure of labour in the first republic / Jill Lewis.
    236p. 21.6cm.
  Includes bibliographical references and index.
  ISBN 0–85496–581–5
    1. Working class–Austria–Styria–History. 2. Industrial
relations–Austria–Styria–History. 3. Fascism–Austria–
History.
  I. Title.
  HD8419.S82L49 1991
  335.6'09436'509041–dc20   90–41438
                                                         CIP

British Library Cataloguing in Publication Data
Lewis, Jill
  Fascism and the working class in Austria, 1918–1934: the
failure of labour in the First Republic.
  1. Austria. Fascism. Political aspects, history
  I. Title
  320.53309436
  ISBN   0–85496–581–5

Printed in Great Britain by
Billing & Sons Ltd, Worcester

Contents

Contents

Preface

The relationship between fascism and workers has long been a contentious issue. The mass nature of fascist movements and the National 'Socialism' of German fascism sometimes lead students to the false conclusion that such movements attracted large scale working-class support. Recent studies of elections in the Weimar Republic have shown that this was not the case in Germany.[1] There are, however, areas in which fascist groups did appear to have relatively large numbers of working-class voters and members. One of these was in Southern Austria, in the iron and steel district of Upper Styria, where, in 1928, a fascist trade union succeeded in replacing the socialist Free Trade Unions as the representative of organised labour in steel mills, iron foundries and mines. Manual workers became members of the Heimwehr (the Austrian native fascist party) in the later 1920s and a fascist deputy was returned to parliament in 1930.

The existence of this nest of working-class fascism in an old industrial region of Austria is at first perplexing. The Austrian working class was particularly well organised in the 1920s. Membership of the socialist party, the Social Democratic Party (SDAP), was unusually high and included over 10 per cent of the country's small population. The party was vibrant and the activities of its council in 'Red Vienna' culminated in a political and social welfare system which seized the imagination of much of the European Left. Support seemed to be growing throughout the immediate postwar years. In Styria itself, metalworkers and miners played an important part in the 1918 Revolution and fought against right-wing groups in 1927, 1931 and in the civil war of 1934.

1. Richard F. Hamilton, *Who Voted for Hitler?* (Princeton, 1982) and Thomas Childers, *The Nazi Voter: The Social Foundations of Fascism in Germany 1919–1933* (Chapel Hill, 1983). For discussions of NSDAP support amongst manual workers, see: Tim Mason, 'National Socialism and the Working Class 1925–May 1933', *New German Critique*, 11, spring 1977; Detlev Mühlberger, 'The Sociology of the NSDAP: The Question of Working Class Membership', *Journal of Contemporary History*, vol. 15, no. 3, July 1980; Max H. Kele, *Nazis and Workers: National Socialist Appeal to German Labor 1919–1933* (Chapel Hill, 1972). This last source uses a very wide definition of 'worker' which includes white-collar workers.

Preface

The purpose of this book is to explain the development of industrial fascism in this region and to identify the weaknesses within the labour movement which prevented workers from resisting employer coercion to join the Heimwehr. The attitude, philosophy and strategy of the Social Democratic Party are considered in detail, in particular the consequences of its policy of municipal socialism on workers both inside and outside the capital. But the main theme is the effect of unemployment on working-class politics in the interwar years. For this reason, the book concentrates on the industrial structure of the province and the effect which war, revolution and economic crisis had on industrial relations.

Research was carried out in Austria, in Graz and Vienna, and was financed at different times by grants from the SSRC (Social Science Research Council), the British Academy, the University College, Swansea, and the Bundesministerium für Wissenschaft und Forschung der Republik Österreich. Much of the material comes from Styrian police reports, formerly held by the Allgemeines Verwaltungsarchiv, but now held by the Archiv der Republik in Vienna, and the published yearbooks of the Bund der Freien Gewerkschaften and of the Austrian Social Democratic Party. The Bibliothek des Österreichischen Gewerkschaftsbundes, the Statistisches Zentralamt, the Verein der Geschichte der Arbeiterbewegung and the Kammer für Arbeiter und Angestellte (Vienna) provided more material, as did the Kammer für Arbeiter und Angestellte (Graz), the Landesarchiv Steiermark and the International Institute for Social History in Amsterdam. The library and newspaper archive of the Viennese Arbeiterkammer was particularly useful. Dr Frey of the newspaper archive introduced me to Willi Scholz and Ditto Pölzl. Professor Steiner of the Dokumentationsarchiv des Österreichischen Widerstand arranged an interview with Otto Fischer. I would like to thank them, in particular Willi Scholz and Ditto Pölzl, who allowed me to listen to and record them talking to each other about their political activities in the 1930s.

The work began as a doctoral thesis under the supervision of Dick Geary. Progress was halted several times and without his patient, thought-provoking and critical encouragement it would not have been completed. Richard J. Evans read the original thesis and offered very useful (and necessary) advice. Both are leading members of the German History Society which sustained my enthusiasm during some bleak periods and I thank all concerned. Several colleagues and friends in Britain have shown great fortitude over the years, offering time and an ear in times of doubt. To

Martin Blinkhorn, Abe Sirton, Chris Gerry, Richard Newman, Noel Thompson and Kevin Lewis I am also indebted, as well as to Dr A.M. El Sharkawi.

Additional material was collected in Vienna in 1986–7 during a sabbatical year, when I renewed old friendships and made new ones. Siegfried Mattl, Karl Stuhlpfarrer, Heinz Renner, Madelene Wolensky and Wolfgang Maderthaner all helped to provide a congenial and stimulating intellectual environment which, I hope, increased my knowledge of Austrian history and society. Willi Trimmel taxed my brain, corrected my German and challenged me to extend my vision beyond the limits of labour history. He still does. Despite this, I am completely responsible for all the views and arguments presented in this book.

Jill Lewis
Swansea, 1990

Abbreviations

Jb BFG	Jahrbuch des Bundes der Freien Gewerkschaften
Jb ö Ab	Jahrbuch der österreichischen Arbeiterbewegung
Präs	Präsidialakten
SDAP	Sozialdemokratische Arbeiterpartei Deutschösterreich (Austrian Social Democratic Party)
Stat Hdb Österreich	Statistisches Handbuch für die Republik Österreich
St AK	Kammer für Arbeiter und Angestellte Steiermark
St LA	Steiermärkisches Landesarchiv
VA Bundes-kanzleramt 22/Stmk.	Allgemeine Verwaltungsarchiv. Wien, Bundeskanzleramt, Staatsamt des Innern und der Justiz 22/Stmk.
WsJ	*Wirtschaftsstatisches Jahrbuch*

FOR

Sarah Ann Lewis

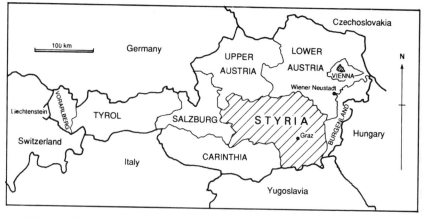

Map 1 The Nine Provinces of Austria

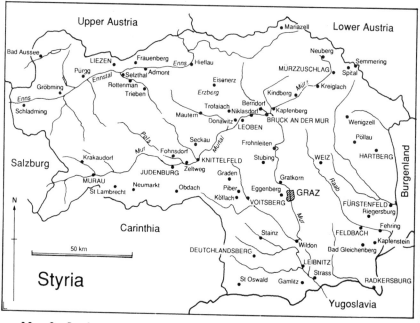

Map 2 Styria

Introduction

On paper it called itself the Austro–Hungarian Monarchy; in speaking, however, one referred to it as Austria, that is to say, it was known by a name that it had, as a State, solemnly renounced by oath, while preserving it in all matters of sentiment, as a sign that feelings are just as important as constitutional law and that regulations are not the really serious thing in life. – There was a parliament which made such vigorous use of its liberty that it was usually kept shut; but there was also an emergency powers act by means of which it was possible to manage without Parliament, and every time when everyone was just beginning to rejoice in absolutism, the Crown decreed that there must now again be a return to parliamentary government. Many such things happened in this State, and among them were those national struggles that justifiably aroused Europe's curiosity and are today completely misrepresented. They were so violent that they several times a year caused the machinery of State to jam and come to a dead stop. But between whiles, in the breathing-spaces between government and government, everyone got on excellently with everyone else and behaved as though nothing had ever been the matter. Nor had anything real ever been the matter. It was nothing more than the fact that every human being's dislike of every other human being's attempt to get on – a dislike in which today we are all agreed – in that country crystallised earlier, assuming the form of a sublimated ceremonial that might have become of great importance if its evolution had not been prematurely cut short by catastrophe.[1]

This sympathetic, if irreverent satire of Imperial Austria, where '[one] spent tremendous sums on the army; but only just enough to assure one of remaining the second weakest among the powers', comes from Robert Musil's *The Man Without Qualities*. Written in Vienna in the 1920s, it reflects a view of the inherent complacency and absurdity of the Empire, a critical reflection which is also found in the more acerbic works of Karl Kraus. The catastrophe to which Musil refers was the First World War and dismemberment of 'Kakania', his mystical name for the Austro–Hungarian Empire.[2]

1. Robert Musil, *The Man Without Qualities*, vol. 1 trans. Eithne Wilkins and Ernst Kaiser (London, 1979), p. 33.
2. The name is derived from k and k (*kaiserlich und königlich* – Imperial and Royal), but also bears a close resemblance to the German slang for human excrement.

He lamented its demise, as did other intellectuals and many Austrian politicians, but his sympathies lay with Kakania's multi-nationalism and lackadaisical political system, rather than the monarchy or dynasty. He regarded the nationalism which destroyed it as a retrogressive step in modern political life. The republic which followed in November 1918, the First Austrian Republic, has since been described as 'a state which could neither live nor die, a state which no-one really wanted'.[3] Viennese crowds did gather to celebrate its announcement on the central Ringstraße, but they were there to fete democracy and peace rather than this new Austria. Not one of the three major parties welcomed the country's birth. German Nationalists yearned for a Greater Germany, while Christian Social members, or many of them, mourned the death of the monarchy. Even the Social Democratic Party (SDAP), which assumed control in the postwar chaos, feared for the political and economic viability of this 'runt' state. 'If we stay independent', the Social Democratic leader, Otto Bauer, wrote in his private papers in 1919, 'then our state will be nothing but a very loose federation of small provinces, and we shall live the life of a dwarf state, cooped up in minute cantons, a life of smallness and pettiness in which nothing noble can prosper, least of all the noblest we know – socialism.'[4] No-one was prepared for the Austria which emerged from war and revolt. The Empire had disintegrated in defeat when the Allied Powers recognised a new political right, that of national self-determination, and extended it to the non-German peoples of Austro–Hungary. Independent states were quickly established in Czechoslovakia, Hungary and Yugoslavia. Austria was, in the words of the French Prime Minister, Clemenceau, 'that which was left over', seven (later nine) provinces, covering 78,061 square kilometres and with a population (then) of 6 million.[5]

One aspect of the political and intellectual disillusion with the new Austria was lack of prestige, post-imperial depression. The influence of the educated German bourgeoisie had extended over much of central Europe and Vienna's cultural flowering at the turn of the century was, to a large extent, the product of middle-class migration from Bohemia, Moravia and the farthest fringes of the Empire.[6] Vienna was a cosmopolitan city, the centre of a European

3. Bruno Kreisky, *Zwischen den Zeiten. Erinnerungen aus fünf Jahrzehnten* (Berlin, 1986), p. 40.
4. Quoted in Karl Stadler, *Austria* (London, 1971), p. 110.
5. Burgenland was incorporated in 1919. Vienna became a separate province in 1921.
6. See Carl E. Schorske, *Fin-de-Siècle Vienna* (London, 1980). For a criticism of

multinationalism which was now dead. In 1918 it became the 'centre' of one of the smallest states on the Continent. But the problem was not just one of size; there was also a lack of cohesion. There had been no 'Austrian' nationalism based on language and culture. The people of the new Austria were German-speaking, with a German culture, but not one which had been part of a specifically German state. German–Austrians had been united politically long before their neighbours to the west and, outside Pan–German circles, support for unification had steadily decreased since the 1880s.[7]

In the truncated 'dwarf state' such support was revitalised. This needs to be put into context. When the Imperial State collapsed in 1918 a provisional government was established, drawn from the elected members of the 1911 parliament and representing the three major parties, the Christian Social Party (72 members), the Social Democratic Party (42 members) and the National Association, an alliance of German–National and liberal parties (102 members). Despite being the smallest party, the SDAP dominated the new government and held most of the important ministries. Karl Renner became chancellor and Otto Bauer, to whom leadership of the party had passed after the death of its founder, Viktor Adler, became foreign minister. Bauer led the Austrian delegation at the Paris Peace Conference which followed the war, where he argued for unification with Germany, supported, naturally, by the Nationalists.

The position of the Christian Social Party was different. The transition from Empire to Republic had proceeded with ease, greatly due to the attitude of the last Imperial government. This had been headed by the Christian Social leader, Lammasch, and had included his successor as party leader, Ignaz Seipel. It was Seipel, a theology professor and Jesuit priest, who drew up the statement of 11 November 1918 in which the Emperor announced that he would

Schorske's thesis and a lucid account of the Jewish influence, see Stephen Beller, *Vienna and the Jews* (Cambridge, 1989). Working-class migration into Vienna was not German, but Slav, Czech, etc., which explains the lack of working-class German nationalism.

7. German nationalism had been a powerful force, culminating in the 1882 Linz Programme. This was drawn up by, amongst others, George van Schönerer and Viktor Adler. Adler later abandoned nationalism and founded the Social Democratic Party, based, theoretically, on Marxist doctrine, at Hainfeld in December 1888. See: Stadler, *Austria*, pp. 82–3; Barbara Jelavich, *Modern Austria. Empire and Republic 1800–1980* (Cambridge, 1987), pp. 69–70. These two books are the best introductions to modern Austrian history. See also Andrew Whiteside, *The Socialism of Fools: Georg Ritter van Schönerer and Austrian Pan Germanism* (Berkley, 1975).

'renounce all participation in state affairs'.[8] There was no formal abdication, only a reluctant acceptance of a fait accompli. The same attitude was again adopted by Seipel, when he pledged the Christian Social Party to the new Republic in these begrudging terms:' The Emperor in advance has recognised the decision which German–Austria will make concerning its future form of government. We do not want to be more imperial than the Emperor, and therefore we submit to the will of the people.'[9] As a statement of support, it could not have been more lukewarm. But the Christian Social Party was a curious creature, an amalgam of monarchist conservatism and Catholic populism, and did nothing to hinder the establishment of the Republic.[10] Nor did the German–National camp, whose aim was still unification with Germany, but whose support had been dissipated by the war and revolution. In September 1920 seventeen nationalist groups formed the Greater German People's Party, but its role in the Republic was limited.

The Social Democratic Party's attitude to the Republic is the most perplexing. Avowedly Marxist since birth, it had played an important role in the Second International and had close links with the trade union movement. Of all Austrian political parties, its links with the Empire were the strongest. There had been Czech, Polish, Slav and Italian sections of the SDAP. Before the war Karl Renner and Otto Bauer had both written at length on the national question, seeking to reconcile the class basis and internationalism of their theory with the popular and powerful nationalist movements in the Empire. Renner's conclusion was that national identity had to be recognised, but should not lead to territorial independence. In this he endorsed the multinational state, but not the Habsburg Empire.[11]

The disintegration of that multinational state destroyed the basis of this analysis. But the SDAP did not criticise the Republic on the grounds of an antipathy to the concept of the nation-state, but due to practical considerations. The 'dwarf state', it argued, was unviable. It was a land of Alpine provinces in the centre and west tacked onto a relatively vast capital and industrial periphery whose economic links stretched north and eastwards. The new Austria was incongruous, its economy disjointed. Having accepted the

8. Jelavich, *Modern Austria*, p. 153.
9. Quoted in Klement von Klemperer, *Ignaz Seipel* (Princeton, 1972), p. 106.
10. Jill Lewis, 'Conservatives and Fascists in Austria, 1918–34', in Martin Blinkhorn (ed.), *Fascists and Conservatives. The Radical Right and the Establishment in Twentieth-Century Europe* (London, 1990), pp. 98–117.
11. Stadler, *Austria*, pp. 74–7.

inevitability of the independence of the Successor States, Otto Bauer argued at the Paris Peace Conference that only unification with Germany could prevent economic and political disaster. It would also further his ambition for socialism by uniting the Austrian working-class movement with the larger and politically mature German movement. This, he argued in the *Arbeiter-Zeitung* in October 1918, would create the conditions in which the Austrian working class could prevail against the resistance of the ruling class.[12] And so the party of multinationalism turned to *Anschluß* as the only pragmatic solution to the predicament in which it found itself in 1918.[13]

The reactions of politicians did not bode well for the First Austrian Republic and their fears were justified. The country was politically divided. The first general election in 1920 was a victory for the Christian Social Party and German Nationalists, who between them won 108 of the 174 seats. The SDAP won 66 and went into opposition, where it remained. But the results indicated a serious geographical division, for the socialists' successes were overwhelmingly in industrial regions and in Vienna in particular, whilst the non-socialist parties were equally strong in the provinces. Although the Christian Social Party, under Seipel's leadership, remained the party of government throughout almost the entire period, it never had an absolute majority and its support declined in the mid-1920s.

Socialist support, however, grew. After 1927 the SDAP needed just 200,000 more votes to win an outright victory. Moreover, both sides were armed. Paramilitary groups mushroomed in the postwar years. On the Right, Seipel fostered and protected the Heimwehr, a group of anti-socialist militias, which were used to break up strikes and socialist demonstrations. On the Left, the socialists organised their own paramilitary, the Schutzbund, which trained, drilled and regulated those very same demonstrations. In Vienna in July 1927 one demonstration left 89 dead (see Chapter 8). Class tensions were heightened and from then on bloody battles between the two sides became weekly occurrences. The Heimwehr regrouped, adopted a crude form of fascism and was taken into government by the Christian Social Party. The fighting continued. In 1933 the government prorogued parliament and ruled by decree, banning strikes and demonstrations and outlawing the

12. Hans Haas, 'Otto Bauer und der Anschluß 1918–1919', in Helmut Konrad (ed.), *Sozialdemokratie und Anschluß* (Vienna, 1978), pp. 36–44.

13. The SDAP maintained a policy of *Anschluß* until 1933, but its enthusiasm waned when the German Socialists failed to maintain power.

small Communist Party and the much larger Schutzbund. In February 1934 the Christian Social Chancellor, Engelbert Doll-fuß, and his Heimwehr State Secretary for Security, Fey, ordered troops to attack Social Democratic offices throughout the country and civil war broke out. The Social Democrats were defeated and outlawed and in May 1934 the government introduced a new constitution based on fascist principles.[14]

The crescendo of violence which became symbolic of Austria in the 1920s and early 1930s cannot be explained adequately in such crude terms. Economic weakness, which the politicians had fore-seen in 1919, underlay much of the tension and caused political polarisation. The Christian Social and Social Democratic parties were divided by more than their attitudes to monarchy and the regional bases and comparable strengths of their support. They had totally opposing views on the nature of the democratic state and, more importantly, the means of solving the chaos of the Republic's economy.

The terms of the Paris Peace Settlement, the establishment of foreign borders just thirty miles from Vienna, cut Austria off from her industrial and agricultural hinterland. The immediate postwar danger was shortage of food, but in the longer term the loss of industrially advanced areas and coal-bearing regions to Czechoslo-vakia hit industrial output and also removed markets for Austrian goods. Before the war the Empire had had one of the lowest levels of foreign trade in Europe; afterwards, Austria was dependent on imported foods, raw materials and manufactured goods. The Viennese administrative and financial sectors had served the entire Empire; in 1919 these also were truncated.

As Karl Stadler has shown, the arguments over Austria's econ-omic viability raged in the 1920s and 1930s and continued into the 1940s.[15] In the 1920s the situation looked bleak, if not dire. In addition to *Anschluß*, there were plans to set up a Danubian Federa-tion, an economic union which would have restored the Empire, to a limited extent. This was favoured by the monarchist wing of the Christian Social Party as well as by some economists, but it came to nothing. Instead, production slumped and inflation hit the econ-omy. Registered unemployment was 16,217 in January 1921, by January 1923 it had risen to 161,227.[16] Between 1920 and 1922 the coalition government tried in vain to raise foreign loans to alleviate

---

14. See Lewis, 'Conservatives and Fascists', pp. 99–103.
15. Stadler, *Austria*, pp. 117–25.
16. See Table 4 in Appendix to this volume, pp. 214–15.

the country's economic problems. In 1922 Seipel became chancellor and by skilful, if at times duplicitous, negotiations with foreign governments he succeeded where his predecessors had failed and obtained loans which were underwritten by Britain, France, Czechoslovakia and Italy. In return he agreed to carry out a series of financial reforms (*Sanierung*) under the direction of the League of Nations. A League representative remained in Vienna overseeing drastic cuts in government expenditure. The economy was stabilised over three years, but concessions which the Austrian public were forced to make in the form of high indirect taxation, unemployment and decreased public services incensed the opposition.

This was the crux of the argument between the government and the Social Democratic Party in the 1920s. The SDAP had gone into opposition in 1920, but only after it had managed to pass a series of laws designed to protect the working class both at work and at home. These conflicted with Seipel's *Sanierung* policy. The most important were unemployment benefit, an eight-hour working day and rent restrictions.[17] Once out of government, the socialists concentrated their efforts on Vienna, the party's main area of support, exploiting the relative economic autonomy which the federal constitution gave the capital. They established an alternative economic strategy, based on high progressive taxation and high public expenditure, which was directly contrary to government policy. Moreover, the parliamentary party consistently and effectively opposed government attempts to cut national welfare expenditure and rent controls, at least for some years.

The Austrian economy did stabilise after 1924, but this was short-lived. Bank scandals in 1924 undermined confidence in the country's financial institutions, precipitating the collapse of a number of small banks and the larger Depositenbank. The banks which survived, including the four largest, Creditanstalt, Bodencreditanstalt, the Wiener Bankverein and the Niederösterreichische Escompte-Gesellschaft, were heavily dependent on foreign investment and closely tied to Austrian industry. In 1929 Bodencreditanstalt failed and was absorbed by Creditanstalt. The subsequent collapse of Creditanstalt itself in May 1931 heralded an economic and political crisis.[18] Between 1929 and 1931 industrial production fell by 39 per

17. The rent restrictions had been set up during the war, but the SDAP fought to retain them in 1919 and thereafter.

18. See Karl Ausch, *Als die Banken fielen* (Frankfurt am Main, 1968) and Edward März, *Austrian Banking and Financial Policy* (New York, 1984). According to Martin Kitchen, Bodencreditanstalt was closely associated with the Christian Social party and the Heimwehr. The government put pressure on the head of Creditanstalt,

cent and unemployment nearly doubled. Attempts to set up a customs union with Germany in 1931 were stifled by the French government and the Austrian economy fell into deeper decline. At the same time, political conflict intensified. The SDAP came nearest to political victory in 1927, when it became the largest single party in parliament, but without an overall majority it remained in opposition. Attacks on its members increased, but the party seemed incapable of defending itself. In 1933 it protested against the suspension of democratic rights, hoping to prevent this by legal and constitutional means. In 1934 it was itself smashed. The 200,000 extra votes it had needed to win power did not materialise, while it had failed to see the growing threat of fascism, even within what appeared to be its own ranks.

From 1928 onwards working-class support for the Heimwehr appeared to have been building in one industrial region of Austria, Upper Styria. The purpose of this book is to examine the failure of the Austrian labour movement in the First Republic, concentrating on this one area. The main thesis is that events in Styria illustrate the fundamental weakness of the SDAP, which never adjusted to its new political situation. The spectacle of workers in Heimwehr uniform and with Heimwehr membership cards was shocking for party leaders, but they did little to counter it. Yet, as events in the industrial centre of Upper Styria show, few joined the Heimwehr by choice, more out of fear of unemployment. Their actions were an indictment of employer policy, but also of the tactics of the party, which said it represented the interests of Austrian workers. To the SDAP's cost, its heart lay almost exclusively in Vienna.

Most modern studies of the Austrian labour movement in the First Republic concentrate on the activities of the Social Democratic Party in Vienna for several valid reasons. In the first place, almost one-third of Austria's entire population lived and worked in the capital, which was not only the major centre of administration and government, but also the largest industrial region in the country.[19] Secondly, the proportion of the city's population which supported and joined the Social Democratic Party was unusually high: in 1930 one in every three adult inhabitants of Vienna was a party member.

Rothschild, to persuade him to take over Bodencreditanstalt. To quote: 'Chancellor Schober announced that he had used a machine gun rather than a pistol to convince Rothschild to acquiesce.' Martin Kitchen, *The Coming of Austrian Fascism* (London, 1980), p. 91.

19. The population of Austria was 6,534,481 in 1923. 1,865,780 people lived in Vienna, 1,480,449 in Lower Austria and 978,845 in Styria. (*St at Hdb Österreich* 1927, p. 2.)

Both the Social Democratic Party and the socialist Free Trade Unions consistently drew over half their respective memberships from within its boundaries.[20] But size alone does not explain the extraordinary dominance which the capital had over the labour movement. There were important political reasons stemming from 1920, when the Social Democratic Party withdrew from the coalition government and went into opposition. From this point on its primary goal was to win an outright victory in a national election and be returned to power. The strategy it adopted, concentrating on the only province it controlled, Vienna, was radical. It sought to create a working model of socialism which would provide voters with concrete evidence that the party's alternative political strategy was not only practical, but also eminently more attractive than that of the national government. The intention was to prove both to supporters and non-supporters that socialism did offer a viable alternative to bourgeois economics.

What began as an election strategy soon escalated. During the fifteen years of the First Republic the city became the main symbol of Austro–Marxism, the attempt to find a midway path for socialism between the Marxism–Leninism of Soviet Russia and the reformism of German Social Democracy. It was the focal point of a major and relatively successful experiment in socialist economics, which stood out in stark contrast to the conservative fiscal policies adopted by most European governments, including Austria's own. This experiment was only made possible by the size and strength of socialist electoral support in the city, which gave the party an overall majority in the council chamber, and by postwar legal reforms, which allowed a considerable degree of financial autonomy.[21] Whilst governing coalitions procured foreign loans in order to stabilise the national economy, the Viennese council pursued a radical and controversial programme of high taxation and high public-sector expenditure, designed to minimise unemployment, improve the quality of life for its working-class supporters and still keep the city out of debt. 'Red Vienna', therefore, played a crucial role in the Social Democratic Party's national strategy for winning power through the ballot box and laying the foundations for a socialist society by democratic means.

As important as the capital was, it still only represented one part of the labour movement, for it should go without saying that if

20. See Tables 1 and 2 in Appendix to this volume, pp. 211–12.
21. Jill Lewis, 'Red Vienna: Socialism in One City, 1918–27', *European Studies Review*, vol. 13, no. 3, July 1983, p. 341.

roughly one half of its membership was found in Vienna, the other half was in the provinces. This is where some of the difficulties for the historian lie, for the cohesion of the socialist movement in Vienna was so great in comparison with the rest of the country that its development was in many ways unique. A study of the Viennese labour movement, or even of its socialist party, cannot offer a full explanation of the fate of the national movement as a whole. The difference between capital and provinces was too great.

The structure of working-class movements in the provinces differed from that of the capital in several fundamental ways. Nowhere else was the Social Democratic Party able to win a majority in a provincial assembly. As a result, economic autonomy, which Vienna enjoyed because of its status as a province, benefited Christian Social and German Nationalist provincial governments elsewhere in the country. There was no opportunity outside the capital for the socialists to put their policies into practice. In addition, of the three other major industrial areas of Austria, only one, Lower Austria, had a large concentration of industrial workers in a single city, Wiener Neustadt. In the other two areas, Styria and Upper Austria, working-class communities were dispersed. This was particularly true of Upper Styria, where small industrial towns were dotted along an industrial belt which ran for over a hundred miles from Mürzzuschlag in the east to Judenburg and Fohnsdorf in the west, and was linked with Graz to the south. As a result, the working-class communities in this area lacked the internal security of the Viennese working class which resulted from its sheer size and the frequent social interaction of its members. Branches of the Social Democratic Party in Styria were small, poorly financed and able to provide neither the array of cultural activities of the capital's party, nor its housing and welfare benefits.

There was a further and more deep-rooted difference between Vienna and industrial areas in the provinces. Trade union tradition, which lay with the skilled sectors of the industrial working class, was noticeably stronger in the capital than it was elsewhere, for economic reasons. The diversification of industry and the high proportion of skilled workers in Vienna created a solid base for trade unionism, which was unrivalled elsewhere. The machine industry of Wiener Neustadt also employed larger numbers of skilled workers, but the scarcity of alternative employment in the area ultimately made the workforce more vulnerable than their Viennese comrades to fluctuation in the domestic economy. Once out of work, it was difficult to find another job without moving.

This situation was even more evident in Styria, where industrial employment was dominated by mining and metallurgy, both of which had a relatively low skill factor, and those industries were in turn partially dominated by a single company, the Alpine Montangesellschaft.[22] The structure of the Styrian labour movement, its size, geographical distribution and economic base, was so different from that of Vienna that it provides a clear contrast for any study of the Austrian working class in the interwar years. Moreover, if the Social Democratic Party was to achieve the electoral success for which it yearned in the 1920s, it needed to expand its support in areas with working-class communities, such as Styria. It could be argued that the party exhausted its electoral potential in Vienna in the 1930 national election, when it polled 59 per cent of the city's total vote, but still failed to gain an overall majority in the country.[23] In the provinces the problems of potential voters were acute, but were different from those in Vienna. The failure both of party and union leaders to address these problems ultimately cost more than votes.

These points illustrate only part of the importance of the Styrian labour movement, for there were other factors which are pertinent to any study of European working-class organisations in the interwar years. The first of these was that trade unionism in the province, which expanded rapidly in the immediate postwar years, was unable to sustain itself. Membership fell drastically in the mid-1920s, long before the international depression of the 1930s which is often cited as the main cause of union weakness between the wars.[24] Secondly, in 1928 the mining and metal districts of Upper Styria became the base of a non-socialist trade union which was closely affiliated to the native fascist Styrian Heimwehr and later to the National Socialist Party.[25] As a result, Styria appears at first glance to provide one of the few clear examples of working-class

22. In 1921 the Alpine Montangesselschaft employed 17,550 workers in Styria. See August Zahlbruckner, 'Die Technische Entwicklung', in Fritz Erben, Maja Loehr and Hans Riehl (eds.), *Die Alpine Montangesellschaft* (Vienna, 1931), p. 61. The earliest available figures for industrial employment in the province are for 1925, when 86,425 were employed in 1,037 plants. *WsJ*, 1925, p. 235. By that time employment in the Alpine Montangesselschaft had fallen to 15,000. (*Der Tag*, 24 September 1925.)

23. *Jb ö Ab* 1930, p. 149.

24. See Table 2 in Appendix to this volume, p. 212.

25. The Heimwehr was not a unified movement, but made up of a number of separate groups. In Styria some were known as Heimwehr and some as Heimatschutz. To avoid confusion the term Heimwehr is used wherever possible in this book. For details of the divisions see C. Earl Edmondson, *The Heimwehr and Austrian Politics, 1918–36*, (Athens, Georgia, 1978).

support for fascism in Europe before the Second World War. Finally, although the organisational structure of the working-class movement was weak in the province, or perhaps because of this, the instances of political violence were unusually high. From 1927 onwards, internal civil conflict raged in Upper Styria. In the civil war itself Styria was the scene of some of the most resolute and determined resistance by members of the working class.[26] This followed a history of armed conflict in the province which dated back to the Revolution of 1918, when Styrian workers took part in strikes and minor riots. In 1927 the socialist council of Bruck an der Mur in Upper Styria was accused of setting up a 'soviet dictatorship' during a national general strike. Nor was militancy a prerogative of the Styrian Left, for the most stridently active section of the Austrian Heimwehr also had its base in Upper Styria, from where it launched a putsch attempt in September 1931. Interspersed between these more important events were numerous battles between Heimwehr and socialist supporters, resulting in a higher level of political violence in this province than anywhere else in Austria.

The Styrian labour movement offers the opportunity to study three important and related aspects of the First Austrian Republic: the impact of structural and crisis unemployment on one region; the rise of industrial fascism; and, finally, the effectiveness, or rather ineffectiveness, of Social Democratic policy outside Vienna. It is a main contention of this book that the policies of the Social Democratic Party, as they evolved both during and after the Revolution, were inapplicable to at least one half of its supporters, those who lived outside the capital; their suitability for Vienna is also questioned. Styrian workers were insufficiently skilled and organised to resist the economic offensive which was waged against them in the 1920s under the guise of rationalisation by intransigent employers. This was the other side of Austrian socialism, the failure of the party to come to terms with the economic realities of its members' day-to-day lives and to check the increasing weakness of its provincial parties. The 'success' of 'Red Vienna' camouflaged these failures and this in itself may have exacerbated them.

The book is therefore a case-study, but one which is set in the context of the development of Austro–Marxism in the interwar period and the initial stages of Austrian fascism. Rather than concentrating on party politics and theoretical debates, I have chosen to investigate the repercussions which both had at the street

26. Ilona Duczynska, *Workers in Arms* (New York and London, 1978), p. 173.

level in a crucial area. This, I believe, reflects the history of Austrian socialism and the First Republic at least as clearly, if not more so, than do studies of Vienna.

The origins of the conflict in Styria lie not only in the politics of the Republic itself, but also in the structure of its industry and the nature of its labour market. For this reason, the book begins with a detailed account of the development of industry in the province before the war and the effect this had on industrial relations and the labour movement. War changed the attitudes of workers, while revolution altered the legal framework of labour relations and for a short time shifted the province's political balance in favour of the workers, as it did throughout the country. It was in this context that the Social Democratic Party produced its programme for the democratic progression to socialism, which culminated in the socialist experiment, 'Red Vienna'. The basis for this programme and its implementation are considered in Chapter 5 and are discussed both as an exercise in social reform and as a wider national policy. At the same time as the party was establishing its citadel in the capital, Styrian workers were losing the limited rights they had won by revolution. By 1927 the working class had been forced into a defensive position. Political violence began as a battle within industry itself over the position of organised labour, fought by workers on one side and an alliance of the employers and the Heimwehr on the other. The early conflict took place in the factories, but when this became legally and economically impractical for workers, fighting spilled out onto the streets and was transformed from a basically industrial dispute with political overtones into a crude battle of class politics which the Social Democratic Party lost.

−1−

The Structure of Styrian Industry

Labour protest in Styria in the First Republic can be divided roughly into two phases. Between 1919 and 1924 the Free Trade Unions mounted an aggressive campaign on behalf of their members to improve wages and working conditions. When this failed it was followed by a period of overt conflict between the industrial and petty bourgeoisie of northern Styria on the one hand and their primary political antagonists, the socialist working class, on the other. Thus one major factor which affected both the level of class conflict in the region and the character of working-class protest was the inability of the trade unions to protect industrial workers against falling wages and worsening conditions. This failure was due partly to adverse economic conditions in the province in the 1920s and partly to a weak local tradition of trade unionism which dated back to the last decades of the nineteenth century. The structure and nature of Styrian industry hindered the early development of a strong trade union movement, despite the size of the industrial proletariat.

In general terms the propensity of a workforce to organise is dependent on a series of factors which include the legal position of trade unions and the extent of their recognised role in industrial relations, the structure and size of industry, the level of skill in that specific industry, the attitude of the employer, and economic conditions such as the level of unemployment. In addition, the presence or absence of a tradition of trade union activity amongst the workers can have an effect on the level of trade unionism. In Styria the tradition of trade unionism was particularly weak in the 1920s. The large units of production which characterised the metal industry in the province were very difficult to organise in the face of concerted opposition by employers which dated back to the days before the First World War. Secondly, the level of skill required by heavy industry was low. As a result the early trade unions, which were chiefly designed to protect the status and income of skilled worker, were less attractive to the Styrian metalworkers, who formed the largest sector of the labour force, than they were to metalworkers in Vienna or Wiener Neustadt. This had been the case in the days of the Habsburg Empire and was also the case during the First Republic. Finally, Styria was an area of heavy industry and was particularly susceptible to fluctuations in the economy, for it was a basic producer of crude and semi-manufactured goods and therefore depended directly on demand from other industrial sectors, most obviously the machine and engineering industries.

The very term 'metal industry' can itself be deceptive for there are two areas of metalwork, the first being metallurgy or metal production, which produced crude iron and steel, and the second being metal processing, that is the work of the engineering works and machine shops which transformed the basic products into finished products. In many regions these two sectors developed side by side in the same geographical location, each dependent on the other and each employing workers who were organised in a common metalworkers' union. However, the level of skill required by the respective industries and, hence, the level of trade union activity found amongst the workforce were notably different. Engineering workers employed in metal processing were more receptive to the ideas of trade unionism than were their colleagues in metal production. These differences were often disguised by the close proximity in which the two sectors operated. However, in Austria, where the two sectors were geographically divided between the metallurgical plants of Styria and the engineering works of Vienna and Wiener Neustadt, the differences were obvious. Both before and after the First World War Styrian metalworkers failed to establish a strong trade union spirit and one cause of this was the structure of the industry in which they were employed.

The mining of iron ore and lignite and the processing of iron and steel dominated Styrian industry. In 1928, despite a recession in the steel industry, 32 per cent of the province's total workforce was employed in heavy industry.[1] Moreover, mining and metal production had a long history in the province and, according to local legend, the iron ore mines on the banks of the river Mur were the gift of Providence. The story is told in this way. In the days of the Roman Empire the area was conquered and its inhabitants were forced to pay homage to the Roman Emperor and his gods. After some time the people rebelled and successfully drove the invaders southwards out of their land. As the last Roman disappeared over the horizon, the Spirit of Good appeared to the people and offered them the choice of three treasures: gold mines for a year, silver

1. *St AK* 1928, p. 197.

mines for twenty years or iron ore mines for ever. The locals, so the story goes, were a canny people: they chose iron for ever.[2]

This is the most attractive account of the origins of the iron industry in Styria. Unfortunately, reality is more bleak. Iron ore had been mined in the region in small amounts for many centuries, as far back as Roman times, but it was overshadowed at that time by the more famous iron-bearing regions which stretched from Schwaz in the Tyrol to Reichenau in Lower Austria, the house of Roman Nordic steel. By 1276, when Rudolf of Habsburg first acquired land in Austria, the northern regions were suffering from a shortage of fuel as many of the forests had been depleted. As a result, ironmasters began to trek south into the mountains and forests of northern Styria, lured by the abundance of wood, easily accessible iron ore deposits and the river Mur, which provided water and transport. The Styrian ironworks prospered and by the eighteenth century they were exporting products as far as France. By 1767, the dawn of the industrial age, Styria was producing as much pig-iron as all the English works combined.[3]

Soon afterwards, the area began to fall into relative decline, caused by a series of debilitating depressions and the technological modernisation in metal production. The first depression came soon after the Napoleonic Wars, when the demand for high-grade steel, suitable for making weapons, dried up and steam power reduced the attractiveness of the area, which had been based on the high grade of its iron ore and the close proximity of wood for fuel. Consequently, during the early decades of the nineteenth century, the area was most noted for its export of skilled craft workers.

The plight of the industry deepened in 1834 with the formation of the German Zollverein, or customs union, from which Austria was excluded, thus cutting Styria off from one of its major markets. As a consequence the industry fell into a deep depression caused not only by the loss of markets and the shortage of skilled labour, but also by the development of new and capital intensive production processes based on steam power and later coke. Although the area had previously had its own domestic fuel, there was no coking coal in the vicinity, and local firms were forced to import supplies at a higher cost. The iron industry fell into a relative decline.

---

2. Hans Pirchegger and Rudolf Töpfner, *Eisen Immerdar* (Graz, 1951), Introduction.

3. Herbert Matis and Karl Bachinger, 'Österreichs industrielle Entwicklung', in Alois Brusatti, *Die wirtschaftliche Entwicklung*, (Vienna, 1973), p. 159.

Another blow fell during the Great Depression of the 1870s, which had a devastating effect on the Austrian economy and forced the state to sell off its interests in the Innerberger company, based near the iron ore mountain at Eisenerz, in order to meet a war debt of 20 million Talern.[4] At first the Styrian provincial government discussed the possibility of buying the company itself, so ensuring the continuation of production by leasing or selling individual works to private investors. But the era of small-scale iron and steel production was already over and the industry was in desperate need of the type of large-scale capital investment which could not be secured by piece-meal measures. This crisis resulted in the amalgamation of the majority of small works in the province into six major companies.[5] This again proved inadequate and by 1881 all six companies were amalgamated into one large firm, the Alpine Montangesellschaft.

By this time, production processes in the industry were archaic. Smelting was primarily fuelled by charcoal: of the 33 blast furnaces the company acquired, 5 were beyond repair, 25 were wood-based and only 3 small furnaces had been converted to coke. The links between wood and the iron industry were also reflected in the company's other holdings: in addition to 37 mines, some of which produced high-grade iron ore and some of which produced useful but relatively unprofitable lignite, the company also owned 24 forest estates, which had provided charcoal for the furnaces.[6]

The long-term aim of the Alpine Montangesellschaft management was to control metal production from the raw materials through the stages of semi-manufacturing and so compete with the Austrian Empire's major steel area in Bohemia. Its first priority was to rationalise, modernise and consolidate its holdings, allowing each plant to specialise in one area of production.[7] Many of the smaller works were closed and a few sold off to neighbouring companies, in particular Böhler in Kapfenberg and the Felten and Guilleaume company in Bruck an der Mur, which continued to

---

4. Pirchegger and Töpfner, *Eisen Immerdar*, pp. 20–40. The Bessemer process was in commercial use in Britain by 1860. It was followed soon after in Germany by the Siemens Martin process.

5. The six companies were: Aktionsgesellschaft der Innerberger Hauptgewerkschaft; Vordernberg-Köflach Montanindustriegesellschaft; Steierische Eisenindustrie; Egyd-Kindberger Eisen und Stahlindustriegesellschaft; Eisen- und Stahlgewerkschaft zu Eibiswald und Krumbach; Neuberger-Mariazeller Gewerkschaft. See Heinz Strakele, *Die Österreichische Alpine Montan-Gesellschaft* (Vienna, 1946), p. 8.

6. Fritz Erben, Maja Loehr and Hans Riehl (eds.), *Die Alpine Montangesellschaft* (Vienna, 1931), p. 46.

7. Fritz Klenner, *Die österreichischen Gewerkschaften* (Vienna, 1953), vol. 1, p. 689.

produce specialised steels. The forest regions were sold and the profit from this was re-invested in the larger plants, in particular the centre of the company's steel production at Donawitz. Coking furnaces replaced charcoal furnaces, and obsolete processes, such as the production of wrought iron by puddling, were abandoned. Fuel remained a problem: lignite was mined at Fohnsdorf, Leoben and Voitsberg-Köflach, but it was unsuitable for smelting, because of the low level of heat it produced. Modern steel production techniques required coal, to be more precise coking coal, and this was unavailable in the area. Whereas the earlier ironworks had supplied their own wood for charcoal furnaces, as well as iron ore, the coal now had to be transported long distances from the coal-fields of Bohemia and Silesia. Twenty years earlier this would have been impossible, but the extension of the railway system simplified transportation and the establishment of the Austrian iron cartel in 1885 eased the transactions. A close relationship then developed between the Styrian and Bohemian iron industries and this was further strengthened in 1897, when the Bohemian steel magnate, Karl Wittgenstein, bought a major shareholding in the Alpine Montangesellschaft.[8] Coal was no longer a problem for the company – until the outbreak of the First World War.

Although amalgamation and rationalisation of the Alpine Montangesellschaft ensured the survival of the Styrian iron and steel industry, it also had a fundamental effect on the structure of that industry in the province, making it increasingly dependent on its prime asset: iron ore and the production of semi-manufactured goods. Between 1825 and 1850 the Alpine regions of Styria and Carinthia had been the major producers of pig-iron in the Empire, amounting to 66 per cent of total production. The new revolutionary techniques of the nineteenth century, which left this area at a definite disadvantage, conversely led to the major development of the large coalfields of Bohemia and Silesia, and in particular of the vast Witkowitz ironworks in Moravia. The plant's first coke smelter in Austria was built in the Witkowitz works in 1836 and a second followed in 1839.[9] In contrast, as late as 1870 Styria was still totally dependent on charcoal smelting. Despite the fact that the Alpine Montangesellschaft's rationalisation plans were based on the rapid modernisation of the charcoal furnaces and the closure of the smaller works, the company's dependence on coal from the north-

8. Erben et al. (eds.), *Die Alpine Montangesellschaft*, p. 50.
9. N.T. Gross, 'The Habsburg Monarchy', in C.M. Cipolla (ed.), *The Fontana Economic History of Europe. Vol. 4. The Emergence of Industrial Societies, No. 1* (London, 1973), pp. 266–7.

ern provinces meant that it had to have something to sell in return. All the Styrians could offer was their high-grade iron ore. In 1882, just one year after the founding of the company, production of iron ore reached a new record of 617,000 tons. By 1900 this had risen to 1 million tons and the region was becoming increasingly dependent on exporting its raw materials to Moravia and Bohemia rather than processing them at home. By the outbreak of the First World War, production had once again doubled to 2 million tons and the iron ore mountain at Erzberg, with its terraces of open-cast mines, was responsible for 64 per cent of Austria's total iron ore production.[10] During these years the Alpine Montangesellschaft expanded its mine holdings until by 1911 it virtually controlled the major sources of raw material in the province, iron ore and lignite.

The consequences of this pattern of industrial development in the region were manifold. The traditional mode of production, based in small workshops which mined, refined and manufactured their products into saleable goods, was superseded by large-scale industrial units, dominated by a single industrial company. In the 1890s the Alpine Montangesellschaft employed 19,500 workers, most of whom worked in the Donawitz plant.[11] In addition, the region's metal industry became increasingly dependent on external sales of raw materials in order to secure supplies of that essential, but locally missing, ingredient in modern steel manufacturing, coke. The province was drawn into the national and international economies as a supplier of raw materials, and so became the first link in the industrial chain. As a result, its economy was particularly vulnerable to fluctuation. If demand for Bohemian or Moravian goods fell, the effect was felt immediately in Styria, where the demand for iron ore also fell. In addition, Styrian production of semi-manufactured goods, such as pig-iron, crude steel, ingots, castings, rails, bars, rods and sheet metal, was completely dependent on supplies of Bohemian coke. If these suddenly stopped, as happened in 1918, the effect on the company and on the entire region would be catastrophic.

The problems of market fluctuations were, of course, not unique to Styria, but were a common feature of industrial economies. However, because of the structure of industry in the province, any downturn in the economy which affected the demand for metal was felt with great force there. One reason for this was the size of the metal industry in relation to other industries in the province.

10. Matis and Bachinger, 'Österreichs industrielle Entwicklung', pp. 164–5.
11. Erben et al. (eds.), *Die Alpine Montangesellschaft*, p. 134.

Mining and metal companies between them employed roughly 33 per cent of the entire workforce in the 1920s, even though heavy industry was in difficulty at the time. The second largest employer was the building industry which employed 13 per cent, followed by the wood industry with 6 per cent.[12] As a result of this concentration or lack of industrial diversification, a crisis in heavy industry which resulted in high unemployment had repercussions throughout the industrial regions of the province. With such a high proportion of the workforce employed in the mining and metal industry, much of the rest of the province's economy, which relied on the domestic market, was thus indirectly dependent on this one industry. A crisis in the mining industry reduced the demand for pit props from the wood companies, affected the building industry, which relied on contracts from the foundries and steel mills,[13] and also the food and clothing industries, which depended to a great extent on the spending power of the industrial workers.

A second reason for the peculiar vulnerability of Styrian heavy industry was the small size of the engineering industry in the region. In 1928, when 21,278 workers were employed in the province's metallurgical industry, there were only 13,486 metal processing workers, most of whom were concentrated in the engineering works in Graz.[14] In Upper Styria, where most of the metalworkers lived and worked, there were even fewer mechanics and engineers and no engineering industry at all. In the Republic the bulk of Styrian metal was exported out of the province to Vienna and Wiener Neustadt and as a result the Styrian metal industry remained a basic producer, unable to develop the type of diversified economic structure which could have cushioned it during periods of economic decline. This can be shown by comparing the size of both sectors of the industry in Styria, Vienna and Lower Austria according to employment. In 1928, when two out of every three Styrian workers in the metal industry were engaged in some form of metal production, ranging from mining to smelting and foundry work, the ratio in Vienna and Lower Austria was drastically lower; in Vienna there were 471 metallurgical workers compared with 70,505 employed in metal processing and in Lower Austria 8,329 compared with 25,205.[15] Whilst Styria remained the major area of metal production in the First Republic, the machine shops and

12. *St AK* 1928, p. 200.
13. This happened in 1930 when many of the steelworks halted production.
14. *WsJ*, 1931–2, Table 73, pp. 136–7.
15. Ibid.

engineering works were found mainly in Vienna and Wiener Neustadt.

This division within the metal industry affected not only the nature of the goods which each area produced, but also the level of skill required and the scale of the units of production, both of which were important for the development of the labour movement. For instance, although both sectors benefited from the massive expansion in demand at the end of the nineteenth century, creating a much larger workforce receiving relatively high wages in comparison with other trades, in metallurgy there were also significant changes in the type of labour required, as the whole process of metal production was modernised. The change in the nature of work from small-scale forge to large-scale plant led to a demand for new skills and an increase in the division of labour. The traditional control which the ironmaster had over the work process was diminished and his importance eroded, to be replaced by a handful of qualified engineers, supported by technicians and white-collar workers, who supplied the scientific knowledge of steel production. The iron was no longer tested by withdrawing a sample and testing it under the hammer, but by consulting a laboratory. At the same time there was an increase in the separation of skills for the manual workers, with a reduction in the number of supervisors in relation to the demand for the physical labour of unskilled workers who carried the ore, limestone and coke to the furnaces. Thus the structure of skill within the metal production process was altered, and the demand for semi-skilled and unskilled workers rose.

The situation in the ore and lignite mines was different. Although miners were technically unskilled, their value rested on experience, the knowledge of where and how to cut stone. As a result of this and the lack of mechanisation in the mines, miners had relatively more job security than metal production workers, for an experienced miner was difficult to replace. However, even in the mines the demand for unskilled labour was high and skills were learnt underground, where lignite was cut, or, in the case of iron ore, on the terraces. A miner, therefore, learnt his trade on the job, and his training was shorter and less specialised than that of a skilled mechanic or turner or many of the other necessary trades in the metal processing industry. Both miners and foundry workers, the largest sectors of the Styrian workforce employed in heavy industry, had relatively less job security than their colleagues in metal processing precisely because of the low proportion of skilled workers who were required. It was easier to introduce new and untrained workers into the mines and steel plants than into the engineering plants of Vienna and Wiener Neustadt.

Thus in Styria the highly skilled sectors of the metal industry, the machine industry, transport production and the electrical engineering industry, employed far fewer people than the mines, blast furnaces and rolling-mills, contrasting greatly with the structure of the metal industry in Vienna above all, where 99.2 per cent of metal workers were involved in metal processing.[16] This was not the only difference, for in addition the average size of firms in the two areas was radically different. For instance, the average number of metalworkers employed in one firm in Vienna was 16.8, compared with 41.2 in Styria.[17] Workshops with fewer than twenty employees employed 20 per cent of the Viennese workforce compared with 5.7 per cent in Styria. Plants with over 500 employees employed 30 per cent of the Viennese metalworkers, compared with 62.4 per cent in Styria. The units of production in the metal producing sector were far larger than those of the metal processing sector. In addition by 1928 ten firms controlled 64 per cent of the entire workforce in the industry in Styria and a rough estimate suggests that one firm alone, the Alpine Montangesellschaft, employed 60 per cent of all miners and metal production workers.[18]

The size of workshops and the lower skill level of the workforce both had an effect on industrial relations in the province before the war. Styrian metalworkers had less job security than their Viennese counterparts and less to gain from trade union membership. They were also more vulnerable to the anti-union tactics of their employers.

16. Ibid.
17. *WsJ* 1928, Tables 106 and 107, p. 181.
18. Official figures for employment at the Alpine Montangesellschaft are unavailable. However, the company history states that 17,750 workers were employed in 1921 (Erben et al. (eds.), *Die Alpine Montangesellschaft*, p. 61). Franz Domes, leader of the Metalworkers' Union, estimated a workforce of 15,000 in 1925. (*Der Tag*, 24 September 1925.)

Labour Relations in the Empire

The scale of industry, the low level of demand for skilled workers and the dominance of the Alpine Montangesellschaft were all factors which hindered the development of trade unionism in Styria before the First World War and later prevented the unions from holding on to their membership in the interwar years. In the days of the Empire the Metalworkers' Union consistently failed to develop a tradition of union membership in Styria, partly because of the opposition of the employers and partly due to the lack of enthusiasm amongst the workers themselves. The nature of the metal industry was such that trade unionism remained weak. In the Republic, after an initial expansion in membership, the Free Trade Unions fell into decline in the mid-1920s, repeating the earlier pattern. The power of the Metalworkers' Union reached its height nationally in 1928, when membership in Austria as a whole reached a level of 80.6 per cent of all those employed in metal trades (see Appendix, Table 5, p. 216). In contrast to this national figure the level of membership in Styria was only 37 per cent. If the miners are included in the total figure of metal trade employees, the Austrian membership rate falls to 78.4 per cent and the Styrian rate to 34.4 per cent. Whereas 20.5 per cent of the national mining and metal workforce was employed in Styria, Styrian workers constituted only 9.03 per cent of the combined memberships of the Metal and Mineworkers' unions. Membership of both unions was uncharacteristically low in the province, due to the state of the economy in the 1920s and also, according to contemporary reports, to a tradition of non-membership.

Both the scale of industry and the skill factor played their role in the lack of a trade union tradition. Small workshops were not only easier for unions to organise than larger plants, but they were more resilient to moves by employers to exclude the union from their premises. This was especially true when the small workshops employed a higher proportion of skilled workers than the larger plants, as was the case in the metal industry, for there is a strong correlation between skill level and trade union membership. Thus in the province, as opposed to the capital, the lower rate of skill found amongst the workers corresponded with a lower rate of trade union membership.

This was not suprising. Traditionally unskilled and semi-skilled workers had less to gain from the unions especially in the early days of industrialisation before the First World War, when the trade union movement was in its infancy. Unlike Vienna, where engineering workers formed the core of the strongest and earliest prewar trade union in Austria, the Styrian metalworkers proved to be notoriously difficult to organise. This was in many ways a reaction to the craft dominance of the early trade union movement which attracted support from skilled workers but not the unskilled, as well as the determined resistance of local employers.

The Metalworkers' Union was the first national trade union to receive legal status in Austria in 1892.[1] Austria's first trade union convention was held by this union in November 1892 in Vienna, although the word 'convention' may be a little too grand to describe a meeting of representatives of nine provincial assemblies and six local associations. Even so, the occasion was of importance, heralding the beginning of a nationally organised trade union movement. Within two months the union's membership had reached 8,500, most of whom came from the engineering industries of Vienna and Wiener Neustadt. This point is important, for although the union later became a national union, recruiting members from all sectors of the metal industry and finally absorbing the mining unions in 1928, its origins lay within the skilled sector, the engineering industry. From this base it came to represent the backbone of the Free Trade Union movement in the First Republic. Theoretically it was not the first workers' association, for workers had had the right to organise themselves into local associations since the relaxation of the labour laws in 1867. There was, however, at least one catch, for local authorities retained the right to ban any organisation which they considered to be a danger to state security, and for some years this provision was unhesitatingly used to curb any embryonic trade union.[2] In addition, the *Gewerbeordnung* (trade regulation) of 1859 effectively outlawed collective bargaining, for no association was allowed to make demands or use threats on behalf of a firm's employees in order to gain improve-

1. Strictly speaking the Metalworkers' Union was not the first trade union in Austria, for several craft unions survived the various bans which were imposed by the government after the 1848 Revolution. It was, however, the first national union.
2. Julius Deutsch, *Geschichte der österreichischen Gewerkschaftsbewegung* (Vienna, 1932), vol. 1, p. 256.

ments in either working conditions or wages. Technically, after the 1867 legislation, collective bargaining was permissible where it was voluntarily recognised by the employer, but it had no legal status. Several craft unions were able to introduce collective bargaining and by 1912 these covered shoemakers, typesetters, watchmakers, painters, as well as railwaymen, tinsmiths and some engineering workers.[3]

In 1890 the Vienna printers' association led a campaign to win the right to recruit and organise members on a state rather than on a provincial basis. In May of that year they blatantly flouted the laws banning national congresses and called a meeting of representatives from printing works throughout the Empire.[4] The meeting passed a resolution urging all members of local printers' groups to establish and support a national union. This, the first real step towards a national trade union movement, soon escalated. By September groups of turners, shoemakers, joiners, hatmakers, textiles workers, foundry workers and miners, bakers and engineering workers had all separately declared their intentions to hold national congresses and each passed resolutions urging local associations to consolidate their struggles for higher wages and better working conditions. Strictly speaking, as both the resolutions and the assemblies were illegal, all participants were risking arrest and even imprisonment merely by attending the conventions. But no arrests were made, indicating that the government's attitude had mellowed. In October 1892 the Metalworkers' Union was formally recognised and its rights to hold national meetings and to organise members from all corners of the Empire were legalised.

This was the initial importance of the Metalworkers' Union. Its members were the first to succeed in a battle which had been initially fought by craft trades – the hatmakers, printers and joiners. But the structure of the union was also important, for although its leadership hoped to straddle the gap between craft associations and industrial unions, which recruited from all sectors regardless of skill, it was initially unable to do so. Many of the more skilled metalworkers resented this form of egalitarianism, and so the union was forced to compromise between the open recruitment of an industrial union and the closed system, which was a legacy of the craft tradition of organisation. An example of this can be found in

3. Ibid., vol. 1, p. 75.
4. 'National' here is somewhat of a misnomer. Membership was not based on nationality, but on occupation. Workers from all nations of the Empire were eligible for membership. However, both 'state union' and 'imperial union' imply government-run bodies and so the term 'national union' remains the most appropriate.

the terms by which the forge workers and moulders, a skilled stratum of the metallurgical industry, were persuaded to take up union membership. Well paid, and with relatively good job security at the time, these men represented an elite within the metallurgical industry and did not consider their interests to be similar to those of the semi-skilled and unskilled workers amongst whom they worked. They agreed to join the union on condition that they remained a semi-independent group within it.[5] So, although the Metalworkers' Union had the potential to become a truly industrial union, drawing members both from the skilled and unskilled workers before the First World War, the divisions within it and the dominance of the engineering workers from Vienna meant that it remained largely the prerogative of the skilled workers and represented the engineering industry in particular, rather than metalworkers in general.

As a result of this dominance, the principal function of the early trade unions was to preserve the position of skilled workers against the encroaching waves of machines and machine tenders. This was particularly true of the Hatters' and Shoemakers' Union, where traditional crafts were being completely replaced by machinery and the prospects for employment were vanishing. The situation in the metal industry was different, because it was expanding rapidly and the demand for labour during the 1890s, when the union was establishing itself, was high.[6] Even so, the craft mentality was still present amongst the turners, smiths and mechanics who formed the majority of the early membership. Many were wary of the employment of semi-qualified workers and the use of apprentices and juvenile workers in skilled jobs. In fact one dominant theme of Austrian trade unionism at the end of the last century was the fiercely fought battle to improve the training of apprenticed labour and prevent its exploitation and the undercutting of wage rates for trained metalworkers.[7] This also reinforced a basic schism between the skilled and unskilled workers, for one result of this was to lower the number of apprenticeships offered. The sentiments of the skilled men naturally found little sympathy amongst the less skilled and none at all amongst the unskilled.

The failure of early trade unions to identify and represent the interests of semi-skilled and unskilled workers was one reason for

---

5. Deutsch, *Geschichte der österreichischen Gewerkschaftsbewegung*, vol. 1, p. 255.

6. P.P. Chladek, 'Geschichte und Probleme der Eisenindustrie in der Steiermark' (unpublished PhD thesis, Vienna, 1955), pp. 133–19.

7. John W. Boyer, *Political Radicalism in Late Imperial Vienna. Origins of the Christian Social Movement 1848–1897* (Chicago, 1981), p. 51.

the low level of trade union membership in Styria before the First World War. The structure of the industry was another, for although there was a long tradition of skilled metalworking in the area, the increased division of labour and deskilling which resulted from the concentration and technological modernisation of production in the 1880s and 1890s fundamentally altered the position of the metal-workers within the industry, limiting the control which they had over the production process and at times rendering specific skills redundant.

The history of the miners was again different. Although the work was technically unskilled, it was highly dangerous and the safety of workers depended on their levels of experience and mutual trust. The evils of coal-mining in the days before electrification and power-driven tools are well known – problems of gas, landslides, coal-dust and the carriage of coal. In addition, lignite has a higher moisture content than coal and the risks of explosion are greater. The Styrian mines were also very deep and the combination of depth and dampness created wretched and dangerous working conditions. Open-cast iron mining was less dangerous, but, as in the lignite mines, the solidarity which might have arisen from the working conditions was disturbed by the owners' policy of employing itinerant workers from the Slavonic regions of the Empire. Despite this the mining communities had a long history of organisation. The Knappschaft, the forerunner of the Miners' Union, had long since established sickness and accident insurance schemes for the workers, which the employers had recognised. However, even in the mines, trade union organisation was difficult, for one major obstacle to working–class organisation was the determined resistance of employers. In Upper Styria the strength of the opposition was unusually great, because the majority both of the metalworkers and mining workers were employed by the same firm, the Alpine Montangesellschaft, which was strongly opposed to any form of trade unionism amongst its employees.

Initially the miners were the first section of the workforce to confront the new company. In June 1889, Viktor Adler addressed a meeting of Alpine workers, many of them miners from Eisenerz, at Leoben at the beginning of a campaign by the Social Democratic Party for an official holiday on May Day, an eight-hour day and a basic minimum wage. One month later miners at Seegraben adopted these demands during a conflict with the management over pay in the pit, when a deputation was sent to put forward demands for a pay increase and for an eight-hour day. The company refused to discuss the demands and the miners went on strike. A number of sympathy strikes followed and the Seegraben miners won a partial victory, not only for themselves, but also for miners at the neighbouring pit at Fohnsdorf. When the Köflacher miners, who were also employed by the Alpine Montangesellschaft, demanded similar improvements and also went on strike, the company resisted and called for military protection against the strikers. It then refused to abide by the agreement reached at Seegraben. In 1890 miners at Fohnsdorf went on strike twice more, demanding yet again an eight-hour day and a minimum wage and also the right to a holiday on May Day. This time the company responded by sacking 180 'trouble-makers'.[8]

The company's response to the 1889 and 1890 strikes provides a classic illustration of its attitude toward organised labour. One of the sympathy strikes which broke out in response to the Seegraben mines took place at Donawitz. At that time the company employed one thousand workers at the plant, which was the nerve centre of its empire. Four hundred men joined in a demonstration outside the director's office, demanding a 15 per cent wage increase, fortnightly rather than the customary monthly payments, and an eight-hour day on Saturdays. The company's initial reaction was a surprise, for they agreed to meet the strikers' demands. But rumours of the Donawitz victory spread to other plants and even other companies. At the Pichling ironworks at Köflach foundry workers laid down their tools, but, before the strike committee had time to confront the management, troops were called in to 'protect property' and 'restore order'. The strike was put down in a manner which one writer has described as 'brutal'.[9] When Slav miners at the Alpine Montangesellschaft mine at Trifail Hrastnigg also went on strike the company persuaded the local workhouse to refuse to provide food for the strikers or their families.[10] Despite this the wave of strikes spread. The government sent several battalions of soldiers into the district, many arrests were made and all public meetings banned. By this time it was evident that the company was not going to honour the agreement it had made with the Donawitz workers and the strike wave crumbled.

In some industrial areas this type of action carried out by employers and supported by the government would have had a boomerang effect, by clearly illustrating the conflict of class interests which local trade union organisers were preaching. This

8. Fritz Erben, Maja Loehr and Hans Riehl (eds.), *Die Alpine Montangesellschaft* (Vienna, 1931), pp. 144–9.

9. Michael Schacherl, *Dreißig Jahre der steierischen Arbeiterbewegung, 1890 bis 1920* (Graz, 1931), p. 20.

10. Deutsch, *Geschichte der österreichischen Gewerkschaftsbewegung*, vol. 1, p. 256.

appeared at first to be the case at the Alpine Montangesellchaft, where local labour leaders attempted to use the fervour which the strike movement had created to resurrect and extend the metalworkers' educational association and create a local trade union. The Styrian metalworkers appeared to be on the brink of organising themselves. However, this proved to be shortlived. The following year the Social Democratic Party organised the first May Day rally in which most industrial branches, including the Alpine miners, were represented. The metalworkers were conspicuous by their absence, for the company had threatened to sack any employee who did not turn up for work on May Day. Over one hundred of the company's miners who took part lost their jobs as a consequence.[11] The metalworkers were more cautious, for in an area which was effectively dominated by one industry and that industry by one firm, once blacklisted, they had little chance of finding alternative work in the locality. The relative solidarity of the miners in the area had made this seem less of a threat for them than it was for the metalworkers. In the end, as the sacking of the miners showed, this was not the case.

And so one additional reason for the weakness of organised labour amongst metalworkers and miners in Upper Styria was the early concentration of the means of production and the relative size of and influence on the area by one company. The employers were not only adamant in their determination to combat trade unionism, an attitude which was not uncommon at the time, but they were sufficiently consolidated to be effective. In addition, they were seldom faced with the shortage of labour which might have forced them to concede and, when such a situation arose, they were able to recruit workers, sometimes from outside Styria, in order to overcome the problem.

The mining and metal industry rarely had to compete for labour, for they paid the highest industrial wages in the area. On the one occasion when the building industry offered higher wages, during the building boom at the beginning of the twentieth century, it was the unskilled and semi-skilled metalworkers who first took advantage of the offer, for they were not tied to the metal industry by trade. However, this did not present acute problems for the Alpine Montangesellschaft, which chose instead merely to recruit migratory labour from Hungary, labourers who had previously travelled to Styria in search of seasonal work which was often found in the building industry. In order to bind these workers more closely to the area, the company developed a policy of company

11. Schacherl, *Dreißig Jahre*, p. 23.

housing, building family units in addition to the barracks in which many single workers had previously been housed.[12] By 1912 there were 1,586 units of housing, most in Donawitz, and this policy had spread to the smaller steel companies in the area.[13] Such inducements to settle may have originally appeared attractive to the workers, but they were a two-edged sword. By the end of the century the level of company housing was higher in Upper Styria than in any of the other eight provinces which later made up the Austrian Republic. The sharp edge of the blade was that if a worker quit his job or was sacked, he lost not only his income but also his home.

These points highlight the main problem of unskilled labour. Workers may have been in a more flexible position than skilled workers to benefit from occasional trade booms in other industries, but they were more dispensable in the eyes of the employer than turners and mechanics, who were able to use their labour power and skills when bargaining with the employer. The skilled worker enjoyed a higher level of job security and for this reason had more to gain and less to fear from joining the union.

A point should also be made about the background of the unskilled as opposed to the skilled worker. The expansion of the metal industry in the 1890s brought with it an influx of new labour into the factory system, workers who had little previous experience of factory work or urban life. This was then extended by the numbers of seasonal labourers whom the employers were successful in persuading to settle. Thus the industry was heavily manned by inexperienced, often young and undisciplined, workers, who were unfamiliar with the ideas of collective action or trade unionism. As such, the Styrian metal industry once again contrasted strongly with the engineering industry in Vienna, many of whose workers had begun apprenticeships whilst in their teens and learned their trade as well as some of their attitudes from old hands in small workshops.

The influence of the Roman Catholic Church may also have been a factor in the lack of trade union fervour, although such an argument is difficult to prove conclusively. The Church had stronger links with rural communities than with urban communities and many new workers coming into the towns to live continued to attend church regularly. Priests rarely hesitated to expound their views on the evils of trade unionists who preached social conflict

---

12. Chladek, 'Geschichte und Probleme', p. 119.
13. Erben et al. (eds.), *Die Alpine Montangesellschaft*, p. 314.

rather than social harmony, and, equally important, whose leaders were often atheists or Jews. In 1891, Pope Leo XIII issued the encyclical *Rerum Novarum*, in which it was argued that the basic misconception of socialism and, by implication, of most organised labour, was the belief that there was a fundamental division between capital and labour.[14] The two, the encyclical argued, were symbiotically related, for capital needed labour and labour needed capital. This encyclical heralded the mushrooming of Catholic trade unions, dedicated to the cause of social harmony in industrial relations, one of the earliest of which was founded in Lower Austria by Lepold Kunschak.[15] This developed into the Austrian Christian Trade Union Movement, which had strong links with the Christian Social Party. The Catholic Church in Austria was attempting to provide an alternative political movement which would lure the industrial working class away from the societies and trade unions of the socialist movement. In 1902, following a recommendation from the Christian Union Congress in Munich, the Austrian Union of Christian Iron and Metalworkers was set up. Two years later this was followed by the Austrian Union of Christian Miners.[16] Thus the opposition of the Roman Catholic Church to the Social Democratic Party and Free Trade Unions may have had some influence on young Styrian workers who crossed from agriculture into industry. By the turn of the century the Church was advocating membership of its own unions rather than no union membership at all.

Thus the Metalworkers' Union was unable to make many inroads amongst the workers employed in Styrian heavy industry. The amalgamation of many of the major employers into a single company, in which the production of basic iron and steel was concentrated, created a situation which was not conducive to strong trade unionism, for the employers were united before the unions could establish themselves and were thus able to use coercion to prevent their employees from joining. In addition, the nature of metallurgical work was such that there were relatively few skilled workers amongst the labour force and a relatively high proportion of unskilled and semi-skilled workers. Finally, the influx of new workers from the countryside at critical times in the

---

14. Fritz Klenner, *Die österreichischen Gewerkschaften* (Vienna, 1953), vol. 1, p. 120. Sidney Pollard and Colin Holmes (eds.), *Documents in European Economic History vol. 2. Industrial Power and National Rivalry* (London, 1972), p. 317.
15. Walter Schwimmer and Ewald Klinger, *Die Christlichen Gewerkschaften in Österreich* (Vienna, 1975), p. 33.
16. Ibid., p. 397.

history of the industry further weakened the position of the un-skilled workers.

It is important, however, to note that the Styrian miners and metalworkers were not opposed to trade unionism in principle. The pattern of union membership was not consistently low, even in the Alpine Montangesellschaft works, but oscillated, subjecting the province's trade unions to frequent and severe fluctuations in membership. To quote from a contemporary source: 'The rise and fall which led to this amazingly strong oscillation between explosion and total indifference is characteristic of Donawitz and to some degree was evident in the Styrian metalworkers organisation in general.'[17]

Long after the introduction of large-scale industrialisation the Styrian metalworkers, and to some extent the miners also, con-tinued to regard the union as a sleeping body of strength, which could be awoken in times of crisis. They flocked to join it when a wage issue arose, or when there was a major dispute over working conditions, and then left again when the issue had been resolved. One example of this was the puddlers' dispute at Donawitz in July 1904.[18] The company had announced a wage cut, which immedi-ately led to a dramatic rise in trade union membership in the plant and to a strike. The wage cut was withdrawn, and, as the battle appeared to be over, union membership fell. Twelve months later the union began a wage campaign within the company, having found a group of supporters from amongst the puddlers, wrought-iron workers whose skill was becoming obsolete. The union won, the increase was conceded, but this time the manage-ment anticipated an immediate fall in membership and refused to implement the agreement. The union stepped in again and in-creased its demands, adding the call for an eight-hour day. At this point the management took decisive action. The director, Köhler, announced that if there was another meeting of shop stewards at the plant, he would sack all those involved. He offered workers the right to come to him personally and individually to air their grievances. Union membership at Donawitz fell to 300.

The discipline of trade union membership was weak in Upper Styria, but this should not be confused with docility. The Styrian miners and metalworkers, particularly those employed by the Alpine Montangesellschaft, joined the union to fight an issue, and

17. Membership of the Styrian Metalworkers' Union: 1897 = 1,155; 1898 = 3,736; 1900 = 1,716; 1902 = 1,472; 1905 = 3,679; 1907 = 4,080. Schacherl, *Dreißig Jahre*, p. 167.
18. Ibid., p. 166.

then left once the issue had been settled, whether they had won or not. The employers' opposition to the union was great and the rewards of membership uncertain.

This does not mean that labour relations remained totally unaltered in the forty-four years between 1870 and the outbreak of the First World War. By 1914 even the autocratic attitude of the Alpine Montangesellschaft had been somewhat tempered by changes in the law and by economic necessity. An example of the former was the law of 1889 which limited the working day to nine hours in the mines. Company housing, which has already been mentioned, was an example of the second. Initially this had consisted of barracks, but by the turn of the century the management began to realise the indirect benefits of this type of investment, which not only tied workers to the company, but also extended the firm's right of supervision from the factory into the worker's home. In the 1920s the problem of company housing became more severe for the trade union movement.

The attitude of the Alpine Montangesellschaft and of the Styrian steel companies in general had not altered fundamentally. They refused to recognise the trade unions and were very reluctant to negotiate with their employees. Troops were frequently used against strikers. However, the economic environment, in particular the periodic shortage of labour, required them to adopt what at first appeared to be a more benevolent air in which they provided a limited number of benefits in return for a labourer's work. There was no room for dispute; when a difference of opinion arose between workers and management, the management was free to sack the worker, just as, theoretically, the worker was free to leave. Any attempt by workers to organise collectively was seen by the employers as an unnecessary upset to the natural and individual relationship between the two.

By 1914 Austrian workers had had the legal right to join a trade union for over twenty years. There was, however, a distinction between winning that right and putting it into practice. In Upper Styria, despite the presence of a large industrial working class, the roots of trade unionism did not sink deep. The area's main industry, iron and steel, was not one in which the early unions found it easy to recruit members. The workers were mainly unskilled or semi-skilled and had relatively little in common with the skilled workers who dominated the trade union movement at the time. Moreover, the control of the industry was dominated by a handful of firms, of which the Alpine Montangesellschaft was not only the largest, but also the most fervently anti-union. The workforce was not by nature submissive to the employers and did take part in a number of strikes, but it was unable to maintain a strong trade union organisation.

Because of the relative size of the iron and steel industry in Upper Styria, few other strong unions developed. The miners, who had had their own form of organisation for many years, were almost all employed by the Alpine Montangesellschaft and membership of the miners' union was low. The only other substantial industries in the region were the wood and building industries, both of which were seasonal. As a result, before the First World War the labour movement in the province was relatively weak, and almost totally confined to Graz and the surrounding area. In Upper Styria when workers did take collective action on their own behalf, it tended to be unorganised, spontaneous and frequently ineffective. The weakness of the union movement and the comparative unity and strength of the employers frequently meant that any agreements which were reached between the two were discarded when this seemed to the employers to be in their interest. The control which the employers exerted rested on two main factors: the lack of working-class organisation and the lack of legal status and protection for the workers. This situation was changed during the war and the Revolution of 1918, but the structural difficulties of the trade unions in Upper Styria reappeared soon after.

-3-

Labour and the War, 1914–1918

Before the outbreak of the First World War, labour relations in northern Styria had followed a familiar pattern. Craftsmen in skilled trades had, for the most part, retained their own organisations, small select groups of established workers joined together into a union which still retained some of the characteristics of earlier craft life, setting standards of work, limiting entrance to the trades by training apprentices. The similarities between these trade unions and the guilds were strong, but the scope for control was very different. Union members were employees, rather than employers, and their organisations also developed many of the features of modern unionism, including, at times, militant action against employers. In contrast, union activity amongst the growing numbers of semi-skilled and unskilled workers employed in the larger industrial plants, woodmills, foundries and rolling-mills was sporadic and weak. These workers had often been recently recruited and were geographically isolated from one another, living and working in the towns of the Mur valley. Their general level of skill was lower than that of the craftsman and so, too, were their levels of pay and job security. They were also frequently faced by strong and determined anti-union employers. The concept of the individual contract between the employer and the workers, which was supported by law, allowed the employer to exert a crude control over the labour force: workers who were dissatisfied with conditions of work or levels of pay were offered a choice between silence and the sack.

This crude but effective control of labour was shattered between 1914 and 1920. The reasons for this were partly local in origin and partly national. At the local level, working conditions during the First World War deteriorated, whilst the supply of labour fell due to competition from the armed forces. This radicalised the Styrian industrial workers and, in particular, those who worked in the very plants which had previously failed to unionise – the foundries and rolling-mills. Most workers suffered deteriorating working conditions during the war. The working day was extended and Sunday working was reintroduced. Food was in short supply by 1916. All essential new industries, including mining and metallurgy, were placed under martial law, with the employer acting as military commander. Riots and strikes broke out in 1915 and again in 1916, sparked off by economic grievances, but soon involved political protest as workers confronted employers and then the state itself. Martial law politicised the strike movement, directing its attack against the authority of the state as well as that of the employer.

When war broke out in August 1914 unemployment immediately rose. The Alpine Montangesellschaft dampened down one blast furnace in the first weeks and then a second. Ten of the sixteen open-hearth furnaces were closed, along with a wire mill and girder works.[1] In Donawitz half the workforce was laid off in the first four weeks and approximately another third was called up.[2] This extreme reaction was based on the misconception, common throughout Europe, that the war would last for a few months at the most. Coke and coal, which had been ordered by the firm to fuel the smelter, were redirected to the railways. Skilled and experienced workers, in particular miners, were conscripted and the union leadership called for 'a united people of brothers fighting on the battlefields against Czarism and barbarism'.[3] By 1915 mine-owners were frantically recalling experienced miners and there were severe shortages of lamp oil, pit props and explosives. The iron foundries, meanwhile, lacked coke.

The Free Trade Unions and the Social Democratic Party, the two formal wings of organised labour, responded to the war with outright support.[4] Unlike the slightly hesitant tone with which the German Trade Union Commission urged supporters to put aside immediate class interests for the duration of the war, their Austrian counterparts argued that it was the duty of every workers' representative to accept those restrictions on trade union activity

1. Viktor Stein, 'Die Lage der österreichischen Metallarbeiter im Kriege', in Ferdinand Hanusch and Emmanuel Adler et al. (eds.), *Die Regelung der Arbeitsverhältnisse während des Krieges* (Vienna, 1927), p. 225.
2. Fritz Erben, Maja Loehr and Hans Riehl (eds.), *Die Alpine Montangesellschaft* (Vienna, 1931) p. 155.
3. Fritz Klenner, *Die österreichischen Gewerkschaften* (Vienna, 1953) vol. 1, p. 401.
4. The socialist trade union federation adopted the title 'Free Trade Unions' in 1928, but for simplicity the term is used throughout this book, to distinguish the socialist trade unions from other unions. See Charles A. Gulick, *Austria from Habsburg to Hitler* (Berkeley, 1948), vol. 1, pp. 285–6.

which the state thought were necessary.[5] The extent of these restrictions soon became evident. In August 1914 the state placed all essential war industries under military law and suspended most existing labour regulations. These included: the ban on Sunday working and regulations on the length of the working day in specific industries, in particular the mines; the ban on night work for juvenile and female labour; laws on apprenticeships; and the law which prevented unqualified or disabled workers from working steam-engines or boilers.[6] Unauthorised mass meetings and strikes became illegal. But the most significant aspect of the war experience for Austrian workers, and the one which differentiated their conditions from those of their contemporaries in Germany and Britain, took place in those plants which were subjected to military rule under the War Service Regulations (*Kriegsleistungsgesetz*).[7] This law applied to munitions factories, mines, factories producing goods for the army, such as medical supplies, and the transport industry. The terms of the regulations were severe and although at first they only applied to able-bodied men of conscription age, this was later extended to all men and even women workers.[8]

As a result of this introduction of martial law into Austrian factories and mines, bonuses for overtime were suspended and all negotiations between employers and workers ceased. Instead pay was regulated by the employer, who was charged with the task of setting a fair rate whilst being theoretically forbidden to reduce wages. However, the extension of the working day and the abandoning of overtime pay effectively reduced real earnings. Hours of work, decisions on Sunday working and even the length of meal breaks were all left to the discretion of the employer, who became the equivalent of a military commander in his own firm, empowered to enforce military discipline on his workers. Employers' power within the factory increased considerably during the war. Workers were forbidden to leave their jobs, but could be dismissed, making

5. Klenner, *Die österreichischen Gewerkschaften*, vol. 1, p. 394.

6. The apprentices' laws were changed in May 1915 to allow apprentices who had completed the first two years of training before conscription to qualify without a further two years of training. Stein, 'Die Lage', p. 255.

7. The *Kriegsdienstleistung* was introduced under the *Kriegsleistungsgesetz* of 1912 and reinforced existing laws of conscription.

8. The conscription laws were extended twice during the war. In July 1914 all able-bodied men between the ages of 20 and 50 were eligible for conscription. In 1916 the age limit was raised to 55 and in 1917 to all able-bodied adults, except those with individual exemptions. Julius Deutsch, *Geschichte der österreichischen Gewerkschaftsbewegung*. 2 vols. (Vienna, 1932), vol. 2, p. 16. Klenner, *Die österreichischen Gewerkschaften*, vol. 1, p. 424.

them eligible for conscription into the army or for reassignment as a soldier worker, on soldier's pay. It became much cheaper to punish a worker than to pay him the civilian rate and only in extreme cases were disorderly workers sent to the front. In theory the relationship between the military and employers was bound by civil law and an employer could be prosecuted for exceeding his powers, but there are no reports of this actually happening.

Military rule was imposed on all workers in heavy industry and mining in Upper Styria, as well as on railway workers. Shipping employees and government workers also lost their coalition rights, but this proved to be less of a deprivation as all public meetings were illegal unless they had prior authorisation from the army. All organised trade union activity on the shop floor disappeared in Styria during the war years.

If military rule had been designed to prohibit labour protest during the war, it failed. The first strikes broke out in the Empire in February 1915 when miners at the Ostraw Krawiner mine in Northern Bohemia walked out for one hour in protest at long hours and poor food.[9] Shortly afterwards, lignite miners at Fohnsdorf in Upper Styria also protested and won concessions from their employers, the Alpine Montangesellschaft, over the provision of food and coal.[10] Throughout the winter and spring of 1915 and 1916 a series of minor strikes and demonstrations took place in Styria, involving miners, metalworkers and railwaymen, all of which were caused by irregular and low food supplies and long working hours. As the war continued into its second, third and, finally, fourth years, conditions in the factories and mines grew steadily worse. The number of industrial accidents rose, many of them caused by unskilled or inexperienced workers who were allowed to handle complicated and potentially dangerous machinery.[11] The level of real earnings fell as a result of war inflation and constant and inevitable falls in harvest. This led to shortages of food and even famine.[12] In the industrial regions the death rate, which had been high before the war, rocketed. General health also declined. Doctors reported a significant increase in cases of venereal disease as well as illnesses caused by hunger and poverty, such as smallpox, anthrax and tuberculosis. Cases of nutritional oedema, a form of dropsy which had previously been

9. Stein, 'Die Lage', p. 203.
10. Erben et al. (eds.), *Die Alpine Montangesellschaft*, p. 156.
11. Stein, 'Die Lage', p. 248.
12. R.W. Rothschild, *Austria's Economic Development between the Two Wars* (London, 1947), p. 15.

unknown in Austria, began to appear.[13] For some reason, the sickness rate amongst railway workers rose particularly, causing much speculation.[14] In addition to actual illnesses there were also problems caused by increased hours of work and fewer rest periods. Several workers in the blast furnacⁿ ; and rolling-mills at Donawitz collapsed and died for no apparent reason: doctors finally decided that malnutrition was to blame.[15]

The deterioration in working conditions precipitated the outbreak of a series of short sporadic strikes in many industrial areas of the Empire in 1915 and 1916. In May 1916 strikes broke out in Steyr, Linz and Prague, as well as Upper Styria. By the end of 1916 the number of strikes had escalated and new demands were being made by protesters. Railwaymen complained about the incivility of their superiors as well as food shortages. Workers at the Skoda works at Pilsen forced the authorities to set up a complaints procedure so that something would be done about conditions on the factory floor. Soon other workers joined in and the boards were extended to cover all factories bound by martial law. By the end of the year clandestine peace meetings were being held in many industrial towns.

Almost all of these early protests began as spontaneous outbursts against working conditions or lack of food. Most lasted minutes, at most an hour, for they were illegal and anyone who was discovered to have taken part, or, more serious, to have organised them was liable to be punished. One consequence of this was that the national trade union executives played no role in the early strike wave, partly because they were reluctant to become involved in illegal acts which might jeopardise their fragile relationship with the state, and partly because what influence they once had over rank-and-file members before the war had gone.[16] This was especially the case in the mines, munitions and metallurgical industries. Here employers had seized the opportunity given to them by conscription to remove any militant trade unionists. Conscription was often very politically selective. In companies such as the Alpine Montangesellschaft, where the employers' opposition to trade unionism

13. Siegfried Rosenfeld, 'Die Gesundheitsverhältnisse der industriellen Arbeiterschaft Österreichs während des Kriegs', in Hanusch and Adler (eds.), *Die Regelung der Arbeiterverhältnisse*, pp. 420–29.

14. Stein, 'Die Lage', p. 261.

15. Ingrun Lafleur, 'Socialists, Communists and Workers in the Austrian Revolution 1918–1919' (unpublished PhD thesis, Colombia University 1972), p. 26.

16. Michael Schacherl, *Dreißig Jahre der Steierischen Arbeiterbewegung, 1890 bis 1920* (Graz, 1931), p. 288. This includes some figures for Social Democratic Party membership before the war. In 1914 it was 9,761, but this fell to 3,431 in 1916.

had been determined, this policy was even extended to cover ordinary union members.[17]

The war also created a change in the character of the labour force. More women and youths were employed, especially during the early war years, when conscription created an immediate and chronic shortage of labour. Despite the usual objections by male workers, many firms were recruiting women by 1916. In the Styrian mines and foundries, where traditionally few women had been able to find work, most employers turned to this pool of labour, paying them wages at half or two-thirds the rate for men and often putting them on permanent night shift, a practice which had been illegal before the war.[18] By 1917, 24.9 per cent of the workers in government-inspected factories were women.[19] This added a new strand to labour protest and to the lives of the women. Very few of them had previously worked outside the home and almost none had any experience of politics or working-class organisation. But the fall in real incomes often affected them more seriously than it did the men. Not only were their wages considerably lower, but many were wives and mothers, whose men had been conscripted and who were now completely responsible for providing for their families. Wages and food became important issues, drawing them into the protest movement. Women were particularly evident during food riots, as they often are: to quote Olwen Hufton's comment on working-class women in a completely different context: 'A food riot without women is an inherent contradiction.'[20]

Grievances were not confined to women. Many young workers, former apprentices and trainees, were called upon to carry out jobs which were beyond their skills and for which they received only a part of the full wage. Apprentices conscripted into the forces were given a two-year training exemption, but this was greeted with outrage by non-conscripts and by the trade unions, which rightly feared a decline in the standard of training.[21] One other group was far from happy. As the shortage of labour increased, the government resorted to a pool of able-bodied men who were beyond the bounds of conscription – prisoners of war. They were originally allocated to the mines to replace female workers, but were later sent

17. Franz Aggermann, 'Die Arbeitsverhältnisse im Bergbau', in Hanusch and Adler (eds.), *Die Regelung der Arbeiterverhältnisse*, p. 210.
18. Ibid., p. 249.
19. Ibid., p. 253.
20. Olwen Hufton, 'Women in Revolution', *Past and Present*, no. 53, 1973, p. 93.
21. Stein, 'Die Lage', p. 255.

to other industries. Understandably they were unreliable and by 1917 the largest group, of about two thousand men, were living and working at the Alpine Montangesellschaft mine at Eisenerz, existing on three-quarter rations and being issued with 'Monopoly' money which the firm had specially printed.[22]

Discontent within all these groups fuelled strikes and demonstrations in 1917. The major issues were food, pay and working hours. Food prices had risen drastically over the previous six months, but allowances for miners and foundry workers had been raised only once. There were complaints, allegations of corruption and sporadic violence. When the Donawitz authorities announced a delay in the issue of rations in February, a crowd of women and youths stormed the Alpine Montangesellschaft offices and attacked company managers, throwing them out of the building. A few weeks later the foundry workers walked out en masse in protest at the size of the rations.[23] The company complained that the military, who were present, did nothing to protect the plant, and one writer has suggested that troops abandoned their posts, presumably in support of the strikers.[24]

Food was not the only issue. In the spring and summer of 1917 protests were triggered by dissatisfaction over pay and working hours, in particular the issue of Sunday working. At the beginning of the year miners at Eisenerz petitioned the War Ministry to have Sunday rest days reinstated, and when this failed they staged a number of protest stoppages. Again the company complained about ineffective military action, arguing that ringleaders were arrested only when prisoners of war joined the local workers' protests.[25] When Fohnsdorf workers demonstrated in April and held an illegal May Day rally in Judenburg, no-one was arrested, but when the same workers went on strike over wages two months later, the military did act. Ringleaders were identified, arrested and sent to the Front. Despite this, the protests continued and even spawned some local organisation. At the end of 1917 a workers' council was set up in Donawitz, under the guise of a workers' club. The company lamented the breakdown of discipline and acknowledged that by early 1918 it had lost control in some of its plants.[26]

The authorities, both civil and military, reacted to the increasing tension amongst the workers with concessions and repression.

22. Erben et al. (eds.) *Die Alpine Montangesellschaft*, p. 157.
23. Ibid., p. 259. Klenner, *Die österreichischen Gewerkschaften*, vol. 2, p. 1049.
24. Lafleur, 'Socialists, Communists and Workers', p. 32.
25. Erben et al. (eds.), *Die Alpine Montangesellschaft*, p. 150.
26. Ibid., p. 159.

Concessions were made after the 1916 strikes when the government increased rations for those workers who were engaged in heavy physical labour. Styrian miners won the right to a minimum wage in 1915, for the first time, and in March and May 1917 new regulations were introduced for militarised factories, to improve conditions. For women the new regulations actually made things worse.[27] By the end of 1917 the workers at Donawitz had coerced the management into at least talking to their representatives. The stick came in the form of reprisals. The Ministers of War and of the Interior drew up a series of new measures to deal with strikes in militarised enterprises and these were published in June 1917. The procedure was as follows: when a strike broke out the government sent a commissioner to the plant in question and ordered the military commander, the owner or manager, to assemble all workers together and order them to return to work; if this failed leaders were 'identified', arrested and, if necessary, drafted into the army. The remaining workers were then read an official order telling them that their strike was tantamount to desertion and ultimately punishable by death.[28] Strikes were treated as mutinies by the military. The response of the Styrian military command to these directions was even more severe. On 15 September 1917 the Graz military commander issued a communique on strikes. Strikers would be punished with heavy custodial sentences and martial law would be declared whenever a strike broke out. Strike leaders who had been condemned to death would be hanged within twelve hours of the publication of the verdict.[29] This extreme reaction followed two strikes in Upper Styria. It was after the first of these in July 1917 in Fohnsdorf that the authorities identified 'strike leaders', conscripted them and sent them to the Front. During the second, in Neuburg in August 1917, metalworkers stormed the manager's office, accused him of neglect and threw him out of his office, to which he never returned. This time the leaders were given long prison sentences.[30]

In the first three years of the war labour protest in Styria had

27. In June 1917 new legislation was introduced reducing the hours which were worked by female and juvenile labour and banning both from night work. As is the case with many apparently humane labour laws on women, the law created problems. The women's working day was cut and the most lucrative shift, the night shift, was unavailable to them. As a result their wages would have fallen. In the event, the law was not implemented. Klenner, *Die österreichischen Gewerkschaften*, vol. 1, p. 427.

28. Lafleur, 'Socialists, Communists and Workers', p. 34.

29. Stein, 'Die Lage', p. 240.

30. Erben et al. (eds.), *Die Alpine Montangesellschaft*, p. 159.

been caused by economic grievances, such as deteriorating food supplies and working conditions. The protest had been localised, sporadic and spontaneous, but had mirrored similar eruptions in other industrial regions of the Empire. Both the Social Democratic Party and the trade unions had effectively been excluded, both by choice and by circumstances. By the end of 1917 things began to change. The shortage of labour and high demand for armaments had given workers in all war industries an economic power which had previously eluded them. Even employers such as the Alpine Montangesellschaft had been forced to negotiate with their workers and to recognise workers' committees, the first of which was set up in Styria at the Donawitz plant. But demands and protests increased. Neither the military authorities nor the management of individual companies were able to contain the situation. Harsher penalties for demonstrating or striking appeared to indicate that the authorities were actually losing control rather than tightening their grip. In 1917 a strike broke out at the Köflach mine, in full view of the army, but no-one was punished. The Social Democratic Party openly organised peace rallies on May Day in 1917, the first time the labour day had been celebrated since the outbreak of hostilities. In Graz the rally took place, but without official permission and again without reprisals.[31]

One reason for the ineffectiveness of army action in Styria was the growing strength of the protest movement itself. Disaffection within the ranks of the ordinary soldiers also played a role. For instance, at Christmas in 1917, sixty-six men from the Fohnsdorf garrison near Judenburg deserted. When news of this spread workers throughout the district called for peace demonstrations in support of the men. Later that year, in May, the entire 17th infantry regiment stationed at Judenburg heard rumours that they were to be sent to the Front and broke out of their barracks, took over the town, looted shops and tore up railway lines in the local station. Miners from Fohnsdorf soon arrived and joined in the foray, with both groups handing out food to local workers and their families. The revolt was finally put down when a large contingent of Hungarian troops occupied the town. Five hundred people were arrested.[32]

The mutinies were particularly important in Styria, although not to the extent that Otto Bauer maintained when he later wrote that 'the revolution in the barracks immediately proved a revolution in

31. Ibid.
32. Lafleur, 'Socialists, Communists and Workers', pp. 107–8.

the factories'.[33] Rather than initiating the strike movement, they encouraged it to continue, by undermining the authority of the state and its ability to enforce regulations not only in the factories, but also amongst its own soldiers. Whereas the main causes of the strikes were food shortages, bad working conditions and antagonism towards the employers and the state, the mutinies were provoked by low morale and nationalism. It had been the policy of the Austro–Hungarian Imperial Army to deploy regiments of non-German-speaking soldiers in German-speaking areas and many of the soldiers stationed in Upper Styria were from Italian and Slovene regions.[34] During the final years of the war, as nationalist demands increased, soldiers deserted and mutinied in large numbers and in Styria they found additional support amongst Slavs who were working in the mines and a substantial number of Slovenes working on the railways.[35]

A second factor which undermined military control of the army in the province was the increased political activity to which the Imperial government was forced to concede in the wake of the Russian Revolution. The combination of uncontrolled strikes at home and revolution abroad forced the government to recall parliament and reconsider its attitude to the Social Democratic Party and the trade unions, allowing them to resume some political activity. In autumn 1917 both the party and individual trade unions were given permission to hold conferences for the first time since the outbreak of war, and at the party conference held in Vienna in October, delegates rejected the previous conformist policies of the leadership and chose instead the more radical platform of the Left Opposition group, led by Otto Bauer, and called for peace.[36] At the trade union conference held the following month, General Secretary Hueber, who had issued the directive in 1914 calling on workers to support the war effort, spoke on the theme of demobilisation and employment, urging an end to war and the restrengthening of trade unions to regain those losses which workers had suffered through employers' abuse of the war regulations. Both conferences congratulated the Russian working class on its victory and demanded

33. Otto Bauer, *The Austrian Revolution*, trans. by J.H. Stenning (abridged New York, 1970), p. 57.

34. Lafleur, 'Socialists, Communists and Workers', p. 107.

35. In 1918 the War Ministry reported that mutinies had broken out in Murau, Judenburg, Rimaszombat, Lablin, Pecs, Rumburg and Radkersburg. Robert Hinteregger, 'Die Steiermark 1918–19' (unpublished PhD thesis, Graz, 1971), p. 19.

36. Klenner, *Die österreichischen Gewerkschaften*, vol. 1, p. 444. Deutsch, *Geschichte der österreichischen Gewerkschaftsbewegung*, vol. 2, p. 44.

that the Austrian government should quickly conclude peace negotiations between the two countries which were taking place at
Brest–Litovsk.

During the autumn and winter of 1917 political tension in
Austria increased. Food supplies dwindled, hunger increased still
further and reports of delays at the peace negotiations found their
way back.' The Social Democratic Party sought to regain the
influence amongst workers that it had lost during the war years,
and organised peace meetings both in Vienna and the provinces.
But whilst putting itself at the head of the peace movement, the
leadership drew a line at adopting more aggressive tactics.[37] Their
argument was for a 'democratic peace', indicating continued caution and a fear that the Austrian working class might follow the
Russian example, 'the most dangerous adventure' as Otto Bauer
described Bolshevik policies on the eve of the October Revolution.[38] Party and union membership both increased over the
winter months, but by early 1918 there were strong indications that
the goals and methods of the party hierarchy were too moderate for
some of their members.

This became evident on 14 January 1918 when the government
announced a reduction in the flour ration for industrial workers in
Vienna and Wiener Neustadt. Workers at the Daimler factory in
Wiener Neustadt sent a delegation to the factory management,
which was responsible for issuing food rations, to say that they
could not survive on the new rate. The management promised to
make representation to the government, but on condition that
work was resumed.[39] The workers refused and went on strike. The
strike spread from Wiener Neustadt, to Vienna and finally to many
of the industrial centres of the Empire, reaching Upper Styria on
17 January. Workers in Bruck, Graz, Kapfenberg, the Erzberg,
Judenburg and Liezen all joined the strike, and on 20 January a mass
rally was held in Graz at which an estimated 45,000 workers were
present.[40]

The strikes began over the issues of food and peace, and these
were the first demands which strikers put forward. But as workers
from most of the industrial regions of the Empire joined the
protest, the scope of demands grew. There were strong calls for the

37. Peter Kulemann, *Am Beispiel des Austromarxismus* (Hamburg, 1979), p. 201.
38. Otto Bauer in a letter to Karl Kautsky 28.9.1917. International Institute for
Social History, Amsterdam. Kautsky Archive KD. 500.
39. Deutsch, *Geschichte der österreichischen Gewerkschaftsbewegung*, vol. 2, p. 46.
Klenner, *Die österreichischen Gewerkschaften*, vol. 1, p. 448.
40. Hinteregger, 'Die Steiermark 1918–19', p. 11.

end of military regulations in factories. In Graz demonstrators carried a banner which read:

> We want peace, freedom and justice,
> We demand that none shall be a slave.
> Work will be the right of all people
> And none shall be denied his livelihood.[41]

The Social Democratic Party's first reaction to the strikes was disapproving, but this quickly changed when leaders understood the size and importance of the demonstrations. The leadership then sought to channel the energies of the protest through its own organisation and set up a central committee of workers' councils comprising of representatives of the Vienna councils and, at first, restricted to party members only. In this way the councils had a central group of spokesmen, but one which was confined to the capital and had been brought under the wing of the party. The party then reinterpreted the strikers' demands and reduced them to four main points: peace negotiations must not be allowed to falter over boundary disagreements; the government should immediately reorganise the conditions of war duty; there should be immediate reform of the franchise both for local and national elections; and military rules in factories should be removed immediately. Armed with these points the leadership appointed a delegation of five – Karl Renner, Ferdinand Hanusch, Karl Seitz, Franz Domes (the leader of the Metalworkers' Union) and Viktor Adler – which began to negotiate with the government in the name of the strikers.[42] An agreement was reached and on 18 January it was brought before a meeting of the workers' council for ratification. Council members greeted it with derision, for it did include any concessions from the government. Each point had been initially accepted by both sides, but government representatives then embellished the details with so many qualifications and delays that the end result was an agreement in which none of the strikers' demands were met. During the debate which followed the party leadership argued that nothing more tangible was possible and reluctantly the motion to end the strike was accepted almost unanimously – 308

---

41. Lafleur, 'Socialists, Communists and Workers', pp. 69–71.
42. There is some disagreement about who was actually present at the meeting. Klenner named the workers' representatives as Viktor Adler, Karl Renner and Karl Seitz (Klenner, *Die österreichischen Gewerkschaften*, vol. 1, p. 451). Deutsch added Domes and Hanusch (Deutsch, *Geschichte der österreichische Gewerkschaftsbewegung*, vol. 2, p. 48.)

votes to 2.[43] But the agreement was not accepted by many of the strikers. Workers in Wiener Neustadt rejected the decision and stayed out for several days. Hungarian workers, who had come out in solidarity with the Austrians, also objected. In Styria labour leaders persuaded workers to return to work, but fresh strikes broke out in Köflach and Voitsberg at the end of the month.[44] Political fever cooled during the next few months as hunger and disillusionment took their toll, but in May riots erupted in Upper Styria. The May strikers reiterated many demands which had been voiced in January, in particular the call for peace, demilitarisation and political reform. Local party officials criticised the renewed disturbances, but then followed the earlier Viennese example and agreed to negotiate with the provincial government on behalf of the strikers. In the negotiations they abandoned the political demands and argued that the strikes were simple wage protests.

The 1918 strikes, and in particular those of January, differed from earlier protests and marked a change in the political strength of the labour movement both at local and at national levels. War conditions had intensified feelings of discontent amongst many workers, but as long as political freedoms were repressed active protest remained local and sporadic. In contrast the January strikes, which came some months after some restrictions had been lifted, were large scale and spread across regional boundaries to involve most industrial regions in the Empire. Communication between workers increased: when the Wiener Neustadt workers came out on strike one of their first actions was to send representatives to explain their actions and ask for support from workers in Styria, Bohemia and Vienna.[45]

The January strikes also demonstrated the growing influence of the Social Democratic Party over the Austrian working class. The party, which had been relatively inactive during the first three years of the war, sprang to life in the autumn of 1917 and increased its support in Vienna and the provinces. The party leadership had successfully called off the strike, despite the misgivings of many participants, and hence the outcome of the strike strengthened its political power. Nine months later, when the Empire disintegrated and bourgeois parties were left in disarray, incapable of assuming power in the new republic, the Social Democratic Party became the

43. Deutsch, *Geschichte der österreichische Gewerkschaftsbewegung*, vol. 2, p. 49.
44. Lafleur, 'Socialists Communists and Workers', p. 88.
45. The Czech workers did not join in the strike. (Bauer, *The Austrian Revolution*, p. 35).

major force in the new government.

But if the January strikes showed the strength of the party, they also indicated a weakness, a gap between the expectations and attitudes of the strikers and those of party leaders. In area after area demands were made which went beyond basic slogans for bread and peace and included vague concepts of 'power' and 'rights' and more direct cries for worker participation in management. The Social Democratic negotiators' interpretation of the strikes was narrower and ignored the allusions to power both on the shop floor and at the national level. Moreover, despite the vast size of the strike movement and the obvious strength of feeling that it produced, party leaders were prepared to abandon it without achieving any of its aims. The strikes and riots of the early summer of 1918 suggest that many workers were not.

Before the war the labour movement in Styria had been relatively weak. Union membership had been unstable, reflecting the uncertainty of workers who could not rely on the success of united action and who feared the consequences of being labelled as activists. The relationship between the employer and his worker was autocratic and only wavered when labour was in short supply. By 1919 the situation was very different. Working conditions had grown steadily worse and the recruitment of new workers had brought instability and even violence into the workplace. Outbursts in 1915, 1916 and 1917 were often spontaneous, at most locally organised and were limited to food riots or work stoppages which lasted for minutes or hours rather than days. Strike committees were elected, often manned by workers who had little previous experience in union or party politics, for the leadership of both wings of the labour movement at first opposed the waves of protest. As a result the strikes and demonstrations gave organisational experience to local men and a handful of women, who had previously shied away from political action. As the authority of the state crumbled, workers attacked first employers, then the state. They became involved in local strikes against what appeared to be local grievances, but were in reality issues affecting industrial workers throughout the Empire. Economic protest escalated into political protest and, by the end of 1917, it seemed to have broken the authority of even the strongest employer. Alpine Montangesellschaft was forced not only to negotiate with its employees, but also to recognise a workers' council. By 1918 some workers were even demanding the socialisation of the company and workers' control. There was little coherence in these demands, almost no consideration of the long-term implications of their success and, until 1917, no organisation. Once the union and party hierarchies acknowledged the existence of the movement and assumed responsibility for the workers' councils, large numbers of people joined both organisations in Styria, whilst still retaining a lack of discipline engendered during the war. In the early years of the Republic the Viennese leadership of the Social Democratic Party, which had assumed leadership of the new Republic on the strength of the class force the war had unleashed, frequently complained about the problems of organising the Styrian workers, and, above all, about the spasmodic support for communism in the province.[46]

46. Hinteregger, 'Die Steiermark, 1918–19, pp. 160–79.

−4−

The Party and the Republic

In his own analysis of the Austrian Revolution Otto Bauer greatly underestimated the significance of labour protest during the war and the role of the strike wave.[1] The Social Democratic Party leadership, in general, continued to do so. When the war ended in October 1918 and the vast Habsburg Empire finally disintegrated, leaving in its wake the small Austrian Republic, the party urged workers to return to their jobs. Notions of a radical seizure of power were firmly rejected as the leadership pledged the party to parliamentary democracy and unification with Germany.[2] This attitude was due, in part, to cautious pragmatism, but it also stemmed from the Austro–Marxist analysis of revolution as developed by Otto Bauer and, to a lesser extent, Max Adler, and from Bauer's belief that once the Empire had fallen, the first revolutionary phase was complete. From that point socialism could develop along a democratic path. His short-term goal was an electoral victory for the party and a series of legal reforms which would protect and extend the rights of the working class within the Republic. His long-term goal was to educate workers in the economic skills necessary to run the economy and transfer economic as well as political power from the bourgeoisie to the proletariat. In practice the electoral victory proved illusory and the complicated economic and political safeguards for the working class floundered. In Vienna, where the socialists held political power, the failure of this policy was not immediately obvious. But in Styria, where workers were in a minority, the victory of 1918 was very short-lived. The complexities of Bauer's philosophy were ill-suited to a politically inexperienced and economically vulnerable working class.

Bauer, who had been a prisoner of war in Russia from 1914 until his release following the February Revolution, became the most

1. Otto Bauer, *The Austrian Revolution*, trans. by J.H. Stenning (abridged New York, 1970), p. 56.
2. In November 1918 the Social Democratic executive voted in favour of a democratic socialist republic which would unite with Germany.

influential member of the party hierarchy on his return to Vienna in September 1917.[3] He was untainted by the wartime appeasement of the party leadership and his politics were more radical than those of Viktor Adler and Karl Renner, more in tune with those of Friedrich Adler, the hero of the anti-war movement.[4] However, Bauer's experiences in Russia had confirmed his earlier distrust of Bolshevik theories of revolution. There were, he believed, two types of revolution in modern society, the political and the social. In the political revolution, which can be completed in a matter of days, the existing state authority and institutions of privilege are overthrown, but economic exploitation remains intact. This, the democratic revolution, whilst making all people politically equal, still leaves them bound by the economic inequalities of capitalism and so only 'inaugurates the struggle for socialism'.[5] Socialism, as opposed to democracy, can only be achieved by years of work and progress within the democratic system.

The overthrow of the Austrian state arose, according to Bauer, from military defeat inflicted by the Entente in the First World War and the successful demands of the non-German nationalities of the Empire for independence. Thus the Habsburg Empire crumbled and fell. The role of Austrian workers counted for very little, he argued, and in his own account of the Revolution the strikes are rarely mentioned. The first strikes which are given the status of revolutionary demonstrations are the January strikes themselves, from which Bauer incorrectly dates the founding of the workers' councils.[6] That this myopic account of the war years belied the actual events is obvious. But it did serve a purpose. By minimising the workers' role Bauer could and did argue that the Revolution arose entirely from external forces – from the mutinies of non-German soldiers in the summer and autumn of 1918. To quote:

In the tumultuous soldiers' demonstrations, which were held daily in Vienna after the gigantic mass meetings of the 30th October, it became plain enough that the National and Democratic Revolution had awakened the Social Revolution and that the transfer of governmental power from the dynasty to the people had set in motion the class struggle within the nation.[7] The social revolution which arose out of the war

3. Bauer was arrested by the Russians on 23 November 1914 and remained a prisoner of war until July 1917. He returned to Vienna the following September.
4. Friedrich Adler, son of the party's founder, shot the chancellor in 1916 in protest against the war.
5. Otto Bauer, *Der Weg zum Sozialismus* (Berlin, 1919), p. 5.
6. Bauer, *The Austrian Revolution*, pp. 60, 84, 86, 130.
7. Ibid., p. 53.

proceeded from the barracks rather than from the factory.[8]

As long as the revolutionary factors were external, the revolution itself remained political rather than social. Bauer could ignore developments within the working class during the war, but he could not remain deaf to demands for workers' control and a dictatorship of the proletariat, which many workers' councils were raising during the early months of the Republic. These he put down to euphoria. 'The semi-revolution arouses the will to total revolution. The political upheaval awakens the desire for a social reorganisation.'[9] But if this were carried out at once, with workers seizing factories, the result would be chaos and the destruction of the economy on which the people depended. The Austrian people were already in dire straits, with no food, machines destroyed and almost no raw materials. Without the expertise of factory managers, technicians, engineers, etc., workers would find it impossible to run complicated works. If workers did attempt to seize the means of production and oust the managers, civil war would break out. Rather than improving the lot of the working man by redistributing goods, the standard of living would fall even lower than it was in the war. 'The people who expected from socialism an improvement in their condition would be terribly disappointed, and this disappointment would drive them into the arms of the capitalists.'[10]

Bauer did not believe that a proletarian revolution could succeed in Austria in 1918–19, nor that the violence which would result from declaring a dictatorship of the proletariat would lead to socialism. His immediate objections, which he later expounded in his book *The Austrian Revolution*, were based on practical considerations. The victors of the war, the Entente powers, would have prevented any attempts by Austrian workers to extend the revolution beyond the introduction of parliamentary democracy. The economic blockade, which had been imposed during the war, would have continued, cutting off essential supplies of food and coal and forcing the Austrian people into starvation. Incursions by Czech, Slovak and Slav troops along disputed border areas would have been encouraged and supported by supplies of Entente arms. 'The dictatorship of the proletariat, would have ended with the dictatorship of foreign commanders.'[11]

8. Ibid., p. 56.
9. Bauer, *Der Weg zum Sozialismus*, p. 7.
10. Ibid.
11. Bauer, *The Austrian Revolution*, p. 91.

In addition to the external threat, Bauer foresaw growing opposition within Austria itself, especially from the peasantry, which
amounted to approximately half the total population of the new
and considerably diminished Austrian state. These people had
initially supported the Revolution, hoping that it would abolish
restrictions imposed on them by wartime military requisitioning of
food. This to them represented the freedom and democracy of the
Revolution. However, chronic food shortages followed the war
and necessitated even stricter requisitioning and rationing, this time
carried out by the workers' militias. Hatred of the military became
hatred of the workers, fuelled by clerical accusations that the
Revolution would destroy the Church. Without the support of
the peasantry, workers would find themselves isolated within the
industrial regions of Vienna, its outlying areas and Upper Styria.
The interests of these two groups were, he argued, diametrically
opposed and 'the economic structure of the country therefore
created an equilibrium between the strength of classes, which could
only have been abolished by force in a bloody civil war'.[12]

Finally, Bauer argued, as we have seen, that dictatorship of the
proletariat would fail because of the poverty and lack of managerial
expertise of the working class itself. It was, he maintained,
impossible to destroy the economic structures of capitalism without first developing socialist alternatives. The result would be
chaos and hardship which would destroy the Revolution. Indeed,
the economic viability of the new Austrian state itself was unlikely,
even assuming the restoration of peace and order, and his major
priority as foreign secretary in the first government of the Republic
was to secure agreement for the unification of Germany and Austria.

When reading Bauer's account of the Revolution, practical and
economic obstacles seem to dominate his arguments against the
dictatorship of the proletariat. In various articles and pamphlets,
most notably 'Bolshevism or Social Democracy' and 'The Path to
Socialism', he developed a more theoretical argument, based on
comparisons between the revolutionary conditions in Russia in
1917 and those in central and western Europe, in particular Germany in 1918. Unlike more reformist socialist leaders, he did not
openly condemn the Russian October Revolution, but took great
pains to distinguish between a political revolution, in which a
revolutionary minority seizes power, and social revolution. The
Bolsheviks, he argued, were attempting to impose socialism on an

12. Ibid., p. 90.

underdeveloped capitalist society, in which the workers formed a minority of the population. The revolution which had brought them to power was not based on the spontaneous actions of the labour movement, but on the direction and leadership of a revolutionary intelligentsia.[13] The net result was a revolution which disenfranchised the majority of the population, the peasantry, by underrepresentation in the soviets, and the bourgeoisie by total exclusion from the political process. Success depended on the immediate socialisation of the means of production directed by a centralised authority. Bauer believed that the Bolshevik strategy raised three major problems which could block the progress of socialism. The first was the agrarian policy, which initially repressed the peasantry, but was later amended to grant concessions in return for food. Without the support of the Russian peasantry the Revolution could not succeed, but the concessions amounted to victory for the economic power of the peasants over the political military power of the Soviet state. The second problem was the role of Russian workers in the new economic system. The Revolution had been fought in their name, but following it they were still untrained and inexperienced in managerial skills. Socialisation did not, therefore, mean industrial democracy or workers' control, but the management of the economy by the Party in the name of the workers. It was not dictatorship of the proletariat, 'but dictatorship of the idea of the proletariat'.[14] This led to the third problem, the increased centralisation and growing power of the bureaucracy. As early as March 1918 he warned that the dictatorship of workers was really a 'dictatorship of the revolutionary secret organisation over the mass movement'.[15]

Despite these forebodings, Bauer defended the Bolshevik state on the grounds that dictatorship of the proletariat was sometimes the only means by which dictatorship of the bourgeoisie could be avoided. In these circumstances the seizure of political power by the proletariat was acceptable as a short-term measure, but only if it led to democracy and, as such, it was not an integral part of the development of socialism, but rather an incident in history similar

---

13. Otto Bauer (alias Heinrich Weber), 'Die Bolschewiki und wir', in *Der Kampf*, March 1918, pp. 137ff. Quoted in Raimund Löw, *Otto Bauer und die russische Revolution* (Vienna, 1980), p. 17. Bauer used two pseudonyms at this time, Heinrich Weber and Karl Mann.

14. Otto Bauer (alias Heinrich Weber), *Die russische Revolution und das europäische Proletariat* (Vienna, 1917), p. 8, quoted in Löw, *Otto Bauer*, p. 62.

15. Löw, *Otto Bauer*, p. 17.

to the Paris Commune.

Bauer's faith in the democratic state in bourgeois society, which appears to be directly at odds with Marx's 'Critique of the Gotha Programme', was ultimately based on his theoretical interpretation of the nature of the state in a democratic republic.[16] There were in fact two interpretations, which, though closely related and sharing similar conculsions about the benefits which democracy would bring to the working classes, were fundamentally different. In 'The Path to Socialism', and more explicitly in 'Bolshevism or Social Democracy', he acknowledged that democracy was an instrument of class domination, but maintained that it was an instrument which could fall into the hands of more than one class. It was, in fact, a mere form (*bloße Form*), an empty shell, which could be filled by capitalist, peasant or proletarian content, depending on such social factors as the numerical strength of the respective classes, their economic position, organisational strength and attitude or consciousness.[17] The concept of the neutral state, whose institutions could be exploited in favour of socialism, was implicit in this first interpretation. It provided Bauer with a justification for his political programme, spelt out in 'The Path to Socialism', which relied on the transformation of capitalism towards socialism by legal and constitutional means. Bauer was acutely aware of the similarities between this interpretation and the revisionist view of socialism, which had almost split the German Social Democratic Party before the First World War, and he took care to point out the differences. His contention was that the revisionists refused to accept the need for revolution in the development of socialism, whereas he fully accepted this as the means by which the working class could achieve political power. Without this political power control of the state would still lie with the bourgeoisie. But he again drew a distinction between political revolution and social revolution. The former had limited capabilities and could only effect political change. Social change would come from social revolution which was a far lengthier business and which could not be accomplished in street battles or in civil war, but only through creative legislation

16. Karl Marx, 'Critique of the Gotha Programme', in *Karl Marx and Friedrich Engels: Selected Works*, with an introduction by V.I. Lenin (London, 1968: original edn, Progress Publishers, Moscow), p. 332. 'Even vulgar democracy, which sees the millenium in the democratic republic and has no suspicion that it is precisely in this last form of state of bourgeois society that the class struggle has to be fought out to confusion. . . .'

17. Otto Bauer, *Bolschewismus oder Sozialdemokratie?* (Vienna, 1920), p. 110.

and administrative work.[18] Seen in this light, the democratic republic was no longer the 'form of a state in which alone the last decisive struggle between proletariat and bourgeoisie can be fought' as Engels had written, but became the foundation on which the new socialist society would be built.[19] More importantly, the relationship between state and class was not based on economic relations, but on social factors: social power as opposed to economic power.

This was the crux of Bauer's first writings on the state after the revolution, in which he saw democracy as 'the state form in which the distribution of power is exclusively determined by the social factors of power and not through the use of the means of material force'.[20] It was also the ideological basis of the Social Democratic Party programme of 1918, which was written by Bauer and which advocated expropriation of heavy industry, landed estates and the banks by law. Without a state which was permanently independent the peaceful transformation of property relations in a society was impossible.

This first view of the nature of the state in a democratic republic, written in the early and more favourable years of the Republic, was later superseded by Bauer's theory of the 'Balance of Class Forces'. No conflict between the two was acknowledged and indeed both theories include the concept of the neutral state. However, in the second and more complex analysis, this neutrality was not inherent within the state, but arose from a balance of class forces. In Chapter XV of *The Austrian Revolution*, Bauer began his explanation of this theory by rejecting his earlier assertion that the state was an instrument of class domination. Whilst accepting that this was the stand most commonly taken by Marxists, he described it as a 'contemporary' interpretation, a crude analysis which 'corresponded to the moral needs of the proletariat, just awakening, organising for the first time, just embarking upon the struggle'.[21] A more sophisticated analysis, drawn from Engels' 'The Origins of the Family, Private Property and the State' and Marx's critique of Bonapartism in the '18th Brumaire', recognised that the state could have more than one form and could, in specific circumstances, maintain an existence which was independent of class domination. This arose where the relative strengths of the opposing classes were

18. Otto Bauer, *Der Weg zum Sozialismus* (Berlin, 1919) p. 8.
19. Friedrich Engels, 'The Origin of the Family, Private Property and the State', in *Karl Marx and Friedrich Engels: Selected Works*, p. 588.
20. Otto Bauer, *Bolschewismus oder Sozialdemokratie?*, p. 109.
21. Otto Bauer, *The Austrian Revolution*, p. 243.

held in balance, preventing the domination of one class over another. It was, in Bauer's opinion, the situation in which Austrians found themselves after the Revolution.

> The state of equilibrium between the strength of the classes was from the beginning based upon the distribution of power between the great industrial district of Vienna, Lower Austria and Upper Styria, on the one hand, which could not be governed in opposition to the workers, and the great agrarian district of the federal provinces on the other hand, which could not be governed in opposition to the peasant.[22]

This balance of class forces, from which the bourgeoisie seemed to have been curiously omitted, resulted in a classless state, in which no single class could dominate the other, but each was forced to share power, to compromise and form a 'People's Republic'. Even after the failure of the first coalition government of Christian Socials, Pan-Germans and Social Democrats a complete restoration of the bourgeoisie was prevented by the strength of parliamentary and extra-parliamentary power of the organised working classes.[23]

Despite his denials, Bauer's 'Balance of Class Forces' came close to equating the power of a class with its numerical strength and ultimately its voting power, whether at the national or local level. The discussion of the state was in effect a discussion of government, the legislative sector, and omitted to take into consideration the executive or, more important, the judiciary. Furthermore, the state which he described was not independent of class control, but unable to fulfil the interests of the dominant class because of the strength of opposition. It was, therefore, not neutral but impotent. Whereas, in his earlier writings, he portrayed the democratic state as a progressive step in the development of socialism, providing the framework for the economic restructuring of society, in the *Austrian Revolution* his belief in democracy was still strong, but its role was to provide the working class with the means to prevent a dictatorship of the bourgeoisie.

The rights and wrongs of Bauer's analysis of the revolutionary potential of Austria in 1918 and his rejection of a dictatorship of the proletariat have been the subject of several books, most of which have approached the topic from the field of political philosophy and are concerned with the nature and basic principles of Austro–Marxism.[24] In a study such as this, the importance of Bauer's thesis lies in its

22. Ibid.
23. Ibid., p. 273.
24. Norbert Leser, *Zwischen Reformismus und Bolschewismus: Der Austromarxismus*

consequences, the impact of subsequent Social Democratic policies on Austrian labour and, specifically, on Styrian workers. The 1919 party platform and the party's attitude to the new Republic were both heavily influenced by Bauer. The contradiction between his two images of the democratic state was one cause of the decline and increasing ineffectiveness of the labour movement, especially in non-metropolitan areas. Throughout the years of the Republic, party leaders retained the conviction that fundamental socialist reform was possible within the democratic system, if only the party could win an election. As a result party members were warned of the dangers of aggression which would bring the walls of democracy crashing down upon them. Bauer may have stressed the difference between class force and electoral power in his writings, but such subtleties evaporated in practice. The conflict between what Anson Rabinbach has called the 'optimistic' and 'fatalistic' attitudes of the leadership dogged the party for the next fifteen years.[25]

Optimism proved to be ill-founded as was shown in the first national assembly election in February 1919. Aside from *Anschluß*, the most important planks in the Social Democratic election campaign were the socialisation of industry and commerce, the re-structuring of the foundations of labour relations, and welfare reforms. Once they were in power, party leaders argued, the social revolution could proceed. But whereas the revolution may have unleashed class forces, the election result depended on votes. The Social Democrats had already lost some support, when the industrial regions of Bohemia and Moravia were incorporated into Czechoslovakia in December 1918.[26] Despite a wider franchise which lowered the voting age to 21 and included women for the first time, the party achieved only a partial victory, winning 69 of the 159 seats.[27] Although this made it the largest single party in the assembly, it was denied an overall majority. The Christian Social Party gained 63 seats, the Pan-Germans 25 and the assortment of smaller parties accounted for two more.[28] As a result of this

---

als *Theorie und Praxis* (Vienna, 1968). Peter Kulemann, *Am Beispiel des Austromarxismus* (Hamburg, 1979). Löw, *Otto Bauer*.

25. Anson Rabinbach, *The Crisis of Austrian Socialism: From Red Vienna to Civil War 1927–1934* (Chicago, 1983), pp. 125–7, 63–6.

26. David F. Strong, *Austria (October 1918 – March 1919): Transition from Empire to Republic* (New York, 1974), pp. 167–73.

27. Officially the assembly had 156 members, elected by proportional representation. However 159 members were returned. *Stat Hdb Österreich* 1920 II.

28. In this election the Pan German Party was an alliance of eleven nationalist groups, including the German People's Party, the German Nationalists and the German Socialist Workers' Party. The 'other' parties included the Democratic

election it did not win control of the state, but was forced to set up a coalition government of all three larger parties, which it could dominate but not control.[29] Local elections were held later in the year and brought more problems when every province except for Vienna produced a sweeping victory for the Christian Social Party.[30] The tenuous hold which the Social Democrats had on the national government was challenged by the overwhelming support for the conservative parties in the provincial assemblies.[31]

Despite these handicaps, the party continued to pursue the programme of radical restructuring which it had advocated in the election campaign. Social welfare measures, some of which had been temporarily passed by the provisional government, were extended and new ones introduced. Laws were passed recognising the basic rights of workers to organise and negotiate collective contracts and creating safeguards for workers and their families in the form of the eight-hour day, unemployment benefit and job-creation schemes. The imperial rent controls of 1917 were strengthened, work books were abolished and many workers were guaranteed holidays with pay.[32]

At that time few of these laws were contentious and the legislation was passed with relative ease. But the Social Democrats had pledged themselves to more radical policies than mere reform. In a series of articles published in the *Arbeiter-Zeitung* a few weeks before the election and written by Bauer, the party executive endorsed a general plan for socialisation to be carried out by law.[33] These envisaged a staggered progression towards the total socialisation of all major industries, banks and landed estates, which would hopefully minimise any disruption of production and hence

---

Alliance, the German Austrian People's Party, the Jewish Nationalists and a Czech party (Die Tschechoslowaken).

29. This became the model for Bauer's theory of 'The Balance of Class Forces'.

30. The Social Democratic party won 100 of the 165 seats on the Vienna Council in 1919. R. Danneberg, *New Vienna*, trans. H.J. Stennings (London, 1931), p. 4.

31. In Upper Styria the Social Democratic Party won a victory, but they were outvoted by the Christian Social Party at the provincial level.

32. Conciliation Offices and Collective Agreements Act, December 1919. The Eight-Hour Day Act was extended during the same month. Abolition of work books, January 1919. Holidays with pay for salaried and waged workers, July 1919. Other major reforms were: State Unemployment Benefit Act, March 1920; Sickness Insurance Acts, February 1919, July 1920, March 1921; Expropriation of Industrial Concerns, April 1919; Community Control Act, July 1919; Factory Council Act, May 1919; Chamber of Labour Act, February 1920.

33. Bauer, *Der Weg zum Sozialismus*. Published originally in 1919 as a series of articles in the *Arbeiter-Zeitung*: 5 January, 9 January, 10 January, 14 January, 16 January, 19 January, 22 January.

aid the recovery of the national economy.[34] The most obvious contenders for socialisation, the banks, would for the time being be left in private hands – any threat to their ownership would undermine confidence and jeopardise any chances of securing credit from abroad. Instead the mines and iron and steel industries would first be confiscated by the state and handed over to the people. Private owners would receive compensation, the costs of which would be borne by remaining property holders through a progressive tax on land and capital. Socialised industries were to be run by boards of governors, representing the state, employees and consumers.

Socialisation was to be limited to large firms and industries, whilst smaller firms would continue to be privately owned. But the power of the owner would be considerably reduced by the reorganisation of such firms and their compulsory membership of industrial organisations. These were to be run by boards of governors similar to those for the socialised industries, but also including the employers. The boards would control all buying and selling, prices, wages and rationalisation and would considerably blunt the power of the employer.

In March 1919 the first socialisation act was passed in the national assembly. It introduced the basic principle that, if socialisation was necessary for the public good, the state could expropriate suitable industrial concerns. It also set up a state socialisation commission to vet individual socialisation bills and coordinate the entire national programme. The first specific bill legalising the expropriation of industrial enterprises became law on 30 April 1919.

Measures such as these, which were designed to redistribute property within the Republic, were only one part of the executive's proposed socialist revolution. A second important factor, which would be part and parcel of the redistribution of power, was the democratisation of the workplace. Every industrial, agricultural, commercial and transport firm employing more than twenty people would be legally obliged to set up a factory council, elected by all employees. These would have widespread powers and, in conjunction with the employers, would be responsible for hiring and firing of workers, setting regulations on wage levels and hours of work and the administration of factory housing, shops, canteens and welfare schemes. Elected representatives could not be sacked unless an independent judge agreed that they had broken trade regulations. The factory councils were not designed to replace

34. For this to succeed, the party considered that unification with Germany was essential.

management, but to work alongside it and ensure the eventual 'self determination in the labour process' which democratic socialism required.[35] In time the companies would be run by boards of governors, as outlined in the socialisation plans, and not by workers themselves, for that, the articles argued, would lead to syndicalism, not socialism.

These three strands of policy, welfare reforms, socialisation and the restructuring of industrial relations, together formed the Austro–Marxist path to socialism, the party executive's alternative to a dictatorship of the proletariat. The social welfare reforms were designed to protect workers and their families from excessive exploitation, the factory councils to give employees practical power on the shop floor and educate them in the skills of management and technology, and the socialisation programme slowly to transform property relations. Socialisation was the key, for without drastic economic reform the other two projects would be ineffective, resulting, at best, in welfare reformism, which Bauer shunned. All three were dependent for their success on the continued dominance of the Social Democratic Party in government and the ability and willingness of the state to enforce radical change. By March 1919, however, the party's political power was already in jeopardy and the independence of the state had yet to be tested.

In practice the theory proved to be flawed. On the one hand, most of the proposed welfare reforms became law by October 1920, although plans for an old age pension were scrapped. The national assembly passed socialisation bills and the factory council act. But on the other hand, the scope of the legislation was limited and progress was hampered by industrialists, trade unions and government ministers. The work of the socialisation commission provides a clear example. This had been instructed to oversee the various socialisation measures and produce a coordinated policy, beginning with the mines and metallurgical industry. The first obstacle to its work was a chronic shortage of coal in postwar Austria. Before the war coal had come from Bohemia, which was now a part of Czechoslovakia, or from Germany. The new Czech government was reluctant to send coal to Austria and German mines had negotiated contracts with a private firm, the Austrian industrial enterprise of Carl Königer. The coal shortage was critical in the first eighteen months of the Republic and the commission decided that proceeding with socialisation in the mines might

35. Bauer, *The Austrian Revolution*, p. 144.

aggravate what was already a grave situation. It therefore agreed to postpone expropriation plans indefinitely. Progress in the iron and steel industry, which was largely located in Styria, fared little better. The commission considered that expropriating firms which were owned by foreign companies was unwise, especially when these were net exporters and so earned vitally needed foreign currency. The Böhler company based in Kapfenberg, the second largest steelworks in Austria, was exempted for it was German-owned and had its company headquarters in Berlin. The wire mills of Felten and Guilleaume and the sheet-metal firms of Styria, Petzold, Gebrüder Lapp, and Vogel and Noot were also considered to be unsuitable, because they exported a large proportion of their products.[36]

This left the Alpine Montangesellschaft, which was not only the largest mining iron and steel conglomerate in the Republic, but also the largest private employer.[37] On 7 April 1919 employees had thrown the management out of the company headquarters in Donawitz and elected a committee of workers to run the firm. They sent a deputation to Vienna to demand immediate socialisation of the company, which was less dependent on exports than was Böhler and was Austrian-owned.[38] In May 1919 the commission began to discuss this, but negotiations were prolonged by the interjection of two deputies, Anton Rintelen, a Christian Social Member from Styria, and Otto Steinwender, a German Nationalist from Carinthia, who argued that the provincial government should take over the company.[39] In the meantime the company's shares, which had fallen in spring because of speculation about the socialisation plans, began to rise and by August 1919 the Italian industrialist, Camillo Castiglioni, had bought a majority holding in the firm. This transaction took place with the knowledge of the Minister of Finance, Josef Schumpeter, who had approved it without informing his government colleagues. The company then fell within the category of a foreign-owned firm and moves to socialise it were abandoned. Schumpeter's explanation for his actions was simple. The Austrian economy, he argued, was shattered after the break-up

36. Rudolf Gerlich, *Die gescheiterte Alternative: Sozialisierung in Österreich nach dem ersten Weltkrieg* (Vienna, 1980), pp. 189–99.

37. Emil Lederer, the chairman of the commission, was against placing so much emphasis on one firm. Ibid., p. 199.

38. Fritz Erben, Maja Loehr and Hans Riehl (eds.), *Die Alpine Montangesellschaft* (Vienna, 1931), pp. 168–9. Bauer, *The Austrian Revolution*, p. 131.

39. Gerlich, *Die gescheiterte Alternative*, p. 202. Michael Schacherl, *Dreißig Jahre der steirischen Arbeiterbewegung, 1890 bis 1920* (Graz, 1931), p. 298.

of the Empire, which had deprived commerce and industry of traditional sources of raw materials and markets. As food was still in very short supply, and whilst the Entente powers were delaying food shipments, the exchequer badly needed the foreign currency provided by the sale. However, this action also meant that foreign capital controlled the most important industry in the new Republic, reducing the power which government had over the economy rather than strengthening it. More important still, the sale of the Alpine Montangesellschaft successfully scuttled Social Democratic plans to socialise the iron and steel industry. In the long term it destroyed the vision of a democratic road to socialism, which had been dependent on the success of this policy. By 1921 few establishments had been expropriated and those that had were of little economic importance.[40]

Spring 1919 brought a second defeat for the Social Democratic proposals, inflicted this time by trade union leaders who had taken exception to aspects of the legislation on factory councils. They agreed with the basic provisions which required each plant or company employing more than twenty workers to set up a council elected by all workers. These were divided into two separate bodies, one representing manual workers and the second representing white-collar workers. They also supported the notion that these bodies should be responsible for supervising the welfare of workers and monitor the observance of labour laws and negotiated contracts by the employers. But they strongly opposed any suggestion that the councils should actually negotiate those contracts or be involved in the process of hiring and firing workers.[41] These functions, they argued, belonged to the trade unions. To delegate them to the councils, which were based on the plant or company level, would lead to syndicalism. National wage negotiations would be replaced by local agreements and the strength of the labour movement would be undermined. When the bill became law on 15 May 1919 many of the original ideas behind it had been dropped by the party. Factory councils were forbidden to negotiate directly with the employers over contracts, but would be consulted by the trade unions, who would conduct the negotiations. The councils could, however, negotiate local agreements and represent workers in discussions with the employers on piece rates. They

40. Max Lederer, 'Social Legislation in the Republic of Austria', *International Labour Review*, vol. II, nos. 2–3, May–June 1921, p. 148.
41. Charles A. Gulick, *Austria from Habsburg to Hitler* (Berkeley, California, 1948), vol. 1, p. 208.

were not involved in hiring and firing decisions, which remained the prerogative of the conciliation boards, bodies which had been set up during the war and consisted of representatives from both employers and employees who sat under the chairmanship of a state official. These boards became both the final arbiters in cases where a worker brought a case of unfair dismissal against an employer, and also the legal interpreters of collective contracts; all such contracts had to be registered with the board before they became binding. In this way collective contracts became legally enforceable in the Republic. Finally, compulsory consultation between the employer and workers' representatives, which had been central to Bauer's scheme, was reduced to a requirement that firms employing more than thirty people provided the factory council with a statement of profit and loss accounts and held monthly meetings with shop stewards. Joint-stock companies were also required to have two factory council representatives at meetings of the board of directors.[42]

The 1919 Factory Council Act considerably reduced the powers of the councils and made them subservient to the trade unions. The councils had sprung up in late 1917 and had led the strike movement of January 1918. In the early months of the Republic they had been largely responsible for maintaining some semblance of order, providing food for workers, and had been a forum for the debates which had raged amongst workers during the Revolution. Bauer had seen them as a functioning organ of labour within capitalist enterprises, protecting workers and educating them in skills which they would later need. In Styria the bill had actually been implemented before it reached the statute books when the Donawitz workers removed the management from the Alpine headquarters and installed their own factory council in its place. Fears of this type of wild socialisation forced the government to pass the legislation with speed, but even before this the Donawitz council had been recognised by both the government and the company.[43] And yet the law itself removed the strengths of such councils and relegated them to the ranks of consultative committees whose major responsibility was for the welfare of their workers. They had little real power.

The Social Democratic Party itself seemed to have been aware of

42. Lederer wrote that they were unpaid directors with the same rights as other directors. (Lederer, 'Social Legislation', p. 18.) Gulick suggests that they were merely observers. (Gulick, *Austria*, vol. 1, p. 203.)

43. Gulick, *Austria*, p. 137 footnote. Erben et al. (eds.), *Die Alpine Montangesellschaft*, pp. 168–9.

the limitations of the Factory Council Act and in February 1920 the national assembly passed a second set of laws setting up separate workers' organisations, the Chambers of Labour. These were modelled on the existing Chambers of Trade and Commerce and were designed to act as information bureaus, collecting data on unemployment, wage contracts, workers' insurance and working conditions and preparing reports for the government on behalf of the labour movement. They were to act as spokesmen for the movement when future legislation was drawn up, but could not participate in industrial disputes. In addition the Chambers of Labour became involved in workers' education, bridging a gap which had resulted from the Factory Council Act. Chambers of Labour were set up in Vienna, Linz, Graz, Salzburg, Klagenfurt, Innsbruck and Feldkirch and were elected by all workers over eighteen who had been employed in the area for more than two months. Candidates for election had to be over twenty-five and to have been trade union members for at least three years prior to the election. As a result of this last requisite, the Chambers of Labour were also dominated by the trade union movement.[44]

By October 1920, when the Social Democratic Party withdrew from the coalition government and went into what became permanent opposition, many major social reforms had become law. If these reforms are compared with conditions in the Empire, it becomes clear that they amounted to a radical change in the legal position of labour. But they fell far short of Bauer's 'self determination in the labour process'. One crucial factor was missing. Attempts to reinforce the changes in labour relations and welfare rights by socialising the basic industries and services and so transferring economic power to the workers had failed. And so the Social Democratic policy created a dichotomy between the legal position of labour and its economic power which intensified rather than reduced conflict on the shop floor. Employers could no longer use the traditional methods of fining and firing troublemakers, in theory, nor could they refuse to recognise trade unions. But workers were still faced with the fact that, in a bid to maintain and even expand profits, labour was one of the first costs which privately-owned industry could and would cut. The activities of the factory councils, in which Bauer had placed so much faith, were restricted to observing the implementation of the law, but they did not include wage negotiations or participation in management and

44. Lederer, 'Social Legislation', pp. 19–20.

did not have powers to enforce the law. This last role was allocated to the conciliation boards, which were controlled by the state. In the following years, as the instability of the Austrian economy led to high structural unemployment swelled by heavy seasonal fluctuations, the labour movement found that the legal protection which it appeared to have on paper gave little or no real protection against job losses and the determination of anti-union employers.

Changes in the economy, deteriorating working conditions and the breakdown of power towards the end of the war had unleashed a crude class force in Austria. This was adopted in the closing weeks of 1917 by a sophisticated and theoretically pedantic party leadership which came to power, temporarily, on the strength of the working class. Under the leadership of Otto Bauer, the party created a legal framework which, it was hoped, would protect workers against exploitation and increase their economic and political power within the Republic. But the machinery it created was too complicated and too cumbersome to be effective. In many areas workers who had had no previous political or organisational experience and almost no training were expected to grasp legal distinctions and procedures. Moreover, the laws had been passed when the political power of the working class was at its height and when the economy was in turmoil. This situation did not last long. In 1920 the Social Democratic Party left the coalition, the bourgeois parties regrouped and the new government began the task of stabilising the economy.

The SDAP's hands were tied, its political power was curtailed and so it was forced to turn its attention from the economic transition to socialism and concentrate instead on the more immediate problem of regaining national power. It did so by focusing on its main area of strength, Vienna, and tackling the problems which faced that city in the wake of the war. As the next chapter shows, a radical policy of social reformism developed out of this and became the hallmark of Austro-Marxism. But the weaknesses which were found in the labour legislation were also evident here. The policy failed to address itself to the wider problems of the Austrian labour movement, which continued unabated, as will be seen in subsequent chapters.

−5−

'Red Vienna'

The Social Democratic leaders crossed over into opposition convinced that the path to socialism went, initially at least, via the ballot box and depended on their ability to win 51 per cent of the vote in a general election. Before the transition to socialism could begin, the party had to be returned to power. This left the basic question of how this could be achieved. Once out of office the socialists' role in parliament would be largely inert, making speeches attacking government policy and defending postwar gains, and biding time until the next general election. Little more could be expected. But outside parliament they had retained one important political asset, for in the 1919 local elections the party gained control of the Vienna city council. If the national path to socialism had been temporarily blocked by defeat in the general election, this smaller local success still remained.

Moreover, Vienna had political potential, as Karl Lueger had demonstrated in the 1880s and 1890s when he launched his Christian Social Party by campaigning and mobilising the city's petty bourgeoisie.[1] Neither war nor revolution had diminished the importance of the capital within Austria. On the contrary, its political position had been enhanced. In 1919 it had a population of almost 2 million, one-third of all Austrians and, despite the economic crisis it faced in the wake of the break-up of the Empire, it remained a commercial and banking centre.[2] By virtue of its size and economic activity alone, Vienna was a major political asset for any opposition. But constitutional reform, passed in 1920 and enforced in 1921, raised its legal status from city to province, divorcing its administration from that of Lower Austria and increasing the powers of the city council to those of a provincial government. These included rights to administer its own budget and levy local taxes, which the national government could incorporate into national taxes, but could not veto. In such a large and economically

---

1. See John W. Boyer, *Political Radicalism in Late Imperial Vienna Origins of the Christian Social Movement, 1848–1897* (Chicago, 1981).
2. Eduard März, *Austrian Banking and Financial Policy* (New York, 1984).

diverse city, where one in ten inhabitants was a Social Democratic Party member in 1919, these constitutional changes enabled the council to raise considerable revenue and gave the party an opportunity to transcend the normally passive role of a parliamentary opposition. Instead party leaders were able to put their policies into operation, albeit on a municipal rather than a national scale. The result was 'Red Vienna', an experiment in city socialism carried out within the parameters of a capitalist economy.

'Red Vienna's' importance between the wars as a citadel of the middle road to socialism, neither Bolshevism nor reformism, and its violent demise in February 1934 have fired the pens of poets and historians ever since.[3] The most recent subjects of discussion have been the Social Democratic Party's ideological debates, the architecture of the council housing projects, which formed the core of its political programme, and the institutional framework of its extensive cultural activities. Relatively little attention has been paid to the practical consequences of the 'experiment' on Austrian interwar politics and the working class of Vienna, let alone the rest of Austria, beyond comments that the existence of such a radical municipal policy in the capital heightened class tensions and therefore contributed to the surge in civil conflict. One exception to this can be found in the work of Helmut Gruber, who has gone as far as to describe the literature of 'Red Vienna' as a 'eulogy', an attempt to produce an icon to Austrian Social Democracy. As a result, he believes 'the institutional cultural efforts of the Austrian Social Democratic Party (SDAP) and Viennese municipality have largely become accepted as the culture of the workers'.[4]

Institutions have taken precedence over people and the success of the experiment has been measured in terms of the number of houses built and the breadth of welfare reforms, rather than the effect these had on lives and attitudes. As an exercise in socialism which sought to transcend pure reformism, 'Red Vienna's' success

---

3. Some examples are: Stephen Spender, *Vienna* (London, 1935); Anson Rabinbach (ed.), *The Austrian Socialist Experiment* (Boulder and London, 1985); Helmut Weihsmann, *Das Rote Wien* (Vienna, 1985); Hans Hautmann and Rudolf Hautmann, *Die Gemeindebauten des Roten Wien, 1919–1934* (Vienna, 1980); Rainer Bauböck, *Wohnungspolitik im sozialdemokratischen Wien, 1919–1934* (Vienna, 1980); Dieter Langewiesche, *Zur Freizeit des Arbeiters: Bildungsbestrebungen und Freizeitgestaltungen österreichischer Arbeiter im Kaiserreich und in der Ersten Republik* (Stuttgart, 1979); Josef Weidenholzer, *Auf den Weg zum 'Neuen Menschen'. Bildungs- und Kulturarbeit der SDAP in der Ersten Republik* (Vienna, 1981): Peter Kulemann, *Am Beispiel des Austromarxismus* (Hamburg, 1979).

4. Helmut Gruber, 'Socialist Party Culture and the Realities of Working-Class Life in Red Vienna' in Rabinbach (ed.), *Austrian Socialist Experiment*, p. 223.

cannot be assessed in this way, nor can the discussion be limited to the capital itself. A major tenet of the Social Democrats' municipal socialism was that it would improve the physical and cultural environment of the Viennese working class and raise self-respect and consciousness to a level which reflected the leadership's view of a socialist society, peopled by 'der Neue Mensch' (the new human being). But this was not its sole nor even its most important purpose. The Social Democratic Party did not intend to create 'socialism in one city', but a working model of socialism which would demonstrate the practical possibilities of its policies and attract new voters, convincing them of the sense of voting for the party in the next general election.[5] 'Red Vienna' was to become living propaganda, 'Propaganda der Tat',[6] the major plank in a recruiting campaign to consolidate working-class support and allay the fears of the petty bourgeoisie, who equated socialism with disaster. In the words of Otto Bauer, 'the class war between the proletariat and ruling classes is all a battle for the souls of the petty bourgeoisie and farmers'.[7] 'Red Vienna' was designed to win those souls for the socialists, or at least to win their votes and so the next election, and for this reason the analysis of municipal socialism must consider the implications of the policy outside the city boundaries as well as within them. The purpose of this chapter is to examine the development of the Viennese programme and its effectiveness both in Vienna and as a national electoral programme.

The municipal socialism of Vienna was not carried out according to a political blueprint. Indeed, in the Empire, party intellectuals appeared to have paid little attention to local politics and the practical considerations of a functioning political microcosm, absorbing themselves instead in broader theoretical questions. But the subject was not completely ignored. Proposals for city council reform were adopted at the 1900 party conference and published in 1914.[8] They included demands for an end to the curia system of franchise, autonomy for Vienna, council housing, progressive taxation, school reform and a city health authority, all of which became important features of the party's future programme.[9]

5. J. Braunthal, 'Auf dem Weg zur Macht', Der Kampf (XVI) 1923, pp. 345–8.
6. A phrase used by Bauer meaning active propaganda or propaganda of action.
7. Otto Bauer, 'Klassenkampf und "Ständeverfassung". Wirtschaftliche Basis und Politischer Überbau', Der Kampf, 27, no. 1, January 1934, p. 1, quoted in Norbert Leser, Zwischen Reformismus und Bolschewismus (Vienna, 1985, 2nd edn), p. 22.
8. Hautmann and Hautmann, Gemeindebauten, p. 54.
9. The curia system, established for municipal elections after the 1848 Revolu-

However, the policy was at an embryonic stage and contained few practical details and no more than a vague outline of the theory or philosophy involved. The failure to incorporate these policies into a broader discussion on the nature of socialism and the role of local politics continued in the interwar years. The party never did develop a theory of community politics, as Hans Hautmann has pointed out.[10] Instead municipal socialism came to mean whatever was happening in the capital. 'Red Vienna' was very much a product of the crisis which beleaguered the city in 1919, when the socialists took over control. In the initial stages, at least, the steps taken to alleviate that crisis were pragmatic and yet many of the most characteristic aspects of the Austro-Marxist's municipal socialism stemmed from that time.

For instance, in the 1920s the council wove an intricate and interconnected taxation and housing policy, maintaining high progressive taxation, low rents and a vast municipal building programme. This policy arose from the appalling condition of housing in postwar Vienna and not from a political principle which saw housing as a fundamental stepping stone on the road to socialism. The roots of the problem lay in the Empire when housing had been an important political issue in Vienna. The nature of the local council franchise, based on a curia system, gave greater political power to those who owned property, particularly landlords.[11] Many city councillors were also landlords and it is therefore not suprising that building and housing regulations, which were controlled by the council, were weak. Working-class housing was particularly bad. Tenements and barracks were built at the end of the last century without adequate light or space and with common lavatories and taps. In 1894, Eugen von Philippovich, the economist, described these buildings as 'miss[ing] everything we are accustomed to regard as the foundation of a healthy existence. The dwelling is merely a shelter from the inclemency of the weather, a night's lodging, which owing to overcrowding, lack of

---

tion, divided the electorate into three categories according to the level of tax payable and educational status. Three curias were created, each electing the same number of delegates. The highest tax-payers voted in the first, the professional classes and small property owners in the second, and artisans who paid minimal taxes in the third. Workers did not have a vote and landlords were credited with the rent tax of their tenants. For this reason, the political power of the Viennese landlords was particularly high before the First World War. See Boyer, *Political Radicalism in Late Imperial Vienna 1848–1947*, pp. 13–17, 285–7, 394–5.

10. Hautmann and Hautmann, *Gemeinde bauten*, p. 90.
11. Robert Danneberg, *New Vienna*, trans. H.J. Stenning (London, 1931), p. 2. See footnote 9 above.

quietness, of air and of cleanliness, can never be a resting place for the exhausted body.'[12]

A 1917 housing survey of four Viennese districts showed that 90 per cent of homes consisted of only a kitchen, main room and a corridor room, or even less.[13] These 'small' flats accounted for almost 75 per cent of all Viennese homes before the war and, even with these, homelessness and 'bed-letting' were rife: in 1900 approximately 3 per cent of the inhabitants of Vienna were classified as 'bed tenants'.[14]

Despite these problems the prewar council refused to intervene in the housing market, beyond providing 250 'units' for those in desperate need. Instead, land and property speculation flourished and rents rose. Philippovich calculated that in terms of rent per square metre many small flats were more expensive than luxury flats on the Ringstraße. Taxes, both local and national, were also levied on rents, with half the city revenue coming from this one source. Viennese housing was the worst in Europe before the war. High rents and overcrowding took their toll on health and Imperial Vienna was known as the tubercular capital.[15] Fear that this situation could incite rebellion persuaded the government to introduce controls during the war, effectively pegging rents at their 1913 level. The measure was meant to be short term, to last for the duration, but it remained in force until 1929, forming the major issue in two general elections and part of the backbone of municipal socialism.[16]

Rent controls did ease some of the pressure on working-class families towards the end of the war, but they did not solve the housing problem. A League of Nations' report published in 1925 stated that 'at the end of the war, the city of Vienna was perhaps in a more difficult position than any other town in Europe. Stocks were exhausted, repairs had not been carried out for years and a considerable proportion of the population was in need of public

---

12. Eugen von Philippovich, 'Wiener Wohnungsverhältnisse', *Archiv für soziale Gesetzgebung und Statistik*, vol. 7 (1894), p. 236.

13. These were known as *Kabinette*. Charles A. Gulick, *Austria from Habsburg to Hitler* (Berkeley, California), vol. 1, p. 409.

14. Ibid, p. 412. A bed tenant rented space in a bed (usually) at night. They were not allowed to enter the room at other times.

15. See Jill Lewis, 'Red Vienna: Socialism in one city, 1918–1927', *European Studies Review*, vol. 13, no. 3, July 1983, pp. 335–54.

16. Rents could only be increased to cover increased costs of maintenance, administration, house tax or mortgage interest. Housing built after the war was exempt. Ibid.

assistance.'[17] Unemployment was also high and growing, as de-mobbed soldiers and immigrants from Bohemia, Moravia and other areas of the defunct Empire flocked into the city, adding to the demand for homes and jobs. There was a chronic shortage of food as supplies from successor states ended and those from rural areas proved unreliable. People were weak from hunger, while the 'flu' epidemic raged and child mortality and deaths from tubercu-losis soared.

This was the situation which confronted the Social Democratic council when it took office in May 1919. Its first priorities were to maintain existing welfare payments and ease the housing crisis. From this the strategy for 'Red Vienna' emerged. Unemployment payments had begun in November 1918, financed by the state. In February 1919 Vienna's interim council began to make additional payments to the families of the unemployed and raised these again at the end of April after violent demonstrations of the Ringstraße.[18] The major problem was finance. Initial funds came from foreign loans which totalled 179.5 million crowns in 1918/19, or one-third of the city's total revenue. Any continuation of this policy was fraught with difficulties; the Österreichische Volkswirt calculated at the time that by 1920 the debt would account for half of all incoming revenue and the proportion could only grow greater, as the value of revenue would fall with postwar inflation and the rent freeze.[19] The new council agreed. It used existing resources to pay off the debt, benefiting from the falling value of the capital sum during a period of inflation, and was then left with an urgent need to increase revenue without resorting to further loans.

The solution came about as a direct result of the constitutional changes outlined at the beginning of this chapter, which allowed the council to administer its own budget and levy new local taxes as a provincial government. Under the direction of Hugo Breitner, an example of that one-time rare phenomenon, the socialist banker, the new council tried to create an inflation-proof taxation scheme which would be economically efficient and politically acceptable to the Social Democratic Party. It aimed to use local taxes to shift the cost of social welfare from the poor to the rich by replacing flat-rate direct taxation with progressive indirect taxation levied specifically on luxury consumption. In the first ten years of the Republic the

17. W.T. Layton and C. Rist *The Economic Situation of Austria. Report to the League of Nations* (Geneva, 1925), p. 158.

18. These were said to have been part of a Communist 'putsch' attempt. See Gerhard Botz, *Gewalt in der Politik* (Munich, 1976), pp. 43–53.

19. Gulick, *Austria from Habsburg to Hitler*, vol. 1, p. 355.

council introduced taxes on servants, carriages, horses, high-class restaurants, cafés and hotels, beer, posters, auctions and amusements. The rationale for some of these taxes was blatantly moral: for example, the tax on amusements, levied on tickets for concerts, operas and cinemas, ranged from 10 per cent to 50 per cent. Cinemas paid the highest rate because the council, and hence the party leaders, wanted to encourage its supporters to indulge in 'higher' cultural pastimes. (This paternalistic aspect of 'Red Vienna' will be discussed later). Other taxes verged on the comical. The dog tax, which had existed before the war, was to have become progressive depending on pedigree, but it had to be dropped after twelve months because the cost of administering it was greater than the revenue it brought in. Such failures were, however, rare and progressive taxation was not confined to luxury consumption. The council retained a tax on rents, but made payment progressive; the higher the rent, the higher the tax payable. By 1927 56.6 per cent of revenue from the rent tax was paid by 1.45 per cent of tenants. A 'welfare' tax on wage bills was also introduced as a means of taxing industry and commerce without falling prey to the problems which profit taxes incurred during periods of inflation.[20]

The combination of luxury welfare and rent taxes became the basis of the Social Democratic Party's radical fiscal policy in Vienna and progressive taxation a key to its municipal socialism. One irony was that both arose from defeat: defeat in the national election and defeat of the party's proposals for a centralised constitution for the new Republic. Indeed, in the postwar constitutional struggles Social Democrats had fought hard for a centralised state with diminished powers for the provinces. When they lost this battle the elevation of Vienna to provincial status was passed as a compromise.[21] Without this the entire policy of 'Red Vienna' would have been a non-starter. For the same reason, the practical application of the policy outside Vienna was also impossible, because the party had no chance of winning a majority in any other Austrian province. Even if it had, the revenue from a non-metropolitan province would have been too small to support the radical policies which its leaders favoured. The situation in Vienna was, therefore, unique and could not be reproduced elsewhere.

Within three years Breitner's taxation system had produced a

---

20. Lewis, 'Red Vienna', p. 345.
21. Maren Seliger, 'Zur Politik des "Roten Wien"', in *Traum und Wirklichkeit – Wien 1870–1913* (catalogue of an exhibition by the Historical Museum of the City of Vienna held in the Künstlerhaus October 1985) (Vienna, 1985), pp. 641–2.

budget which was balanced and remained so, despite rampant inflation and the collapse of the currency in 1922. Moreover, to quote again the 1925 League of Nations' report, '[in] contrast with the finances of the state, the finances of Vienna throughout the period of inflation were handled in a way which maintained equilibrium'.[22] The contrast between state and council continued. In 1923 the government negotiated loans through the League of Nations to finance currency restabilisation. In so doing they agreed to abide by a supervised and deflationary economic programme. The city avoided further loans and outside political interference and was able to spend its revenue as it saw fit – on the reconstruction of Vienna.

The political consequences of this were problematic and 'Red Vienna' became one of the most contentious issues in the First Republic. Opponents accused the council of 'tax sadism' and 'tax bolshevism', of bleeding dry the bourgeoisie, forcing businesses into bankruptcy and workers into unemployment. Political venom was directed at the luxury taxes, but the economic arguments revolved around the welfare tax which, the Right maintained, was an attack on jobs. The socialists responded by arguing that employers regarded any tax on their activities as a tax on jobs, because all taxes added to costs. A profit tax might have been marginally more palatable, but it had serious drawbacks, foremost of which was the problem of collection. A profit tax could only be assessed annually when companies filed their returns and so during periods of inflation the value of its revenue fell. It was also susceptible to the vagaries of clever accountancy. A tax on wages could be collected monthly and was less vulnerable to falling value during inflation. The jobs created by the council and financed from this tax would, they also argued, more than compensate for any job losses in the private sector.[23]

But the council's critics were not confined to the political Right. In 1922 a series of strikes broke out amongst its own employees – gas and electricity workers, the fire brigade, city administrators and tramworkers – sparked off by a refusal to increase pay in line with inflation. In its attempts to maintain a balanced budget, the council had decided to enforce a rigid control on expenditure, including wages. It was a paradoxical situation for the labour movement. The country's largest union, the Metalworkers', had fought for and won a sliding scale of wages linked to the price index and based on

22. Layton and Rist, *The Economic Situation*, p. 41.
23. Lewis, 'Red Vienna', pp. 346–7.

a proposal put forward by Karl Renner in 1919.[24] Other unions had tried to negotiate similar agreements, but these were strongly resisted by employers, amongst whom the socialist Viennese council could now be counted. The party press berated striking tramworkers for being led astray by Communists and Catholics.[25] A party leader accused strikers of shortsightedness and jeopardising the long-term benefits which municipal socialism would bring for the many for short-term gains in the pay packet. The party knew best, a theme which persisted throughout the days of 'Red Vienna'. But the fact the strike had taken place at all indicated the deeper dilemma arising from the Austro-Marxist shift from economic socialism to social welfarism. In 1918 the party had championed socialisation of the economy, democratisation of the workplace and welfare reform. By 1922 it was left with welfare reforms on a municipal scale and tinkering with mechanisms of taxation within a capitalist economy to finance them.

On the other hand, Hugo Breitner's taxation system was an imaginative solution to Vienna's immediate budgetary problems. By 1924 it was generating enough income to maintain the city's budget at its prewar level, despite drastic reductions in allocations from national revenue, and so was able to finance major municipal investment on housing – the second major problem which confronted the council in 1919. Indeed, the solution to the housing crisis came to symbolise 'Red Vienna'. But, like the taxation policy, it arose initially from necessity rather than ideology. The plight of Viennese housing has already been described. The council's first step to alleviate the crisis was to make liberal use of national requisitioning laws, taking over any surplus living space, including single rooms in bourgeois homes. It was a controversial measure which forced some middle-class families to endure the same indignities which poor families had experienced for years when letting out beds – having to have a stranger live in one's midst. It was also unsuccessful in solving the housing crisis. The council turned to house-building in 1920. In 1923, having completed over 7,000 flats, it launched a campaign to build 25,000 more over five years, its major platform in the council elections. These were finished a year early and a plan for 30,000 more was announced before the 1927 elections. By 1933 64,000 units of council housing had been built, paid for almost entirely out of the council's

24. März, *Austrian Banking*, p. 415.
25. Karl Weigl, 'Die Organisationskrise bei den Wiener Straßenbahnern', *Der Kampf* (XVI) 1923, pp. 220–2.

budget. The Austrian Social Democratic Party, which had been renowned for its theorists before the war, became the forerunner of modern council housing and community politics.

At the centre of this lay the 'superblocks' or 'workers' palaces', built along main roads and railway embankments leading into the city on land the council acquired in the early 1920s when land prices fell. These massive estates eventually housed over 50,000 families, 1,325 of them in a single complex, the Karl Marx Hof, which spanned almost a kilometre between the Danube Canal and a northern main road. This six-storey building with its turrets and arches resembles a large, solid fortress, a point which did not escape the socialists' political adversaries. Architectural plans were chosen by tender, but had to conform to rigid guidelines. Actual buildings were restricted to one-third of the total site, leaving open space for recreation. Flats were small with a kitchen, hall and one or two bedrooms. Each had a toilet, but bathrooms were not included on the grounds of cost and also, some argued, because communal bathing fostered a stronger community spirit. But to allay any fears that the party was encouraging immodesty, it should be pointed out that these facilities were strictly segregated according to sex. Indeed, the laundry rooms, where tenants could wash their (white) clothes on specified days only, were barred to men, ostensibly to protect the women from embarrassment. Needless to say, it also protected the men from the arduous task of sinking their elbows in suds.[26] Flats had running cold water, gas and electricity, but no hot water or central heating. The larger blocks also had libraries, kindergartens, medical centres and shops on site and each bore a plaque proclaiming that it had been built by the Vienna council and paid for out of the building tax.

The Social Democratic Party was intensely proud of the Viennese housing. In 1930 Karl Renner remarked that the 'workers' palaces' would stand as a monument to the party long after the present occupants had died.[27] But, as with the taxation, the schemes had their critics. Landlords and right-wing politicians accused the council of destroying the private housing market and pauperising landlords. Their attacks were directed at the rent

---

26. This is not a flippant point. A questionnaire carried out among 1,320 female factory workers in 1931 revealed that many were sole breadwinners. Their lives were hard and Käthe Leichter, who carried out the survey, pointed out that the party did little to address their needs. Käthe Leichter, *So Leben Wir. 1320 Industriearbeiterinnen berichten über ihr Leben* (Vienna, 1932).

27. Quoted in Norbert Leser, *Zwischen Reformismus und Bolschewismus: Der Austromarxismus als Theorie und Praxis* (Vienna, 1968), p. 220.

protection legislation, which the Social Democratic Party defended in the national parliament, and the council, which voluntarily enforced an identical rent policy even though its own housing was exempt. As a consequence of this and the scale of council housing, it was no longer profitable to rent out accommodation. The designs of the flats were also attacked by the Right, as mentioned earlier, and the Social Democrats were accused of building along main transport routes into the city as part of a long-term plan to launch a revolution. When the civil war broke out in February 1934 and the fiercest fighting in the capital centred in and around the 'workers' palaces', the government felt such charges had been vindicated. But these were political accusations hurled by people who fundamentally disagreed with any and all aspects of socialism. Nearer to home there were other critics. The first announcements in 1920 provoked a demonstration of 50,000 outside the town hall demanding houses and gardens rather than blocks of flats. The cost of extra land plus new roads, sewerage, electricity and gas was prohibitive the council argued, but when an international conference of town planners reiterated this complaint in 1926, a compromise was announced. Blocks built after 1926 were landscaped and a number of small garden estates were also built. A second more crucial criticism, that the flats themselves were too small, was not solved.[28]

This brings us to the central questions of the role of council housing in the ethos of municipal socialism and Austro-Marxist philosophy and the impact of these on the lives of Viennese workers. The answers, for there are definitely more than one, are not easy to deduce, despite rivers of ink which have been spilled on the subject of 'Red Vienna'. Most sources are found in party journals and reports which outline in detail the benefits the system brought to the Viennese. Without a doubt these were impressive. In addition to the housing, the council built swimming baths, libraries, gymnasiums, kindergartens and childrens' refuges. It planted new parks and reorganised street cleaning to provide a healthier and safer environment, initiated campaigns against tuberculosis, venereal disease, smallpox and alcoholism and bought five grammes of radium to treat cancer victims. Counselling was provided for the latter and for the mentally ill, deaf and blind.

28. Flats built before 1926 were of two sizes: 75 per cent were 38 sq.m., the rest were 48 sq.m. After 1927 there were four categories: 21 sq.m. for single occupants, 40 sq.m., 49 sq.m., and 57 sq.m. For details of the architectural controversies see Weihsmann, *Das Rote Wien*, pp. 166–90.

Heated rooms were opened for those without homes or heating. Free milk and warm midday meals were available in city schools, which were reorganised and modernised. Children under three were entitled to places in kindergartens run on Montessori methods. District welfare committees were set up to coordinate the council's welfare work with private agency programmes. Special attention was given to mothers and babies; new clinics offering nutritional and health advice were opened and children who were judged to have special problems – having been orphaned or coming from single-parent or poor or violent homes – were monitored. Child mortality dropped from 158 deaths per thousand live births in 1918 to 60 per thousand in 1933.[29]

The council's programme, which had begun with pragmatic responses to fiscal, housing and welfare problems, soon swelled into a host of social welfare organisations, each intended to offer guidance, support and, if necessary, instruction to individuals or families in difficulties. The entire edifice was controlled from the centre by the council and, for the most part, financed by it. Drawing on the expertise of some of Vienna's most eminent experts – Otto Glöckel for education, Julius Tandler for social welfare and Hugo Breitner and Robert Danneberg for economics – the council had indeed created a model social welfare system. But aspirations went further, to create a new culture, a new society, 'der neue Mensch' (the new human being).

At this stage of the discussion it may be useful to be reminded of the original grounds on which the party had turned to municipal socialism. This was to establish a working model of socialism in order to increase electoral support and win a general election. It was a step towards socialism, taken in the face of defeat when more favoured paths, such as the socialisation of property and the democratisation of the workplace, had been blocked. In the early years at least, it was not seen as a goal in its own right. However, the success of the council's work, coupled with the expanding activities of the Social Democratic Party in the city, altered this attitude, even distorted the vision of some party leaders, giving them a misplaced faith in the potential of their experiment. In 1931 the party's newspaper, the *Arbeiter-Zeitung*, proclaimed Vienna to be 'a social democratic city. Its pores seeping with socialist spirit, with proletarian will – a red city through and through, not only at skin level and in its administration as in some other cities, but in its

29. Gulick, *Austria from Habsburg to Hitler*, vol. 1, pp. 509–15.

life, its blood and its nerves.'[30] Twelve months earlier the party's slogan in the national election had been 'From Red Vienna to Red Austria'. Robert Danneberg was more cautious. In the same year he wrote: 'Capitalism cannot be destroyed by the town halls. But large cities are able to create a sound piece of socialism within a capitalist society.'[31] He was not alone. The party had come a long way since 1919, when it supported unification with Germany on the grounds that Austria could not survive as a socialist island in a capitalist world, to this praise of Vienna as a 'piece of socialism', a socialist island in a capitalist country. Economics had been the key to the earlier concept. In the second the economics were overshadowed, almost fully hidden behind the city's social and cultural achievements. Social welfarism and a strong and active socialist movement were being confused with socialism itself. Clear examples of this can be found in the leadership's pursuit of 'der neue Mensch', a proletarian culture which was distinct from its bourgeois counterpart, but had little to do with the street culture of most Viennese working-class families. Social Democratic leaders had a vision of creating a socialist class-consciousness within a working class which still contended with a capitalist economy. And what is more, that capitalist economy was in crisis and the working class in question was only one section of the party, albeit a large one.

The concept of 'der neue Mensch' stemmed from the party's cultural and educational traditions in general and Max Adler's writings in particular. Adler, a relative maverick within the party hierarchy, rejected what he saw as the 'economic determinism' of the prewar leadership and argued that progress towards socialism would only take place with the aid of socialist education. He warned of the dangers of party instruction rather than education, arguing that the objective was not to direct workers, but to develop their critical faculties. This, he pointed out, could also be a problem for the party, for it would lead to self-criticism and so criticism of both the party and its leaders. This, too, was a necessary step towards socialism.[32]

Although the phrase 'der neue Mensch' passed into the party's vocabulary in the 1920s, Adler's thesis was only partially accepted. Education did become a major issue, both as council policy

---

30. *Arbeiter-Zeitung*, 19 July 1931.
31. Robert Danneberg, *Das Neue Wien* (Vienna, 1926), p. 80.
32. Max Adler 'Neue Menschen', reprinted in Alfred Pfabigan (ed.), *Vision und Wirklichkeit. Ein Lesebuch zum Austromarxismus* (Vienna, 1989), pp. 89–97.

through Glöckel's school reforms and within the party itself, through childrens' associations, parents' clubs, youth and student groups, as well as the vast array of lectures the party organised throughout the city.[33] But the emphasis was on moral and political instruction, not self-criticism. Indeed, as Anson Rabinbach has shown, party leaders were 'always sceptical that too much political discussion and activity would lead to increasing autonomy on the part of the youth organisations and sought to limit them to purely educational concerns'.[34] This was in line with the underlying commandment of Austrian Social Democracy – unity within a mass party which preached mass participation, but only up to a point. Education in this sense was the process by which the party broadened the outlook of its members, absorbing them into an environment which would strengthen their resolve and raise their cultural values. 'We need new human beings who will build a better world with intelligence, energy and idealism.'[35] A new people, a new culture, but a culture for the people, not of it. For Tandler, Danneberg and others the object was to raise the standards in working-class communities and divorce them from the contamination of bourgeois association and those retrogressive aspects of working-class life which were condemned as petty bourgeois. The ideal working class for whom 'Red Vienna' was designed was politically conscious, politically organised, culturally sophisticated and, above all, disciplined. It was fundamentally strong. The actual Viennese working class may have been relatively more advanced than its provincial comrades, but it remained weaker than the party leadership acknowledged. Its culture remained that of the street, the Beisel (pub), the family, workplace and, as the 1920s progressed, the dole queue. But it was politically organised and this gave the illusion of strength, nurturing the leaders' faith in their own experiment. They confused working-class strength with party organisation, a confusion which arose from the astounding success the council and party appeared to have in organising working-class life in the city, and a myopic view of the lives of the men and women who made up the movement. It was a consequence of what

33. For details of this see Langewiesche, *Zur Freizeit des Arbeiters*, and Weidenholzer, *Auf den Weg zum 'Neuen Menschen'*.

34. Anson Rabinbach, *The Crisis of Austrian Socialism* (Chicago, 1983), p. 65.

35. Otto Glöckel, quoted in A. Pelinka, 'Kommunalpolitik als Gegenmacht: Das 'rote Wien' als Beispiel gesellschaftsverändernder Reformpolitik', in K.H. Naßmacher (ed.), *Kommunalpolitik und Sozialdemokratie: Der Beitrag des demokratischen Sozialismus zur kommunalen Selbstverwaltung* (Bonn, 1977), p. 71.

Helmut Gruber has called the 'socialist paternalism' of the party.[36]

The organisational strength of the movement lay in the close relationship between council and party. At times any distinction between the two became blurred, for the council housing schemes were the spawning grounds of the new socialism. The estates were an integral part of the party's overall strategy of recruiting members and maintaining disciplines, for they brought working-class families together, literally, providing communal space, communal activities and, it was hoped, a communal class spirit. The council provided, the party organised. The first stage was the housing list. Flats were allocated on a points system which took into account an applicant's health, existing housing, family circumstances and origin (a Viennese birth certificate was four times more valuable than Austrian citizenship). The homeless, war invalids and unemployed were given priority. But adherence to the system was not always rigid: party members, particularly party workers, could expect special consideration.[37] This was one benefit of Social Democratic Party membership in the city.

It is important to clarify this and avoid the impression that the housing system was primarily a means of buying support. Party membership in Vienna rose from 123,684 in 1920 to 418,055 in 1929, an increase which belies such superficial explanations. In addition, despite the political significance of 'Red Vienna' in national politics and the determined efforts of the Christian Social Party to uncover chronic mismanagement in council affairs, little evidence of corruption in tenancy procedures came to light. Nevertheless, there were material advantages to being a party member in Vienna which were not found elsewhere in the country. This must have some bearing on the discrepancy between the surge in membership in the capital and its decline in the provinces. Between 1921 and 1929 membership outside Vienna fell from 302,771 to 300,001.[38] It was the growth of the party in Vienna which gave the impression of a strong and expanding Austrian working-class movement. But size was not the only indication. The level of party membership in some working-class districts was astounding: in Brigittenau, Simmering and Florisdorf 48 per cent of those eligible to vote in 1927 were members.[39] The party yearbook reported that no other party in the International could

36. Gruber, 'Socialist Party Culture', p. 231.
37. Weihsmann, *Das Rote Wien*, p. 40.
38. See Table 1, Appendix to this volume, p. 211.
39. *Jb ö Arb* 1927, p. 33. *Arbeiter-Zeitung*, 24 April 1927.

boast membership figures comparable with Vienna, self-praise which was understandable but exaggerated; as a national party the SDAP itself fell far short of this level of success, for nowhere else in Austria was it so large, so well organised, so structured and so visible. But for those whose vision extended little further than the city boundaries, the party seemed invincible. Each May Day hundreds of thousands of workers and their families marched into the Ringstraße from every district, with banners, flags and bands, all celebrating the strength of the movement. Party festivals became a part of working-class life, at least for the politically active, on Republic Day, International Women's Day and on 15 March in memory of the 'victims of 1848'. The city was strewn with posters and slogans lauding the success of modern Vienna and decrying the drudgery of the Empire. Each new council building was opened with the razmataz of a ship's launch – speeches, ribbons, balloons and revelry. Sports festivals were held in the districts and at the annual Workers' Gymnastics. In 1931 the city staged the second Workers' Olympics. From ward level to city level, every opportunity was taken to bring members onto the streets in celebration, as long as the occasion was organised and stewarded by the party.

This workers' 'culture of festivals' (*Festkultur*) was supported by a vast network of party clubs and societies, which had been extensive before the war, but now seemed to engulf the workingclass. Children joined the Red Falkans, older brothers and sisters joined one of a number of youth organisations. Parents campaigned for welfare and education reforms through the 'Childrens' Friends'. Members of 'Flame' fought for the right to cremate their dead. Freethinkers attacked religious influence on education and public life and organised non-religious festivals. Women's groups campaigned for reform of the abortion laws. There were socialist organisations for teetotallers, stamp-collectors, chess-players, gardeners, aethist and religious socialists. There were singing groups, political cabarets, esperanto groups and a workers' orchestra. Sports clubs provided facilities for football, handball, cycling, fishing, swimming, walking, hiking, gymnastics and ju-jitsu.[40] After 1923 there was also the workers' paramilitary, the Schutzbund. Whatever the activity, somewhere in the party someone would organise it. But only up to a point. There were no party drinking clubs, at least not officially. The Beisel, that very Viennese institution which combined pub, café, and eating house and was the working man's equivalent of the bourgeois coffee house, had no

40. Langewiesche, *Zur Freizeit des Arbeiters*, p. 388.

place in the party's concept of the new socialist culture. None were built in the 'workers' palaces'. In theory the party was an alternative to the Beisel, but in practice workers continued to eat and drink in them as before and certain establishments were still considered 'socialist' territory.

The Beisel illustrates yet again the SDAP leadership's paternalistic attitude towards members. 'Social Democratic leaders had little knowledge of the workers as they really were and refused to accept their indigenous subcultures as points of departure.'[41] Active members could fill their spare time with a great array of recreational pastimes at very little cost, but they did so under the umbrella of the party organisation and the critical eye of party officials. Working-class culture had to be politically acceptable. Sport was encouraged as long as it was participatory and did not encourage individualism. Football, in particular, was the subject of rigorous analysis, in which party intellectuals differentiated between bourgeois ideals of commercialised sport and socialist ideals of courage and team discipline. But directives forbidding members from belonging to sports clubs outside the party fold fell on deaf ears and in 1932 the party executive was forced to compromise, banning members from holding office in bourgeois sports clubs and SDAP functionaries only from actually joining them.[42] The fact that the executive concerned itself with such apparently trivial matters as these should not be surprising for, despite its mass nature, few decisions were left to rank-and-file members. In theory policy was set at the annual conference, but party newspapers carried little or no preliminary discussion of motions, there were few pre-conference meetings at street level and, in practice, recommendations from the executive were seldom criticised and never rejected. It was a situation which led Max Adler to conclude that party officials had a 'fear of discussion'.[43]

The gulf which lay between leadership and membership was critical. Bauer, Renner, Seitz and the other seventeen members of the committee intended to create a politically sophisticated working class, but lack of internal party discussion meant that ordinary members had little idea of political debate or decision-making. At the street level the party was primarily an election and recruiting machine, maintaining frequent contact with members, but severely

41. Gruber, 'Socialist Party Culture', p. 238.
42. Langewiesche, *Zur Freizeit des Arbeiters*, pp. 382–3.
43. Max Adler, 'Parteidiskussion?' (1932) reprinted in Alfred Pfabigan and Norbert Leser (eds.), *Max Adler: Ausgewählte Schriften* (Vienna, 1981), pp. 304–18. He was particularly worried by the lack of democracy in the Jungfront. See pp. 315–18.

limiting their actual involvement in its running. It was organised into four tiers, the Wahlsprengel, covering a group of approximately one thousand voters, the ward, the district and the city. Vienna's dominance within the party meant that the city personnel overlapped the party executive. Karl Seitz, the mayor of Vienna from 1923, was chairman of the national party. The district organisations consisted of ward representatives, district officials and union representatives. They were responsible for party education, running advice centres, local party offices and libraries. For the vast majority of members contact was maintained through the lowest tier, the Wahlsprengel and its representatives (Vertrauensmänner), who distributed newspapers and journals and collected party dues. Each representative was obliged to visit the homes of members in his block or street at least once a month, enabling the party to function without members having to attend meetings. The wards did hold monthly meetings, but evidence suggests that relatively few members went regularly: a questionnaire answered by 1,320 politically active female factory workers in 1931 showed that only 46.8 per cent of them attended.[44] Rank-and-file attendance was much lower and for these people the representatives were their one link with the party.[45]

It was this widespread organisation, coupled with cultural activities and the council's programme, which enabled the party to grow so rapidly in Vienna and sustain that growth. All of these were dependent on factors which were specific to Viennese life and could not be reproduced outside. The size of the city, its economic base and legal status all combined to create the conditions in which the socialist experiment could, for a time, flourish. But there were weaknesses within the system even in Vienna. The lack of internal party democracy created tensions within the youth movement in particular but also amongst the party representatives.[46] In 1925 the writer of an article in the party's monthly journal wrote: 'We representatives, who only carry out technical tasks [*technische Arbeit*], feel the need to actually take part and the lack of opportunity to do so is very painful. The machines we handle in the factory during the day, should not be substituted by the party machine in the evening.'[47] Events in July 1927 would show that the leader-

44. Leichter, *So Leben Wir*. See footnote 25.
45. Kulemann, *Am Beispiel des Austromarxismus*, p. 309.
46. Rabinbach, *The Crisis of Austrian Socialism*, chap. 3. Ernst Fischer, *An Opposing Man*, trans. Peter and Betty Ross, with an introduction by John Berger (London, 1974), pp. 181–223.
47. Quoted in Kulemann, *Am Beispiel des Austromarxismus*, p. 310.

ship's failure to consult its rank and file was dangerous.

The second weakness was the shifting goal which the party set itself in Vienna. What began as an election strategy, grew into an exercise in social reformism and became an idealistic attempt to create a new working-class consciousness. The party succeeded instead in creating a vast organisation which also gave the impression of a changed consciousness and working-class strength. Under the surface old values and beliefs survived. Käthe Leichter's 1931 survey of female factory workers clearly shows the limited impact which 'Red Vienna' had on everyday life.[48] Few sent their children to kindergarten or children's centres, for a variety of reasons. For some the hours were incompatible, as work started at seven, the kindergarten opened at eight and provision had to be made for child care during Easter, Christmas and summer holidays. For others the cost, which was very low in comparison with private kindergartens, was still prohibitive. Many of these women were sole breadwinners and any fee would have been too high. The most revealing answer given was that the women preferred to leave their children with relatives or friends rather than strangers. Leichter commented that the mothers could not or would not accept the socialising advantages of pre-school education.[49]

Few married women took part in outside activities. There was little time, for on average they were away from home for eleven or twelve hours a day, and used evenings and weekends to carry out housework, which remained a female responsibility even when the male partner was unemployed. Single women fared better, allocating Sunday as 'their' day. Many were members of socialist sporting clubs, youth movements or nature and walking groups and spent Sunday afternoons walking in the Viennese woods. Even amongst this group the most popular recreation, dancing, was not party organised, and women as a whole spent much spare time listening to the radio.[50]

The questionnaire does not provide conclusive evidence, nor was it representative of the Viennese working class. Women were underrepresented in the party and Leichter herself fought hard to awaken the leadership to the particular problems of female members and to their potential as activist and voters. However it does provide some much-needed insight into the real social history of 'Red Vienna', the lives of the members, and it reveals a degree of

48. Leichter, *So Leben Wir*.
49. Ibid., pp. 95–6.
50. Ibid., p. 114.

scepticism and suspicion which cannot be found in the party press. It also suggests that the scope of party activities was irrelevant to many members, who did not have the time or inclination to join in organised pursuits. Books which faithfully list the number of clubs and societies often omit to point out that many had very small memberships; ju-jitsu and tennis sometimes had fewer than 500 in 1927, stamp-collecting, chess and fishing under two thousand.[51] These may be relatively impressive in their own terms, but as part of an all-embracing political and cultural structure, their role was marginal and their existence revealed more about the breadth of the party organisation than about the cultural life of the Viennese working class. The works of both Helmut Gruber and Dieter Langewiesche suggest that the main benefit which 'Red Vienna' brought to workers was material.[52] There was relatively little change in their values and attitudes. Even the material successes have sometimes been overestimated. Despite the vast building programme, homelessness and overcrowding still occurred in the city. In Leichter's sample, 1.3 per cent rented bed space and 35 per cent shared their sleeping area with more than two other people. When asked what they desired for their children, the most common reply was 'their own bed'.

To some readers these criticisms of 'Red Vienna' may appear unduly harsh considering the undoubtable progress which was made in economic and social reforms. In comparison with the activities of other Social Democratic parties in Europe at the time, and many since, the Austrian Social Democrat's experiment was radical, imaginative and successful in improving the lives of many people in the city. But it should not be judged purely on reformist terms, for these were not the goals which the party had set for itself. In speeches and pamphlets the leadership rejected reformism for its own sake, warned of the dangers of complacency and urged workers to be prepared to fight in defence of party, city and Republic. Yet they preached caution and, above all, discipline and after 1927 repeatedly retreated when attacked by the Right. This contradiction between revolutionary theory and reformist practice has been the major criticism levelled at the party in recent years.[53] But an equally important weakness lay in the leadership's view of the party, its relationship with its own membership and its inability

51. Langewiesche, *Zur Freizeit des Arbeiters*, p. 389.
52. Ibid. Gruber, 'Socialist Party Culture'.
53. Leser, *Zwischen Reformismus und Bolschewismus*; Rabinbach, *The Crisis of Austrian Socialism*; Hautmann and Hautmann, *Gemeindebauten*.

to distinguish between short-term strategy and long-term goals. 'Red Vienna' had developed in response to the needs of the Viennese people, coupled with the need of the party to win votes. In later years ordinary party members found it more difficult to express their problems, and the goal of winning votes was superseded by a wider vision which was fed by the apparent success of 'Red Vienna'. But the impracticality of such a policy outside Vienna was important for it is very doubtful that a general election could have been won on the strength of the Viennese electorate alone. The aim had been to woo provincial votes by example, but both membership and voting figures suggest that this failed and that the flamboyant spectacle of the Viennese party masked a crisis in the provinces. Social Democratic Party membership throughout Austria more than doubled between 1920 and 1929 from 335,863 to 718,056.[54] But within these figures there is an underlying trend, a growing disparity between capital and province. Between 1920 and 1922 membership rose by 65.5 per cent in Vienna and by 64 per cent in the provinces. It doubled between 1922 and 1928 in Vienna and continued to rise until 1930, when it amounted to 60 per cent of the entire national membership. In the provinces it fell by 25 per cent between 1922 and 1926 and then rose slowly until 1929, reaching a peak which was still 14 per cent lower than that of 1922. The boom in party membership which national figures show is misleading. The party's policies in the 1920s did attract new members, but only in the capital. Whilst the Viennese party was growing, the provincial parties stagnated.

In terms of its own aims, the Viennese dominance was not necessarily a disadvantage, if it led to electoral victory. After all, elections are won by votes not party cards. The Austrian electoral system was based on proportional representation which meant that a geographical concentration of votes was not inevitably damaging. In two elections – 1923 and 1927 – the party did win a higher proportion of the votes, culminating in a moral victory in 1927, when it became the largest single party in parliament. Even though the vote fell in 1930 the number of Social Democratic deputies elected actually rose by one.[55] So it could be argued that the strategy was partially successful and could have led to victory had the parliamentary system survived. But the disparity between capital and the provinces which was evident in the membership figures is found again in the voting figures. The party won 47 per

54. See Table 1, Appendix to this volume, p. 211.
55. *Stat Hdb Österreich* 1927, p. 189; 1930, p. 207.

cent of votes in Vienna in 1920. By 1927 this had risen to 60 per cent. There were meagre gains in the provinces of 3.5 per cent and only once did the party capture more than one-third of the total provincial vote. In terms of pure numbers, an election victory required more provincial votes. The relative size of the capital distorted the national figures transforming a Viennese trend into a national one. Even with 60 per cent of the Viennese electorate in 1927, the party did not secure a victory.

The electoral system may not have penalised geographical concentration, but there were long-term political consequences resulting from the dominance of 'Red Vienna' which damaged both the party and the labour movement. The first, the impossibility of recreating such a system outside Vienna, has already been discussed. The second was that the entire policy of municipal socialism marked a switch of party strategy away from the economic sphere – the factories and workplaces which had been the focal point of the 'Path to Socialism' – to the home and environment, the domestic sphere. This came at a time when the economy was hit by hyper-inflation and high unemployment and meant that inadequate attention was paid to issues such as worker participation, the eight-hour day and trade union rights. As unemployment grew, trade union membership fell and with it worker protection. In 1923 and 1927 the Social Democratic Party fought elections on the platform of rent controls and educational reforms, both issues which were more important to the Viennese experiment than to the workers of Styria. In Upper Styria the weakness of the labour movement was crucial to the build up of fascism in Austria, as subsequent chapters will show. This weakness became most apparent after 1923, when Vienna was beginning to bloom and the 'workers' palaces', the extensive party network, the marches, rallies and international gatherings gave the pretence of invincibility. Meanwhile the labour movement in Styria was confronting new problems which neither the party nor the Free Trade Unions were able to address.

−6−

Stabilisation and Unemployment, 1919–1923

War and the Revolution had shattered the political inertia of the industrial workers of Styria and fundamentally altered the basis of industrial relations in the province. In the Republic most employers were legally compelled to recognise the rights of their employees to join trade unions and by 1921 many unions had successfully negotiated an index linking wages to fluctuations in the price of basic commodities. For several years local union branches in Upper and Middle Styria maintained an aggressive stance, calling strikes in support of wage demands, defending members who were unfairly dismissed and mounting campaigns against any shopkeeper or farmer who was rumoured to have food hoards, for food was in very short supply. For the first few years of the Republic the policing of the area was carried out by a people's army, the Volkswehr, made up almost exclusively of socialists and workers. As the role of this body diminished, and was replaced by a professional and more right-wing police and army, political violence between workers and the anti-marxist paramilitary, the Heimwehr, became rife in the region, culminating in a rising in Judenburg in 1922.

Labour organisation had also come to Styria. Membership of the two wings of the labour movement, the Free Trade Unions and the Social Democratic Party, flourished in Styria in the early years of the Republic, creating one of the few areas of socialist support in Austria outside the capital. But this expansion was short-lived. By 1925 Styrian membership of the Social Democratic Party had fallen by 40 per cent, and although it began to increase again thereafter, it never regained the early high levels.[1] The Free Unions fared even worse, losing almost half their membership in the first seven years of the Republic, compared with a national loss of 25 per cent.[2] This apparent fickleness on the part of the Styrian workers was, in fact,

---

1. See Table 1, Appendix to this volume, p. 211.
2. See Table 2, Appendix to this volume, p. 212.

the result of a series of different factors which, when combined, served to weaken the labour movement in the 1920s before the onslaught of the 1929 depression, and unleashed an atmosphere of political violence in the province which intensified in the 1930s.

Throughout the 1920s the strength of the trade union wing of the Styrian labour movement was undermined by a combination of factors, some of which were peculiar to this province and others which were felt to a greater or lesser degree elsewhere in the country. The first and most peculiarly Styrian problem was the early and strong alliance or anti-socialist forces which emerged in the immediate postwar months and resulted in characteristically high levels of organised violence, both locally and provincially. Political violence only became a significant aspect of national politics after 1927, but it plagued Styria for many years before this.

The origins of the anti-socialist alliance lay in the economic and political turmoil of the first months and years of the Republic when urban communities were faced with lack of both food and shelter. Because of mountainous terrain in the north of the province, the industrial regions had relied on supplies of fresh food from the southern plain and grain, fat and sugar from Hungary, Croatia and Bohemia before the war.[3] By 1919 much of the plain was incorporated into Yugoslavia and the little which remained was the scene of border disputes between Yugoslav and Austrian troops. In addition Hungary, Croatia and Bohemia were no longer part of the Empire, but formed separate states and had problems feeding their own populations.

This led to a chronic shortage of food in Styria and throughout 1919 and 1920 supplies in the towns were strictly rationed to a bare minimum; half a kilo of flour per week, 150 grammes of meat, 750 grammes of sugar and 120 grammes of lard. Fresh milk was reserved for children under two and the chronically ill, condensed milk for children under three and the less chronically ill; potatoes and, later, sugar were only available on the black market and at very high prices. Even at these levels supplies could not be maintained. By the middle of October 1919 there was no white flour, no coal, meat or fat in most towns and starvation was ultimately avoided by the timely arrival of emergency supplies of food brought in by American relief agencies for the children. To make matters worse, when the bread ration re-emerged, heavier maize

3. *Lebensnot, Wohnungselend und Hilfsbedürfigkeit in Graz. Bericht verfasst über Auffordung eines Schweizer Hilfsausschusses von Gemeinderat Engelbert Rückl* (Graz, 1920). International Institute for Social History, Amsterdam.

flour had replaced wheat, reducing the quality of a loaf.[4]

Food shortages were not the only difficulty. Basic necessities such as sheets, towels, clothes and shoes were unavailable, even in the depths of midwinter. In 1920 one official reported that doctors would soon be wrapping orphans in paper. In Graz these problems were exacerbated by the influx of people from the new states of Yugoslavia and Hungary, as well as a constant stream of ex-soldiers returning from the war or from prisoner-of-war camps. The city's population grew from 151,781 in 1910 to 155,837 at a time when the populations of other cities in the country were actually falling. On the other hand, the housing stock remained static and even shrank as the authorities closed unsafe and unsanitary buildings. By 1920 over 5,000 people were living in former barracks, another 300 in railway carriages, whilst the desperate had taken to living in cellars, without light or water and in constant fear of rats attacking the children. In one case it was reputed that fourteen people were living in a kitchenette which measured six metres by five.[5]

The cold, malnutrition and homelessness set their mark on the health of the community. Doctors' reports gathered in Graz in the spring and early summer of 1919 showed that of 17,000 children of school-age who had been examined, 230 were already in hospital, 9,897 were suffering from severe malnutrition, a further 5,784 had less serious signs of malnutrition and 80 per cent (ca. 13,600) had bronchial tuberculosis. The average weight of fourteen-year-old girls had fallen by 8.2 kilos since 1914. Tuberculosis was also taking its toll amongst the adults, for the number of patients in the lung hospital rose from 2,000 in 1918 to 5,000 in 1919. There were outbreaks of chronic diarrhoea, skin diseases, rickets and oestomaticis, the last of which affected two-thirds of the total adult population.[6]

Hunger and poverty did not lead directly to violence between urban and rural communities, but indirectly they resulted in a mushrooming of paramilitary groups in the early years of the Republic. On the workers' side was the Volkswehr, the successor to the Imperial army, which was initially led and manned by members and supporters of the Social Democrats, and the Arbeiterhilfskorps, set up by the workers' councils and comprised of unemployed workers and ex-soldiers.[7] The opposition consisted of

4. Ibid.
5. Ibid.
6. Ibid.
7. Robert Hinteregger, 'Graz zwischen Wohlfahrtausschuss und Räteherrschaft',

various factions of the Heimwehr supported by the provincial government, farmers, members of the petty bourgeoisie, and industrial employers. This political polarisation came to light in the conflict of 1919–20, as both the Revolution and the shortage of food shortened tempers and heightened tension. Non-socialists blamed the socialists for the economic chaos and socialists blamed farmers and shopkeepers for hoarding food. In June 1919 housewives attacked market sellers in the central market in Graz for raising the price of cherries, overturning their stalls and looking for food. The police were called out and quickly opened fire when they were met with a barrage of flying stones and anything else which came to hand. Seven people died instantly and five more did not recover from the wounds they received. Three months later crowds ransacked the city's pharmacies, inflamed by rumours that these were being used to store sugar for the black market. The following February, after a reduction in the bread ration, about 700 people stormed the distribution centre in Donawitz in the vain hope of finding supplies of flour.[8]

Hunger led to food riots, but these did not escalate into full-scale rebellion, nor did they form the picture of a battle between town and country which emerges from some histories of the period.[9] Fighting in the towns was directed mainly against shopkeepers and the police, whilst examples of townspeople running amuck in open fields are notably absent. The workers were distanced from the farmers by the Volkswehr and the Arbeiterhilfkorps, who organised searches for illicit stores of food and requisitioned cattle and grain from farms, by force when necessary – and force often was necessary. The number of cattle fell by 90 per cent after the war – government prices for meat did not compare with those offered on the black market. Many farmers were issued with guns by the provincial government to protect themselves from bands of ex-soldiers who were passing through the countryside on their way home after the war and who took food wherever and whenever they could find it. The farmers saw little difference between these groups and the workers' militias and organised themselves into community defence units, the original Heimwehren, to defend themselves, their property and their land. By 1919 it was reported

---

Historisches Jahrbuch der Stadt Graz, 7–8 (1975), p. 234.

8. Michael Schacherl, *Dreißig Jahre der Steirische Arbeiterbewegung, 1890 bis 1920* (Graz, 1931), p. 300.

9. Bruce F. Pauley, *Hahnenschwanz und Hakenkreuz*, trans. Peter Aschner (Vienna, 1972).

that approximately 70 per cent of all communes had raised such a unit and links were established between these groups and others fighting the Yugoslavs on the southern borders.[10]

This was the origin of one faction of the Heimwehr, but not the one which later concerned the labour movement. A second group emerged from the urban communities themselves and was less intent on defending the position of the farmer than on attacking all forms of socialism. Events in February 1919 brought about its birth. On 20 February members of the newly-founded Communist Party addressed a crowd of soldiers and ex-soldiers at a meeting in the Freiheitsplatz in Graz. The meeting had been called to discuss the food situation and the plight of ex-soldiers. Two Communist speakers urged those present to give an ultimatum to the provincial government demanding increases in food rations and demob pay. Rintelen, the Christian Social provincial governor, interpreted this as a call to arms and immediately asked the national provisional government to send in troop reinforcements, alerted regular and irregular forces within the city and imposed martial law, including a curfew and a general ban on all political meetings.[11] Despite these measures a crowd gathered again in the square two days later, when the ultimatum was up. A scuffle broke out as government forces tried to disperse the crowd and escalated when they opened fire, killing four people. The next day many known members of the Communist Party were arrested and the police, Volkswehr, Arbeiterhilfskorps and other irregulars patrolled the streets, setting up guards outside important buildings.[12]

There were two important features of this event. The first was the role of the local Social Democratic Party. At the first meeting, on 20 February, the leader of the soldiers' council, Oberzaucher, a Social Democrat, attempted to convince the crowd that Communists were consciously inciting violence by making demands which could not be met. He was shouted down by the crowd. Kaan, the leader of the Social Democratic block in the provincial government, then tried to negotiate with the Communist spokesmen, Brodnig and Maresch, without success. Finally, the two Social Democrats ordered their own militia to join the police in restoring order, confirming at the local level a national party decision to oppose Communist attempts to push the revolution further to the

10. F.L. Carsten, *Fascist Movements in Austria: From Schönerer to Hitler* (London, 1977), p. 43.

11. St LA, Präs. E.91/3416–1918. Police report.

12. *Arbeiterwille* 23 February 1919.

Left.[13] Bauer's policy of directing and controlling the revolution was in force in Graz. However it must be pointed out that, despite the size of the Communist support in the city, there was no immediate reaction to the heavy-handed tactics of the provincial government and Communist activity in the city waned thereafter.[14]

The second point concerns the non-socialist irregulars who were called up by Rintelen. These came from two main sources: a paramilitary group made up of local farmers and ex-army officers, which Rintelen himself had set up in December 1918 as a counter force to the Marxist threat he felt was growing all around him; and members of the university's student battalion, a body renowned for its racial nationalism.[15] As with the Freikorps in Germany, this irregular unit was not only non-socialist, but stridently anti-socialist and anti-democratic. It was this group, rather than rural-based defence leagues, which later formed the basis of a radically nationalist and increasingly authoritarian faction of the Heimwehr led by a Judenburg lawyer, Walter Pfrimer.[16] By calling them out in support of the regular police, and by providing them with arms which were not subsequently withdrawn, the provincial government conferred a degree of respectability and legitimacy on these units which was later exploited to the hilt. It did not disturb Rintelen, who shared their beliefs and used the precedent time and again when he felt the police were in need of support.[17] But it proved ironic for the Social Democratic Party, whose leaders had tacitly endorsed the decision in 1919, but whose own members became the target of later attacks. By 1922 'the Heimwehr had acquired about 17,000 rifles with the necessary ammunition, 286 machine guns, 12 pieces of artillery and even aeroplanes, largely by ruse from Volkswehr depots'.[18] In addition, the faction led by Walter Pfrimer was employed by the provincial government to break strikes and was also receiving financial support from Styrian industrialists.[19]

13. Hinteregger, 'Graz zwischen Wohlfahrtausschuss', pp. 231–2.
14. A police report, dated 1.3.1919, put the official membership of the Communist Party in Graz at 600, with 3,000 sympathisers. St LA, Präs. E.91/3416–1918.
15. Pauley, Hahnenschwanz, pp. 39–42.
16. Carsten, Fascist Movements, p. 44.
17. In 1935 Rintelen was sentenced to life imprisonment for his part in the Nazi Putsch attempt of July 1934. Charles A. Gulick, Austria from Habsburg to Hitler (Berkeley, California, 1948), vol. 2, p. 1707. Anton Rintelen, Erinnerungen an Österreichs Weg (Munich, 1941), pp. 305ff.
18. Carsten, Fascist Movements, p. 44.
19. Ernst von Streeruwitz, Springflut über Österreich (Vienna, 1937), pp. 213, 216.

This early and strong alliance of anti-socialist forces was peculiar to Styria, for although the Heimwehr was found in other provinces, its organisation elsewhere was dominated by rural groups with memberships drawn largely from farming communities. In no other province were there such strong links between industry and the movement. Within Styria the Pfrimer wing developed its own version of Heimwehr philosophy and the movement spread amongst the urban petty bourgeoisie, protected as it was by local business and the provincial government. Styrian industrial communities were also more vulnerable to attack from right-wing units than other industrial regions, simply because of their geography. Unlike Vienna, Wiener Neustadt and even the smaller industrial area in and around Linz, the Styrian industrial belt was spread out along two lines from Mürzzuschlag in the east to Judenburg in the west and from Graz in the south to Eisenerz in the north. The largest single conurbation was Graz, with a population of 152,706 and a mixed economy. In this city Social Democrats competed for power with the German National and Christian Social Parties. Elsewhere the largest towns were Donawitz with 18,121 inhabitants and Eggenberg with 15,267, whilst Bruck, which later became the stronghold of socialism in the province, boasted a total population of only 11,275.[20] These isolated industrial communities were seldom large enough to mount a successful defence against outside attack by right-wing armed militias.

The effectiveness of such an attack was illustrated in Judenburg in November 1922, as was the ambivalent attitude of the provincial government towards paramilitary units; those of the Left were condemned as a threat to public order, whilst those of the Right were extolled as upholders of that same public order. The incident began on the evening of 2 November when a crowd of 200 workers armed with guns and sticks took over the small village of Waltersdorf near Judenburg and carried out a search for illegal weapons.[21] They had been riled by similar searches made in workers' homes by right-wing students from the Mining College in Leoben and by reports that the Heimwehr was increasing its stock of arms.[22] The village was cordoned off, rifles, pistols and ammunition for which the owners could not produce permits were removed and most deposited with the police in Judenburg.[23] After some of the in-

20. Die Ergebnisse der österreichischen Volkszählung vom 22 März 1934. Table 2. Figures for 1923.
21. St LA, Präs. E.91. E.Nr.2050, 5 November 1922. Report to the county court from mining inspector Anton Untersteggaber.
22. Gulick, *Austria*, vol. 1, p. 130.

truders were identified as workers from the Alpine Montangesellschaft steelworks at Fohnsdorf, the police arrested six men, including the local Social Democratic Party secretary, Chlaponka. On
15 November, as these men were taken to Graz for trial, steel-
workers came out on strike and made their way into Judenburg. Many of them were armed. Workers' representatives were
negotiating with the police when reports of strikes came in from
Zeltweg, Knittelfeld and Wasendorf, industrial towns which were
between 7 and 20 kilometres away.[24] News also came that Pfrimer
had alerted the Upper Styrian Heimwehr and was waiting with
6,000 men outside the town. At this point accounts differ. According to Rintelen's memoirs, this was when he decided to enlist
Pfrimer's men as auxiliary police, fearing that the regular police and
reinforcements who had already been sent in would not be able to
contain the crowd.[25] A police report dated 17 November stated that
negotiations between the workers and police had resulted in a
compromise, whereby the workers would disarm and both illegal
forces would leave the town, separated by the police and soldiers.
The Heimwehr was enlisted after the workers had laid down their
arms. The reaction amongst the crowd was noisy, but ineffective.
There were cries of 'Let's set fire to the buildings', but the only
action taken was by the bakers who refused to sell bread to the
Heimwehr. Despite differences over timing, both Rintelen and the
police report agreed on one thing: the presence of the Heimwehr
had persuaded the workers to give up their arms and return to
work. The police report ended by repeating Pfrimer's warnings
that the Heimwehr would not permit further 'outrages' by workers
and recommended that the provincial government should increase
its support of Pfrimer's men by issuing them with more weapons.[26]

The legal issues raised by the Judenburg affair were complex.
The original action of the workers' militia at Waltersdorf had been
against the law, for they did not have the right either to search for
weapons or to carry arms. The close relationship between the army
and the unofficial workers' units had evaporated when the Social
Democrats withdrew from the national government and Julius
Deutsch handed over control of the Volkswehr, renamed the
Bundesheer, to the Christian Social Minister of Defence, Karl
Vaugoin. However, the provincial government had turned a blind

23. St LA, Präs. E.91. E.Nr.2050 as footnote 21.
24. St LA, Präs. E.91. Police report (no number) from Abteilung Nr.7 Judenburg, 17 November 1922. 'Unruhe in Judenburg'.
25. Rintelen, *Erinnerungen*, pp. 132–3.
26. St LA, Präs. E.91. Police report as footnote 24.

eye towards the large numbers of weapons which were in circulation after the war and at this time arms searches were carried out by the various paramilitary groups. By prosecuting Fohnsdorf workers and ignoring similar actions by the Leoben students, the provincial government had shown a clear bias towards the Right. But this was just a small violation in comparison with their attitude towards the Heimwehr at Judenburg, for here both workers and the Heimwehr were breaking the law by carrying arms and gathering together with the obvious intent of disturbing the peace. Rather than arresting leaders on both sides, the authorities chose instead to deputise the Heimwehr and glorify them as heroes of the hour. A clear distinction had been drawn between the rights of the labour movement and those of the Heimwehr to carry arms.

More important than the legal questions, Judenburg had raised acute political issues for the labour movement. On their own the Judenburg workers were heavily outnumbered by the Heimwehr and the regular troops. Support from the large works at Zeltweg and from Knittelfeld would have improved the balance, had they arrived. But the journey from these towns was undertaken on foot, leaving the authorities enough time to quell the disturbance and also giving them ample opportunity to stop outsiders from reaching the town. Without their own organised paramilitary units workers in Styrian towns were an easy prey for their opponents, as it was obvious to all that they would not be able to count on the support of either the police or the provincial government to protect them. It appears that the Social Democratic leadership had reached the same conclusion, for in 1923 a second workers' army, the paramilitary Republican Schutzbund, was founded, the first Styrian unit of which was set up in Leoben in July.[27]

Finally and most obviously, the Judenburg incident further strengthened the provincial alliance of anti-socialist forces. Following this victory, Walter Pfrimer was elected leader of the Styrian Heimatschutz, giving him overall control of Heimwehr units in the provinces.[28] His reputation had been made at Judenburg, where, according to the conservative press, he had put down a workers' rising.[29] The ease with which the strike had been broken also made a firm impression on the provincial government and employers and under Pfrimer's leadership the Heimatschutz

---

27. Ilona Duczynska, *Workers in Arms* (New York and London, 1978), pp. 58–9. St LA, Präs. E.91 21 Vst R/41 1366 8 July 1923. Police report of Schutzbund founded in Rottenmann, 24 July. E.91. E.Nr.1391.

28. Pauley, *Hahnenschwanz*, p. 44. The election was in the autumn of 1923.

29. *Tagespost* 14 November 1922.

continued to pay close attention to the activities of the industrial workers in the province. Five years later Pfrimer's group founded the euphemistically named 'Independent Unions'.

The early existence of a unified anti-socialist front obviously presented problems for the young labour movement. The presence of a right-wing militia, which was politically committed to the use of violence in order to break strikes and which was supported both by the provincial government and by employers, was bound to affect the character of political and class conflict in the province, for it inevitably increased the likelihood of violence. Workers who decided to go on strike were aware that there was a distinct possibility that members of the Heimatschutz would intervene, as had happened in Judenburg. They also knew that neither the provincial government nor the police were likely to come to their aid in defence of the rights to strike or to join a trade union and, as a consequence, there was little confidence in or support for the provincial government in the industrial communities. And yet it would be a mistake to overemphasise the importance of the anti-socialist victory in 1922, for far from stifling labour demands or reducing the level of strikes in the province, the Judenburg incident was followed by an unprecedented eruption of labour protest in 1923; more Styrian workers went on strike in that year than in any other year during the Republic.[30] By 1923 the Heimwehr had become a thorn in the side of the labour movement, but a second and major threat to union strength, unemployment, was growing by the day.

At this stage of the discussion it is necessary to comment on some of the criteria which can be used to judge the relative strengths and weaknesses of a trade union movement. As Dick Geary has shown, many of the more common indices which are used by labour historians to indicate labour militancy, such as the level of trade union membership or the number or scale of strikes, can be misleading if looked at in isolation.[31] This is certainly the case in Styria. A cursory glance at the strike statistics for 1920–3 suggests that the labour movement was increasing its activity in the workplace.[32] However, the figures for Free Trade Union membership for the same period show a fall from 1921 onwards, with a loss

30. There were 23 strikes in 1923 involving 22,497 workers (96.2 per cent of the workforce involved). *Stat Hdb Österreich* 1924, vol. 5, p. 103.

31. Dick Geary, 'Identifying Militancy: the Assessment of Working-class Attitudes towards State and Society', in R.J. Evans (ed.), *The German Working Class 1888–1933* (London, 1982), pp. 220–46.

32. See Table 3 in Appendix to this volume, p. 213.

of 25 per cent between 1922 and 1923. The explanation for this apparent contradiction is twofold. Firstly, trade union membership can relate both to economic and political factors, the number of people who are in work and are able and willing to pay weekly union dues, and the confidence which they have in the union to provide them with personal and/or class rewards. Although trade unions are primarily economic organisations, there can be no doubt that at least some of those who rushed to join in the early years of the Republic were caught up in the political euphoria which followed the Revolution. The loss of at least some of these members may account for the fall in union membership in Styria between 1921 and 1922 of 320 members (0.25 per cent), which, although small, did reverse a trend towards union growth.[33] The larger fall the following year coincided with an escalation in unemployment resulting from the currency crisis of the summer and autumn of 1922, which affected the whole of Austria.[34] The reduction in membership in Styria was, however, 10 per cent higher than the national average, suggesting that local factors were accelerating the move away from the unions. Thus the fall in trade union membership in 1923 indicates that unemployment was beginning to reduce the strength of the labour movement. This point is actually borne out by the pattern of strike activity in the province, for, although the number of workers who went on strike increased from 1922 to 1923, the character of the strikes themselves changed. Between 1920 and the summer of 1922 many of the strikes were short and aggressive, arising from demands for wage increases, improvements in working conditions and demonstrations against food shortages and political victimisation. By late 1922 the majority of strikers were engaged in defensive struggles against wage cuts and large scale redundancies. The shift in the character of strikes from 1920 to 1923 confirms the view that the position of labour and hence the strength of the union movement had been weakened by unemployment. Thus the second explanation for the apparent contradiction between union membership and strikes is that the strike statistics camouflage a change in the nature of strikes.

A comparison of two strikes in the Alpine Montangesellschaft mines in 1922 and 1923 illustrates this point well. Both concerned accusations of political victimisation, but the scale and outcome of the two protests graphically display the change in the strength of one union, the Miners' Union, over a period of nine months. In the

33. See Table 2 in Appendix to this volume, p. 212.
34. See Table 5 in Appendix to this volume, p. 216.

first example, miners at the iron ore mine at Eisenerz went out on strike for one day in September 1922 in defence of a colleague who had been sacked for insubordination. This was the third incident at the mine in that year. In the spring miners had been involved in a national strike for higher wages which had been resolved by government intervention. A compromise had been reached between the union and employers which the Alpine Montangesellschaft management then refused to accept, compelling their own workers to stay out on strike in order to force a concession.[35] Some weeks later, when the management rejected the results of the factory council elections at Eisenerz, the union took out a lengthy but successful court case against them. The third incident followed at the end of August when a temporary overseer had a row with a turner, resulting in the latter's immediate dismissal. According to both the Miners' Union and the Metalworkers' Union, which also had members on site, this was a clear case of political victimisation, for the turner was a shop steward, one of those who had been re-elected in the disputed ballot, an experienced and skilled worker with a good record, who was an active and leading member of the local branch of the Social Democratic Party. Union officials attempted to negotiate with the management for his reinstatement and when this failed a crowd of about 2,000 gathered outside the mine office and harangued those inside.[36] Members of the management were manhandled, furniture and windows were broken and five men were arrested. Despite this the management reopened negotiations with union officials that night and made several concessions. The sacked worker was reinstated pending an appeal to the industrial commission in Leoben, the overseer was removed and the management agreed to ask the court to deal leniently with the men who had been arrested. However the greatest victory for the union was an agreement reached between the Free Trade Unions, the Christian Trade Union and the management that henceforth the mine would only recruit members of either of these two unions.[37]

35. Fritz Klenner, *Die österreichischen Gewerkschaften* 2 vols. (Vienna, 1953), vol. 1, p. 531.

36. St LA, Präs. E.91 2V. 180 Bh. Report by the local secretary of the Miners' Union on the workers' demonstration, contained in a report from the Bezirkshauptmannschaft, Leoben, 7 September 1921.

37. Similar demands had been made by metalworkers at the Graz engineering firms of Puch and the Weitzer Waggon und Maschinenfabrik in February 1921. St LA, Präs. E.91. ZL. 2360/47. ZL. 2360/49. Police reports to the Styrian provincial government, 25 February 1921 and 4 May 1921.

The grievance which led to the strike in the spring of 1923 was similar, but more extreme. In the autumn of 1922, during the depths of the currency crisis, the company closed down two works at Zeltweg and Neuberg and laid off workers in other plants, including mines. Those who remained at work were put on short time and subjected to a wage cut. In spring 1923 the company began to recruit miners once more, but they were selective in their choice. Lignite miners at the Karlsschacht who lived near the mine and been laid off the previous winter were not reinstated, but were replaced by non-union miners from the neighbouring Graz-Köflach company. This action led to a strike on 17 March which spread throughout the lignite mines. On 5 April police were called in to protect persons and property. The strike was broken two weeks later.[38]

The comparison between these two strikes is revealing. In the first case, when the victimisation was directed at one individual, there was a high level of solidarity in the mine and surrounding area which enabled the unions to exploit the situation in order to win concessions for a limited closed shop. This exceeded their legal rights.

In the second, when larger numbers of workers were involved and the presence of the Free Trade Unions itself was under threat, the solidarity was not so great and the mines remained partially open. The attitude of the management had also changed. Although this was not the first time that the Alpine Montangesellschaft had asked for police protection, such requests previously had been milder and had not been part of a policy to break a strike.[39] By 1923 management was more determined to destroy the base of Free Trade Union support within the mines and later this policy spread to the rest of the company.

The power of organised labour had diminished considerably not only in the mines but throughout Styrian and, more generally, Austrian industry between the summer of 1922 and the spring of 1923. The first indication of this was an attack on wage indexes which escalated during the second half of 1922. Indexes had been introduced in the winter of 1919–20 in an attempt to curb labour

38. Fritz Erben, Maja Loehr and Hans Riehl (eds.), *Die Alpine Montangesellschaft* (Vienna, 1931), pp. 178–80.
39. The Alpine Montangesellschaft had asked for increased police presence in Leoben in August 1922 after a strike at Donawitz over lunch-time breaks. However the request came after the strike had ended in the workers' favour. Letter to the Bezirkshauptmannschaft Leoben from Zahlbruckner, 28 August 1922. St LA, Präs. E.91. Z1. 1361/22. Dated 2 September 1922.

unrest over the growing shortages of food and rising prices.[40] Wages were divided into two parts: a fixed wage, which all workers received irrespective of skill or experience and which was usually linked to government figures for the rise in the price of basic commodities, and a variable rate based on the skill of the worker. The index was not legally compulsory, but a voluntary agreement between individual unions and employers, the rates of which were set during the normal negotiations over wages.[41] During the early postwar inflation the index scheme successfully protected most workers in large firms, where collective bargaining was in force, from the full impact of rising prices. But there were problems. Firstly, not all workers were covered by a wage index and civil servants and council employees resented their exclusion as we have already seen. Secondly, as inflation rose the index system tended to erode the differentials between skilled and unskilled workers, for the skilled variable rate did not rise as fast as the fixed rate. Thirdly, from the winter of 1921 to the autumn of 1922 inflation did not just rise, it galloped, sending the currency exchange rate between the crown and the US dollar up from 142.2 crowns to one dollar in January 1921 to 3,308 crowns in July 1922 and, further, to 14,153 in September 1922.

Official figures for the cost of living based on a 1919 mean of 100 rose even faster, from 92.18 in January 1921 to 6,035.35 in July 1922 and 15,029.78 in September 1922. As the fixed wage was reviewed every two months, real wages fell.[42] This problem was then compounded by the increasing reluctance of employers to pay the full amount calculated according to the index. In June 1922 a government announcement that railway employees would receive only part of the inflation increment provoked a national rail strike which spread to the post office and telephone workers, who feared that they too would lose the relative security of the index. The strike began on 24 June and the government capitulated two days later.[43] But the struggle was not over. In August the railwaymen were told that their wages would not be paid on time and as prices were rising hourly rather than daily, there was once again a call to strike.[44]

By this time, however, many workers were facing an even more critical problem. The value of the crown fell dramatically in August

40. Eduard März, *Austrian Banking and Financial Policy* (New York, 1984), p. 414.
41. Gulick, *Austria*, vol. 1, p. 152.
42. März, *Austrian Banking*, pp. 416, 424.
43. Klenner, *Die österreichischen Gewerkschaften*, vol. 1, p. 543.
44. Police report 1 September 1922. St LA, Präs. E.91. Z1. 3304/36.

1922 and panic set in. In the uncertain economic climate of that autumn companies laid off large numbers of workers and even closed down entire works. In Styria many glass manufacturers went out of business as both the domestic and export markets disintegrated.[45] The Alpine Montangesellschaft put out three of its four blast furnaces at Donawitz and closed the works at Neuberg and Zeltweg. Employment at the rolling-mills fell by 50 per cent.[46] In the machine shops at the Finze ironworks at Kalsdorf employees were offered a choice between a 25 per cent wage reduction or a 31-hour week; the net result for the worker in terms of pay was the same, a reduction in income.[47] Shop stewards called an unofficial strike but it failed and this defeat was then cited by shop stewards in other companies as proof that resistance was futile and was being used by 'Communists'.[48] In November 1922 the iron and steel employers announced a national wage reduction of 12.5 per cent and immediately threatened to introduce a further reduction of 15 per cent.

The bargaining power of the trade unions temporarily collapsed that winter as registered unemployment rose in Austria as a whole from 33,355 in June 1922 to 141,222 in January 1923 (423 per cent). Heavy industry was particularly hit by the currency crisis, for it depended on imported raw materials and foreign markets and, as a result, the official figures for Styrian unemployment were even more drastic, showing a rise of 13,549 from 985 in June to 14,534 in January.[49] The true scope of the problem was even greater than this, for the figures excluded those who were not eligible for unemployment benefit, such as casual workers, assistants and apprentices, women who often did not register because they were rarely entitled to benefit and workers who were employed outside the industrial areas. This last group was not restricted to workers in agriculturally-based industries or small-scale manufacturing, but included employees of larger firms, such as the Finze company at Kalsdorf, which was in Middle Styria, outside the industrial areas of Graz and Leoben.[50] In addition to those who were completely without work, many workers were on short time; in December

45. St AK 1921–6, p. 25.
46. Erben et al. (eds.), *Die Alpine Montangesellschaft*, p. 62.
47. St LA, Präs. E.91. Z1. 948/7. Police report dated 4 January 1923 on a meeting of Finze workers.
48. St LA, Präs. E.91. Z1. 470/11. Police report dated 28 November 1923 on a meeting of shop stewards from the Styria-Durkoppwerke.
49. See Table 4 in Appendix to this volume, pp. 214–15.
50. The fact that the Finze workers were not covered by unemployment insurance partially explains their stand against redundancies.

1922 this included over half of the province's metalworkers. At the same time unemployed workers were accusing those who were still in work of adding to the problem, by agreeing to work a ten- or twelve-hour day.[51] Divisions developed between the employed and the unemployed in the province which employers were quick to exploit, as the recruitment policy of the Alpine Montangesellschaft at their Karlsschacht had already shown.

On a broader level, the economic crisis and inability of the trade unions to defend their members encouraged employers to try to cut production costs by attacking the national welfare reforms which had been imposed on them after the Revolution and which, they maintained, were crippling economic recovery. Their objections to the cost of these measures were not new, neither were violations of the labour laws. Immediately after the introduction of the eight-hour day, many firms had attempted to win exemption by arguing that the provisions of the act only applied to factories and not smaller units of production. The Styrian paper industry fought for a general exemption for all its members on the grounds that their industry could not survive without a twelve-hour working day.[52] Applications for exemption were made to the provincial government, but cases against employers were judged by the industrial courts. Before the large-scale unemployment of 1922 most reported violations took place in small workshops employing young workers and members of the employers' own families. The major preoccupation of larger firms was to gain exemption. After 1922 this changed as the unions' resistance to longer working hours waned and employers became aware of the financial advantages of defying the law. Theoretically an employer could face three months' imprisonment if found guilty, but in practice the industrial courts imposed fines which were so low that they were ineffective. By 1926 the Styrian Chamber of Labour reported that it knew of no cases in which the authorities had successfully enforced the eight-hour day.[53]

Many larger firms were now openly ignoring the law, more so since the employers' contribution to the unemployment levy had been increased by the government in January 1923 as part of its

51. *WsJ* 1925, p. 198, Table 169. St LA, Präs. E.91. Z1. 634/7. Police report dated 13 January 1923.
52. Karin Schmidlechner, 'Die Situation der steirischen Industriearbeiter zwischen 1918–1934' (manuscript of social conditions in Styria for the exhibition, 'Für Freiheit, Arbeit und Recht – Die steirische Arbeiterbewegung zwischen Revolution und Faschismus (1918–38)', co-ordinator, Robert Hinteregger, February 1984).
53. St AK 1921–6, p. 65.

policy for economic restabilisation. This was dubbed an 'employment tax' by the conservative press, just as the Viennese building tax had been, for it was levied on the wages of those in work. Employers reacted to the increase by arguing that the social cost of labour was now unrealistic and would lead to long-term economic decline, unless employers were compensated by a reduction of costs in some other form, e.g., an extension of the working day. In spring 1923 Styrian employers wrote to the Metalworkers' Union asking for an agreement on this. When it was rejected some firms took their own action by announcing, at a time when there was a surplus of labour, that workers who did not agree to a longer working day would be sacked. This was not restricted to small or even middle-sized firms; in January 1924 the Alpine Montangesellschaft informed its workers that overtime was no longer voluntary.[54]

In addition to the law on the eight-hour day, collective bargaining was also attacked. According to the law of 1919, collective contracts between workers' organisations and employers were legally binding and covered all workers in a company whether they were union members or not. Contracts had to be lodged with the conciliation commission and only came into force after the commission had announced them publicly. Any subsequent alterations went through the same process.[55] As a result, employers who had entered into a collective contract with their workforce could not change the terms of that contract arbitrarily. Despite this, in the spring of 1923 the Graz engineering employers announced a new contract drawn up without union consultation and reducing both the wages and the rights of the employee. The announcement was withdrawn when the national Metalworkers' Union threatened an all-out strike, but shortly thereafter the employers consolidated their strength by delegating the Employers' Association to represent them in wage negotiations in which more than one union was involved. According to Fritz Klenner this action united the employers, whilst highlighting the many differences between the unions, and so helped to alter the crucial balance of power in wage negotiations in favour of the employers.[56] Although the legal status of collective contracts survived these attacks, the number of Styrian workers who were covered by them fell in 1923 from 85,525 to

---

54. Klenner, *Die österreichischen Gewerkschaften*, vol. 1, p. 618.

55. *Arbeiterwille*, 8 February 1924. Klenner, *Die österreichischen Gewerkschaften*, vol. 1, p. 660.

56. Klenner, *Die österreichischen Gewerkschaften*, vol. 1, p. 619.

53,088 and the following year to 44,000, despite a slight improvement in employment figures. The total number of contracts in the province also fell from 254 in 1922 to 68 in 1924, suggesting that, although some of the reduction was due to the decrease in the number of people in work, other factors, such as the growing resistance of employers to collective contracts, were also responsible.[57]

The crisis unemployment of 1923 undermined the strength and bargaining power of the trade unions and lost them members. Some people left simply because they could not afford to pay union dues out of their meagre unemployment pay. Others became disillusioned as the business at branch meetings, which had previously provided the link between the union organisation and the rank-and-file member, became increasingly irrelevant to those who had been out of work for many months and saw little chance of finding a job. A conflict of interests began to arise between those in work and those on the dole, for the unemployed frequently complained that the unions were only interested in preserving jobs, even if this was done at the expense of the jobless, by extending the working day.[58] In this way the fluctuations in union membership in Styria in 1923 were no different from elsewhere in Austria, for union membership fell throughout the country in that year, and although the level of Styrian losses was 10 per cent higher than the national average, this only reflected the province's level of unemployment, which was also higher than the national average. Differences between the Styrian and the national trend did emerge in 1924, when national membership began to even out, but Styrian losses continued to rise; between 1923 and 1926 Styrian membership fell by a further 32 per cent, compared with a national loss of 16 per cent.[59] The experience of the Metalworkers' Union was even more disastrous, as comparisons with Wiener Neustadt show. Both the size of the workforce and union membership in the metal industry in these two areas had been roughly similar in 1922, when both had been hit by heavy unemployment. By 1924 the Styrian branches had lost 70 per cent of their members and only half the workers still employed had retained their union membership. In Wiener Neustadt union membership fell by only 41 per cent, whilst 98 per cent of the employed metalworkers were still in the union.[60]

57. *Stat Hdb Österreich* 1924, vol. 4, p. 92; 1924, vol. 5, p. 95; 1925, p. 119; 1926, p. 115.
58. St LA, Präs. E.91. Z1. 634/7. Police report dated 13 January 1923.
59. See Table 2, Appendix to this volume, p. 212.
60. *WsJ* 1925, p. 196.

The figures for Vienna, the country's major industrial area, showed even fewer losses than Wiener Neustadt.

The decline of the Metalworkers' Union in Styria had a profound effect on the entire labour movement in the province and highlighted the peculiar difficulties which faced it. This union was the largest and most powerful in Austria and, because of the dominance of heavy industry in Styria, its membership had accounted for a full 20 per cent of the province's trade unionists in 1922. By 1924, despite declines in other unions, this proportion has fallen to 10 per cent. One obvious reason was unemployment, for as has already been shown, heavy industry fared particularly badly during the currency crisis. But although this may explain the relative decline in the fortune of the Metalworkers' Union as opposed to other unions in the province, it does not explain why the Styrian section should have suffered more severe losses than other industrial regions. Wiener Neustadt was also affected by the crisis and the proportion of metalworkers who were out of work was actually higher than in Styria in December 1922 and of those on short time only marginally lower.[61] Whereas the union was able to sustain its membership in the Wiener Neustadt plants, it blatantly failed to do this in Styria.

This leads to the conclusion that, although crisis unemployment provided the catalyst which sparked off the decline in the labour movement in Styria, it cannot alone explain the severity of this decline. In the case of the Metalworkers' Union the solution lies once more in the structure of the industry and the attitude and determination of the employers, and in the lack of a strong tradition of trade union membership. In other industrial areas, such as Wiener Neustadt and Vienna, this tradition was embedded in engineering companies, supported by the skilled workers who had been the strength of the prewar labour movement. Union membership tended to come with the job and, on the basis of this, the union was able to re-establish itself in the years of partial economic recovery from 1924 to 1928. For the majority of the country's skilled metalworkers, who lived and worked in Vienna, the Social Democratic Party also played an important role in alleviating the burden of unemployment and improving the standard of living of many of its members through the policy of 'municipal socialism'. None of this was possible in Styria, where political power was in the hands of the opposition and large-scale trade union membership was a fairly recent phenomenon. Most union members in 1922 had

61. *WsJ* 1925, pp. 281–2.

been recruited in the early years of the Republic, when the authority of the employers appeared to have been curbed by the united strength of the working class, and it seemed that this position was permanent, enshrined in law. The expansion of the union was due to the recruitment of semi-skilled and unskilled workers and depended on its ability to improve wages and conditions for its members by negotiation, or, at the very least, to protect their living standards and legal rights by collective action or recourse to the law. Whilst the union fulfilled its side of the bargain membership grew, but in 1923, when the union was unable to stop wage cuts and could not even prevent this victimisation of its own shop stewards, it fell. The battle at the Karlsschacht had clearly shown that union membership could cost a worker his job, for even though the victimisation in this case had been directed against miners, the company which was involved was the Alpine Montangesellschaft, the major employer of metalworkers in the province.

7

The Debilitation of Labour

High crisis unemployment in 1922–4 and its effect on the Styrian union movement suggest that structural problems which had beset labour before the war still existed. The dominance of heavy industry continued to hinder trade union growth in the province. For example, in 1921 the three largest unions in Styria were the Metalworkers', which had 21,985 members the Miners', with 17,575 members, and the Railway Workers' Union, which had 15,835 members. By 1925 the Metalworkers' and Miners' Unions had fallen to second and third places, with 7,899 and 3,564 members respectively, whilst membership of the Railwaymen's Union, the only one of the three which did not draw its members from heavy industry, had fallen by only 17 per cent.[1] Mining and metallurgy still remained the chief industries in the province, relying heavily on semi-skilled and unskilled workers. Moreover, although ownership of the Alpine Montangesellschaft had passed from Austrian to Italian and then into German hands, it remained the largest private employer in both the province and the country, with 15,000 workers in 1925, and retained considerable political influence. During the dispute which followed the announcement of a ten-hour day in February 1924, the company successfully called on the government to provide police protection for strike breakers, despite the dubious legality of the announcement. Indeed it even gained tacit government support, by arguing that the only viable alternative to extending the working day was to 'rationalise' its assets still further, by shutting down the works at Kindberg.[2] At the same time it won a campaign to alter national tariffs and fought a second campaign to force the national railways to buy domestically produced rolling-stock. All of this was taking place at the same time that the Alpine Montangesellschaft management was leading the attack on the eight-hour day and the right of the Free

1. *Stat Hdb Österreich* 1923, p. 103; 1924, vol. 5, p. 105; 1925, p. 130; 1926, pp. 126–7.
2. Eduard Straas, 'Der Achtstundenarbeitstag', *Arbeit und Wirtschaft*, 1 April 1924, p. 10.

Trade Unions to represent their members within the mines and foundries.[3] These various strategies were part of a wider rationalisation policy which the company adopted in the 1920s in order to increase productivity whilst lowering labour costs.

Rationalisation and, more specifically, the high structural unemployment which it helped to create, provide the second major key to the weakness of the labour movement in the 1920s. Although the currency crisis, which had led to the first wave of job losses, ended in 1923 after the government had secured foreign loans and introduced the schilling, unemployment in Styria continued to rise each year from 1923 to the end of the Republic, with one slight fall in 1926. Between January 1924 and January 1925, when the level of insured unemployment in Austria rose by 156 per cent, the rate in Styria was 219 per cent.[4] Although all industrial areas in Austria experienced high unemployment in the 1920s, only Linz had a level which was comparable with this. In addition to the actual numbers who were out of work, there is also evidence that Styrian workers were suffering from unusually long periods of idleness. Before the 18th amendment to the Unemployment Insurance Act was passed in July 1924, unemployment benefit was issued only for 30 weeks. This was later extended indefinitely, at the discretion of the industrial commission and according to the needs and family status of the recipient.[5] In January 1924 24,089 unemployed people in Styria registered with the authorities, but of those only 4,609 were entitled to benefit. Twelve months later, when the amendment was in force, 29,226 were registered and 24,380 were receiving benefit, which indicates that over 15,000 people had previously been ineligible for the dole, because they had been out of work for longer than the stipulated period.[6] This large discrepancy between the numbers of registered unemployed and those receiving benefit occurred only in Styria and Linz.

The Free Trade Unions attributed this high level of structural or long-term employment to industrial rationalisation. Despite the frequent use of this term, which became politically fashionable in the 1920s, its exact meaning in this context remained unclear. In general it refers to the more rational use of resources, whether of materials, time or labour power. An increase in productivity per worker per shift or per year would normally indicate this, but

3. Ibid.
4. See Table 4, Appendix to this volume, pp. 214–15.
5. Charles A. Gulick, *Austria from Habsburg to Hitler*, 2 vols. (Berkeley, California, 1948), vol. 1, p. 231.
6. See Table 4, Appendix to this volume, p. 214–15.

without detailed production figures or a precise knowledge of the structure of the labour force in a specific plant and time, it is difficult to assess the actual impact of any rationalisation plan.

Some general comments can be made using figures which are available for production in mines and blast furnaces in Styria in the 1920s. Between 1921 and 1927 the number of lignite miners employed in Styrian mines fell from 13,124 to 7,624, a reduction of 42 per cent, whilst production fell by only 1.4 per cent.[7] During the same period employment in the blast furnaces also fell from 1,208 to 788, whilst the production of crude steel rose by 86 per cent and cast iron by over 300 per cent.[8] The uncertain state of the market in 1921 and a shortage of coking coal led to unusually low production in the postwar years and this obviously had some impact on the production of basic metals. But this does not detract from the fact that there was a general trend during the 1920s towards an increase in labour efficiency. Figures for annual average output per worker per shift in the mining and metallurgical industries published by the Chamber of Labour in 1927 confirm this. Calculated in tons for the years 1922 to 1927, these show a rise from 0.982 to 1.440 in lignite mines, 2.109 to 3.489 in iron ore and manganese mines, 44.17 to 85.17 in steel and 12.4 to 23.96 in the manufacturing in rolling-mills, forges and steelcasting works.[9] Although these figures refer to the national averages, they do also relate to Styria, which produced 60 per cent of Austria's lignite, 90 per cent of its iron ore and manganese and all of its crude steel.[10] A report on rationalisation by the International Labour Office in 1931 published these figures and concluded that in Austria 'rationalisation has been systematically carried out during recent years'.[11] It is worth noting that in the more detailed sections of the report, which showed which types of rationalisation were introduced in specific countries and industries, no reference to Austria was made. This is important, for the way in which a company or industry rationalises, and the state of the market when that rationalisation takes place can have a profound effect on labour power, as Doreen Massy and Richard

7. *Stat Hdb Österreich* 1923, p. 27; 1924, vol. 4, p. 31; 1924, vol. 5, p. 35; 1925, p. 44; 1926, p. 42; 1927, p. 61; 1928, p. 64.

8. *Stat Hdb Österreich* 1923, pp. 28–9; 1924, vol. 4, pp. 32–3; 1924, vol. 5, pp. 36–7; 1926, pp. 46–7; 1925, pp. 44–5; 1927, pp. 63–4; 1928, pp. 65–6.

9. *WsJ* 1927, pp. 166–7.

10. *Stat Hdb Österreich* 1923, p. 28; 1924, vol. 4, p. 32; 1924, vol. 5, p. 36; 1925, p. 45; 1926, p. 43; 1927, p. 62; 1928, p. 64.

11. International Labour Office, *The Social Aspects of Rationalisation. Introductory Studies* (Geneva, 1931), pp. 77, 206.

Meegan have shown.[12] For instance, the introduction of new technology into an expanding industry can result in rationalisation which improves the wages and working conditions of the employees. The streamlining of production by closing less profitable plants and concentrating production in fewer areas can also be of benefit to workers if they are redeployed at the same or better levels of pay and conditions. Improving training and efficient organisation, thus removing tedious and unnecessary labour, both of which the ILO report cites as methods of rationalisation, are yet further examples of forms which could improve the position of labour. However, if rationalisation merely increases production per worker without any corresponding increase in income or reward, the net result can be a further weakening of the bargaining power of labour, as the proportion of industrial costs which are allocated to labour falls. Rationalisation in this case can lead to increased unemployment and competition amongst workers for the jobs which remain.

The major factors in a rationalisation programme are technological improvements, which increase mechanisation, streamlining of industry, concentrating production in fewer sites, and reorganisation of the work process to speed up production. There can be little doubt that some technological rationalisation did take place in heavy industry and mining in the province, although the exact extent is more difficult to assess. To take the case of the Alpine Montangesellschaft once more, according to the conservative press, major investment was made in the 1920s to increase production and lower costs.[13] This was especially true in the company's mines, where the introduction of electricity to all five major plants in 1925 led to the mechanisation of ore crushers, sorting machines and dressing plants, tasks which had previously been performed by hand or with the use of compressed-air machines. Two conveyor belts were built at Erzberg to remove sinter from the furnaces and a funicular rail to remove slag from the furnaces at Donawitz. All of these investments resulted in a speeding up of the work process and a reduction in unskilled labour, which had formerly carted waste material away. New cutters in the iron ore mines, most of which were powered by compressed air, but two of which are electric, improved efficiency, but these were still operated by labour and so did not directly add to the numbers of unemployed. The company

12. Doreen Massey and Richard Meegan, *The Anatomy of Job Losses* (London, 1982).
13. *Neue Freie Presse*, 18 June 1927; *Neues Wiener Tagblatt*, 10 November 1928.

also streamlined its metal production by closing the ironworks at Neuberg and the plate-rolling-mill at Zeltweg in 1923, transferring many workers to Donawitz. Apart from these changes, most investment went into technological improvement which increased production, but did not reduce the demand for labour. There were major innovations in lignite drying, which reduced the company's dependence on imported fuel, and a new ore roasting process. An electric arc-furnace was built in Donawitz in 1927 in addition to two new smaller solid-fuel furnaces at Eisenerz.[14] However, the extensive rationalisation which had already taken place in metal production in the United States, involving electric trolleys, overhead mechanical ladles and rising and falling tables, was a thing of the future in Austria. It was these techniques which had considerably reduced the numbers of workers in American foundries and steel mills.[15] The more limited investment of the Alpine Montangesellschaft increased the productive capacity of plants, but did not substantially reduce the demand for labour.

Streamlining and technological rationalisation therefore had some impact on labour in the mines, foundries and rolling-mills, but they cannot fully explain the extent of the reduction in the labour force which actually took place. Between 1922 and 1926 employment in the company fell by 30 per cent, from 16,605 to 11,722, rising slightly thereafter to 13,400 in 1929. The number of foundry workers fell by 33 per cent. In contrast, production of lignite, pig-iron and crude steel, iron ore and rolled steel rose steadily from 1922, falling for a short period in 1924.[16] One other possible explanation, which also falls within the category of rationalisation, remains: the reorganisation of the work process. This can range from improvements in the organisation of the shop floor, improved technological training for management and workers, new incentive payments, to increased supervision, small work teams and a clampdown on all types of wastage. The introduction of some or all of these, combined with the modernisation of machinery, could radically improve efficiency, as Frederick Taylor had shown at the Bethlehem Steel Works in the United States.[17]

14. Fritz Erben, Maja Loehr and Hans Riehl (eds.), *Die Alpine Montangesellschaft* (Vienna, 1931), p. 58, 64, 66.

15. Katherine Stone, 'The Origins of Job Structures in the Steel Industry', *Review of Radical Economics*, vol. 6, no. 2, 1974, pp. 61–97.

16. *Neues Wiener Tagblatt*, 10 November 1928. In 1928 Alpine Montangesellschaft bought the Graz-Köflacher Company.

17. Harry Braverman, *Labor and Monopoly Capital* (New York and London, 1974), pp. 102–6.

There is no evidence that the Alpine Montangesellschaft radically altered work processes and, although a new pay incentive scheme was introduced in 1927, this was too late to have been a cause of increased productivity. On the contrary, wage levels at the company were notoriously low, both before and after 1927.[18] Supervision on the shop floor was intensified in the 1920s, as frequent complaints from the Free Trade Unions about intimidation and company spies indicate.[19] In 1928 a conference of Free Trade Union shop stewards passed a resolution denouncing what was described as the atmosphere of terror in the company and accusing the management of mounting a systematic campaign against its workers. The level of company housing, which was higher in Styria than most provinces in Austria, led to one other major grievance, for the Alpine Montangesellschaft alone owned 7,000 units of housing and was accused of threatening Free Trade Union members both with the sack and with eviction from their homes if they insisted on remaining in the union.[20] These allegations implied that the company was using reorganisation to increase control over workers rather than to rationalise production.

The final area of possible rationalisation, modern scientific management and training, seemed to be adopted by the company in 1926 when it opened the first of five company schools for the vocational training of selected youths between the ages of fifteen and twenty. The first school at Zeltweg concentrated on training joiners, carpenters, turners, fitters and smiths and was soon followed by a second at Fohnsdorf, which specialised in mining.[21] However, the schools were not designed exclusively as skill centres, for the four-year course also included intensive courses in physical education and the euphemistic subject of 'civics'.[22] The

18. In 1926 a hewer in the Upper Austrian mines earned 12.28 schillings per shift and an ordinary adult miner 9.94 schillings per shift. In 1928 this fell to 11.83 schillings and 10.61 schillings respectively. In 1926 in the Upper Styrian lignite mines a hewer earned 8.74 schillings per shift and an ordinary adult miner 7.57 schillings. By 1928 the gap had narrowed slightly to 10.16 schillings per shift for a hewer and 8.73 schillings for an ordinary miner. Rates in the middle Styrian field were even lower. Verband der Bergarbeiter Deutschösterreichs in Leoben, *Bericht des Vorstandes für die Berichtsjahre 1926–28*, pp. 20–5. (Kammer für Arbeiter und Angestellte, Wien II 5861).
19. A resolution at the executive conference of the Free Trade Unions in May 1928 referred to 'factory terror' at the Alpine Montangesellschaft works. *Jb BFG* 1928, p. 43.
20. Karin Schmidlechner, 'Die Situation der steierischen Industriearbeiter zwischen 1918–1934', p. 41.
21. Erben et al. (eds.), *Die Alpine Montangesellschaft*, p. 197.
22. Ibid., p. 202.

former, which included competitive team sports, hiking, skiing and gymnastics, fostered group loyalty: students were divided into small groups, each with its own leader and tutor, and competed for school trophies and prizes. Tutors also gave 'spiritual guidance' to students and demanded complete obedience and discipline. This permeated down throughout the whole school. Courses in civics included instruction in maths, economics and a liberal dose of political propaganda emphasising the unity and interdependence of the company and its employees.

At face value it may seem that the work schools were the product of a clear recognition of the need for highly-skilled labour which could liaise between management and workers, for the students were selected and trained to become future shop floor supervisors. However the technical side of the training was only one of its functions and, as it transpired, a minor one. In addition, the schools formed the centre of a wider company campaign to influence the political attitudes and behaviour of workers, for although they were nominally independent of the company, the teaching staff were all company employees, engineers and managers, who were seconded for a limited period. The body which supervised the running of these and five similar schools in Styria, was the Austrian Association for Technical Training (DINTA). This institute had been founded in Düsseldorf in 1925, under the auspices of German heavy industry, including the Thyssen concern, which controlled the Alpine Montangesellschaft. In 1927 the founder of DINTA, Dr Arnhold, set up the Austrian Association in Leoben with the full support and cooperation of the Alpine Montangesellschaft management.[23]

The purpose of the DINTA was not simply vocational training, but was linked to a wider philosophy of industrial harmony which it was hoped would woo workers away from any commitment to socialism. German trade unions had dubbed this the mission to win the souls of the workers.[24] Students at the school were encouraged to discuss their training at home and to bring their parents to evening classes, where the older workers also heard the message of peace and prosperity for both workers and the firm. The image of the company as a vast family made up of members of different ages and grades dominated much of the teaching. Students were encouraged to suggest improvements in production and management based on their own work experience, which was carried out within

23. Ibid., p. 197.
24. Paul Lazarsfeld, 'Dinta', *Arbeit und Wirtschaft*, 1927, p. 438.

the steelworks and mines under the supervision of their tutors. In an article in *Arbeit und Wirtschaft*, the Free Trade Union magazine, published in 1927, Paul Lazarsfeld quoted from the programme of the DINTA: 'The worker must learn to understand that in the production process one must give more than receive.'[25] In the German original, this phrase became a play on words, for the word to receive also means to earn. Loyalty to the company combined with German nationalism was a central key to the training and, as a result, these company schools soon became centres of Heimwehr activity in the province.

In addition to this programme of political and vocational training of future workers, the company also took steps to influence the political attitudes of its existing workforce. From 1926 it produced its own weekly newspaper which was issued free to all workers. The paper's format was more like a magazine than a newspaper, containing many photographs and drawings which emphasised the spiritual, as opposed to the material gains which work provided. The paper included romantic stories about the history of the region, with little reference to mining or steel, and homilies on safety at work, obedience to parents and love of the fatherland, by which the writers meant Germany rather than the Austrian Republic. The front cover of an edition published in 1927 showed a picture of Hindenburg, alongside the words and music of 'Deutschland über alles'.[26] There was also a births, marriages and deaths column and advice on Do-it-yourself. The paper's obvious message was pride in the factory, pride in the company and opposition to all who threatened it. For older workers the company set up 'voluntary' weekly evening classes preaching the same message.

As part of a rationalisation process, the schools were established too late to have been effective, for the first graduates did not emerge until 1930, when production had already fallen. But as part of the DINTA programme they illustrate the company's changing attitude to industrial relations and its increasing involvement in German nationalism in the province. The policy of crude repression with which the company had controlled its workers before the war was replaced by more sophisticated techniques of sociological and psychological manipulation, designed to woo workers into identifying their own interests with those of the company. Workers were told that, although the company was amongst the

25. Ibid.
26. *Alpine Post*, October 1927.

most successful in Europe, its progress was stifled by national politics and regressive economic policies.[27] The 'Führer Prinzip', which was such an integral part of fascist philosophy, was expounded at all levels throughout the company, starting in the schools and evening classes. Physical prowess, teamwork and discipline were, Erben wrote in 1932, the only way in which the Austrian and German people would successfully compete with the new world leader, America.[28]

Increased productivity and falling employment in the Alpine Montangesellschaft cannot simply be attributed to rationalisation. New investment did improve the production process, but only to a limited degree; many of the investments merely extended existing techniques without decreasing demand for labour, whilst the newer labour-saving techniques, such as the electric arc furnace, were only just in operation before the crash of 1929, when production fell. New management techniques were introduced, but these were not linked to a reorganisation of shop floor practices. The most important factors in increased production were, therefore, the extension of the working day and greater supervision of a traditional kind. The company succeeded in increasing the pressure of work by intimidation and ignoring legal regulations which had been imposed after the war. The high level of unemployment in the region produced a surplus of labour which was exploited in order to defeat organised labour within plants. Success was not, therefore, due to rationalisation, but a reaffirmation of the control of the company over its workforce. However, the situation had not completely reverted to the days of the Empire, for industrial relations had been transformed by the Revolution and the company was forced to negotiate with the elected representatives of its workers. But the law did not stipulate that these had to be members of any particular union and the management soon realised that there were alternatives to the socialists, who had dominated the factory councils in the early years after the war. If negotiations were inevitable, it was better for the company if shop stewards believed in peace and harmony on the shop floor, rather than in the philosophies of class conflict. As a result, from 1925 onwards, the Alpine Montangesellschaft management sought to 'win the minds of its workers' and encouraged first the Christian Unions and then the Heimwehr-sponsored Independent Unions in opposition to the socialist Free Trade Unions.

27. Ibid.
28. Erben et al. (eds.), *Die Alpine Montangesellschaft*, pp. 207–9.

The first evidence of this appeared in September 1925, when foundry workers at Donawitz rejected a pay offer which increased the level of piece rates but barely affected the level of basic wages.[29] A strike broke out, spread throughout the entire plant of 4,000 workers and finally resulted in a lock-out at Eisenerz.[30] The strike lasted for four weeks and resulted in a substantial, though not a total, victory for the workers, who forced the company to raise basic wages by between 5 per cent and 10 per cent, the rate varying according to grade. However, the 1925 strike was significant for more than just this, for only 400 of the strikers were union members and therefore entitled to strike pay. Non-union members were at first forced to rely on their own resources, garden produce and local support, whilst the Free Trade Union leaders chastised them for their folly at not staying in the union.[31] This attitude changed after one week, when the Metalworkers' Union leader, Franz Domes, acknowledged the importance of the battle at Donawitz and authorised the establishment of an extraordinary fund to support the strikers. One notable feature of this strike was the discipline and solidarity of the strikers. A strike committee, which was controlled by the Free Trade Unions, imposed a ban on alcohol, organised local meetings and leafleting campaigns to ensure that the strikers were kept informed of what was going on. Throughout the four-week strike railway workers prevented trains from delivering goods to the plant and the strike remained solid until it was called off on 17 October. In a plant were union membership was particularly weak, this was a major achievement. But there was a second aspect to this dispute which was even more significant. When negotiations between the company and the Free Trade Unions initially broke down on 20 September, the management attempted to reach a settlement with the small Christian Union of Metalworkers, which at that time had only a handful of members. The Christian Union leaders had agreed to this, but the attempt to isolate and ignore the Free Trade Union backfired when Christian Union members ignored their leaders' call to work and walked out.[32]

29. Fritz Klenner, *Die österreichischen Gewerkschaften*, 2 vols. (Vienna, 1953), vol. 1, p. 689.

30. *Arbeiterwille*, 27 September 1925.

31. Ibid. A bulletin issued by the provincial trade union commission not only commented on this, but also warned strikers of the dangers of being led astray by Communists.

32. Klenner, *Die österreichischen Gewerkschaften*, vol. 1, p. 690. *Arbeiter-Zeitung*, 23 September 1925.

The 1925 strike marked a significant point in labour relations for the Alpine Montangesellschaft. The management had tried to ignore the larger Free Trade Union and, when this failed, it ordered the strikers to return to work or be sacked. The attempt to establish a working relationship with the Christian Union also failed, not because of the organisation itself, but because of the antipathy of its members. From this time onwards, the management instigated its campaign of workers' 'training' and sought to foster splits within the workforce, so drawing itself ever closer towards the Heimwehr.

One final question remains before turning to the more overtly political battles of 1927 to 1934. Why was it that the Free Trade Unions and their shop stewards were unable to resist the erosion of their power and the rights of their members in the years before the 1929 depression? The most important reasons, the level of unemployment, the structure of Styrian industry, the concerted opposition of employers and the wavering attitude of the workers themselves, have all been discussed. There was one further problem which was pointed out in the 1926 yearly report of the Styrian Chamber of Labour.[33] In 1919–20 the Social Democratic Party had produced a plan which envisaged an industrial system whereby shop stewards would systematically increase their knowledge of industrial management by practice and ultimately take control of the economy. When the Factory Council Act and the act establishing the Chambers of Labour were finally passed,[34] the role of the shop steward had been reduced to that of a negotiator with the management, over wages and conditions, and of a monitor, observing that the law was actually followed. But this still presented major problems for shop stewards in Styria, who often lacked both negotiating experience and detailed knowledge of the laws. One of the main functions of the Chamber of Labour was to provide training and information on industrial relations for shop stewards, but after 1923 employees at the Chamber noticed that interest in the law had been superseded by a more basic concern over wage levels, earnings and unemployment. The threat of long-term unemployment swiftly removed workers' determination to improve their working conditions. The lack of political opportunity was evident when, for instance, shop stewards demanded an increase in company housing to reduce the problems of homelessness.[35] In this case there was little alternative: housing could not be provided by

33. St AK 1926, pp. 73–4.
34. See Chapter 4, pp. 60–1; 63–4 above.
35. St AK 1926, p. 8.

the community, as was happening in Vienna, so who else could finance new building projects other than the employers? But shop stewards also urged their members to leave the government insurance schemes; this smacked of a lack of political experience rather than expediency.[36] By 1924 some local union leaders were even suggesting that the level of unemployment benefit was too high, a point with which the employers were in total agreement. The Chamber of Labour became increasingly exasperated with the shop stewards, which was understandable. But then, the shop stewards themselves were in a difficult position, for many no doubt felt it was better to win short-term financial gains as real wages fell, rather than hold out for distant and less tangible rewards. As a result, the period of trade union militancy in Styria came to an end in 1923.

Styrian trade unionism fell prey once more to the uncertainties of high unemployment and a lack of job security. From 1924 until 1928 the Free Trade Unions maintained their presence in the area through the factory councils, but the province never saw the high levels of trade union membership of 1921 and 1922. The reasons for the lack of trade union commitment in the prewar period re-emerged in the 1920s; the trade unions were less geared towards the provincial unskilled and semi-skilled worker than they were to the skilled workers of the capital and Wiener Neustadt. Despite the rapid drop in union membership in the province there was no campaign to draw the Styrians back into the fold. The province's unemployment was higher during the currency crisis than elsewhere and so the fall in union membership was inevitably greater. However, there was one other explanation. The structure of the labour legislation was designed for an area in which there was already a strong trade union movement. The legislation was complex and sophisticated and required a labour organisation which could swiftly cope with specific problems of law. Although such a labour organisation existed in Vienna, and to some extent in Wiener Neustadt, it was missing in Styria and particularly in Upper Styria.

For the Austrian economy and labour force, 1923 was a crisis year. It was also election year. As the eight-hour day, union representation and union rights came under attack, the Social Democratic Party fought a campaign on the Tenants' Protection Laws and increased its votes. It then launched an agricultural programme to win over small peasant support from the Christian

36. Ibid., p. 33.

Social Party. No initiative was taken on Styria. Some union leaders criticised the party's stance and its refusal to re-enter a coalition government. But the unions' response was also weak. In 1923 they called for increased education and training of members and issued a new directive on strikes, hoping to bring them under greater control. But in Styria the problem was not one of undisciplined trade unionists, but their dwindling numbers.[37]

---

37. Klenner, *Die österreichischen Gewerkschaften*, vol. 1, pp. 626–7.

8

The Year of the General Strike, 1927

At this point it is necessary to widen the discussion once more, for the year 1927 marked a turning-point in the political history of the labour movement, both nationally and provincially. 'In April 1927 Austrian labour and with it Austrian democracy had reached the peak of power. In July 1927, both crossed this peak.'[1] The ostensible cause of this change took place on 30 January in Schattendorf, a small town in Burgenland with a population of 2,500, close to the Hungarian border. On that day notice was given of two separate political meetings which were to take place in the village, one to be given by the paramilitary Association of Frontline Soldiers (Frontkämpfervereinigung), and the second by the Social Democratic Party. Party politics was unusual in Burgenland because of its vulnerable geographic position; having been part of Hungary before the First World War, it was ceded to Austria in 1919 by the Entente, following demands for a plebiscite, and had since been a point of dispute between the two countries, with both demanding the right to govern. Hungarian propaganda flowed into the province and the Austrian government frequently accused Hungary of attempting to provoke violence in Burgenland in order to reclaim it. This situation led to a working agreement between the Social Democratic Party and the Christian Social Party, which was designed to avoid conflict; the provincial government was a coalition of the two parties, and both agreed to refrain from introducing their paramilitary wings into Burgenland.[2]

In practical terms this meant that in 1926 Burgenland was the only Austrian province which did not have a Republikanische Schutzbund movement. The agreement was jeopardised at the beginning of November 1926, when the Association of Frontline Soldiers began to set up branches, including one in Schattendorf. This was a predominantly socialist town and a Schutzbund unit was immediately organised in response. The Social Democrats

---

1. Charles A. Gulick, *Austria from Habsburg to Hitler*, 2 vols. (Berkeley, California, 1948), vol. 1, p. 771.
2. Ibid., p. 726.

viewed the very existence of the Association of Frontline Soldiers as an act of provocation. When they heard that a large meeting was to be held, drawing supporters from the surrounding districts and addressed by the national leaders and the chief commander Hermann Hiltl, they decided to hold a counter-demonstration of Schutzbund strength. A call went out to neighbouring villages and on 30 January at least 200 Schutzbund members were in town.[3]

Contemporary accounts of the events which followed were both emotional and confused. According to one Styrian newspaper, 200 Schutzbund members attacked a small group of Frontline Soldiers and two people were killed.[4] The *Arbeiterwille*, the paper of the Styrian Social Democratic Party, described the deaths as 'Workers' murder', in which a war invalid and a young boy were shot dead during an attack on a socialist meeting.[5] The story which emerged from the trial differed from both accounts. The meetings had both been scheduled to take place at 3 pm in two separate inns. The Association of Frontline Soldiers met in the Tscharmann inn and the Schutzbund at the Moser inn along the street. At 11 am, as rival supporters were arriving, a group of Schutzbund men went into the Tscharmann inn. Whether they sat quietly and drank wine, as the Social Democrats later maintained,[6] or whether they demanded the cancellation of the Frontline Soldiers' meeting and threatened violence if their own meeting was disrupted, is immaterial.[7] The Schutzbündler were challenging the Frontline Soldiers just by being there, as the Frontline Soldiers had challenged them by calling the meeting in the first place. A conflict developed of a kind which was to become increasingly common over the next few years. There was a stormy exchange of words in the inn and the police arrived to oust the Schutzbund men. Shortly afterwards a troop of 200 Schutzbündler marched to the railway station at-Loipersbach, met the train on which were the leaders of the Association of Frontline Soldiers either persuaded them or forced them to return from whence they had come. It seemed that a fight had been avoided and the Schutzbündler marched back to the Moser inn with a sense of victory. As they passed the Tscharmann inn several shots were fired from a window. Seven people were wounded and two stragglers, who had been trying to keep up at the

---

3. *Neue Freie Presse*, 1 February 1927.
4. *Grazer Tagblatt*, 31 January 1927.
5. *Arbeiterwille*, 1 February 1927.
6. Gulick, *Austria*, vol. 1, p. 727.
7. Ingeborg Messerer, 'Die Frontkämpfervereinigung Deutsch-Österreich' (unpublished PhD thesis, University of Vienna, 1963), p. 20.

back of the column, were killed. One, Matthias Csmaritas, was a war invalid and the other an eight-year-old boy named Grossing.[8]

The deaths of Csmaritas and the boy were not the first examples of political killings in Austria, for bloody fights between rival groups were becoming more common.[9] The most notorious death prior to Schattendorf took place in the Viennese district of Mödling in May 1925, when a Social Democratic city councillor named Müller was beaten and stabbed to death by members of an ex-servicemen's organisation.[10] However, the reaction to the Schattendorf deaths was intensified by various factors. There had been no serious attacks on Social Democrats in 1926 and almost all the previous incidents had taken place in industrial areas. Schattendorf was just a small country town. Secondly, the deaths took place at the beginning of the election campaign, when the Social Democrats hoped to win power, and boded ill for such a victory. Finally, the victims in this attack were not robust party members, who could, theoretically, defend themselves, but a cripple and a child.

The murders were therefore emotive and editorials in the bourgeois press were often callous, but the reaction of the industrial workers in January 1927 was disciplined and peaceful. On 31 January workers in factories throughout Burgenland and in neighbouring Wiener Neustadt laid down their tools. The response was spontaneous.[11] Neither party nor union had ordered it, although they assumed joint leadership as soon as the news reached Vienna and directives could be issued. On 1 February work continued as normal, but the following day, the day of the funerals, the Social Democratic Party executive and the Trade Union Commission[12] issued a joint order for a fifteen minute general strike in commemoration of the dead and to demand the dissolution of the Association of Frontline Soldiers.[13]

There was no unofficial action in Styria on 31 January but on 2 February the general strike was carried out throughout Upper Styria and in Graz. There was local resentment in Graz at the city's trades-council, which held a meeting on 31 and passed a series of

8. *Neue Freie Presse*, 1 February 1927.
9. Gerhard Botz, 'Gewalt und politisch-gesellschaftlicher Konflikt in der Ersten Republik (1918 bis 1933)', *Österreichische Zeitschrift für Politikwissenschaft*, 1975, pp. 511–34.
10. Gulick, *Austria*, vol. 1, p. 719.
11. *Arbeiterwille*, 3 February 1929.
12. Prior to 1928 the socialist trade unions were organised under the Trade Union Commission (Gewerkschaftskommission). In 1928 this was renamed the Bund der Freien Gewerkschaften Österreichs (Free Trade Union Commission).
13. Gulick, *Austria*, vol. 1, p. 730.

anti-Jewish and anti-socialist resolutions. The council expressed admiration for Lueger and his attack on Jewish capital, blamed the collapse of the Lower Austrian Farmers' Bank on its connections with Jewish financiers, passed vitriolic condemnations on the 'Red Council' in Vienna, and agreed that the fight against Socialism was to be supported, whether led by the Christian Social Party or by the German Nationalists. This was on the very evening of the murders at Schattendorf. In Graz and the outlying districts of Eggenberg, Andritz and Puntigam, the strike was heralded at 11 am by the sound of sirens. Factories and trams stopped. In Andritz, paper workers gathered in a square outside the factory. Heissler, an official of the Trade Union Commission, addressed a meeting at the Grazer Waggon- und Maschinenfabrik AG, whilst two national parliamentary deputies, Ludwig Tuller and Franz Schaffler, spoke at the Puch works and the Styria Durkopp works. The railwaymen at the central station in Graz sounded the train whistles on the stroke of 11 and it was reported that not a single train moved anywhere in the province.[14]

The strike was a success in the eyes of the local Chamber of Labour, party executive and union officials, for it was a clear expression both of party and union policy. Despite revolutionary rhetoric, which the union and party leadership still used, neither intended that their verbal fighting should be taken out of the meeting halls and become physical in the streets. The following motion had been passed at the Linz party conference in 1926: 'The Social Democratic Party defends the right of manual workers, white-collar workers, and government employees to organise. It places its political power in the service of the organised struggles of the manual, white-collar workers and government employees.'[15] For some it was a welcome response, however late in coming. But the principal weapon to be used in 'the organised struggle' was the general strike, a peaceful and highly disciplined action designed to illustrate the power of the labour movement, to flex its muscles without delivering a blow. A blow was violence and: 'Violence means civil war. . . . Civil war means famine, destruction of economic life. . . . Civil war means that Socialism, even in the case of victory, cannot improve the economic conditions of this genera-tion of workers, but must worsen them, because the devastation of economic life means incomparably more than the confiscation of

14. *Arbeiterwille*, 3 February 1927.

15. Fritz Klenner, *Die österreichischen Gewerkschaften*, 2 vols. (Vienna, 1953), vol. 1, p. 713.

surplus value.'[16] Violence was the very last resort, to be employed only when all other tactics had been seen to fail and the working class was pushed back into the defensive position. Until such a time the policy of the party and their unions was one of passive resistance.[17]

In practice the general strike became the ultimate weapon. The general strike was, and still is, a radical action. As an economic tactic, it could be used by a disciplined and well-organised labour movement to disrupt an economy and bring a government to its knees. The Austrian labour movement preferred to confine the strike to short periods of minutes, hours or days, and use it as a threat, a symbolic gesture demonstrating the power of the working class. The professed aim was to disrupt the economy as little as possible. But in this role the general strike only remained effective when it reflected this actual power available, and when the opposition was aware that the power would be unleashed if it was thought necessary. When employers and right-wing groups in Austria realised that the strike was the ultimate deterrent, and that they could defy it, faith in the general strike became dangerous.

Prior to 1927 employers had shown some tolerance of national stoppages and these had passed without serious reprisals. During the strike which followed the Schattendorf murders the policy of sectors of Styrian industry hardened. This was an indication of the aggressive tactics used by employers to call the bluff of the labour leaders, to attack the movement and finally to defeat it. On the day before the official strike, the Graz section of the Confederation of Styrian Industry and the Association of Metal Industrialists advised their members to forbid workers to switch off machines during the fifteen minute strike.[18] One reason for this, the time and energy needed to restart the machines after they had been stopped, appears to be reasonable until it is remembered that this advice was new, and was described by the *Arbeiterwille* as an act of intimidation (*Hemmungsaktion*). As it had presumably been policy in the past to

16. Otto Bauer's speech at the Linz Party Conference, quoted in Gulick, *Austria*, vol. 2, p. 1391.

17. This declaration by the leaders of the Social Democratic Party was, according to one member, 'the expression of the best hopes of a class-conscious working class and the indirect means of their destruction', but was described by critics as a direct challenge to the democratic republic. In July 1927 a coalition deputy in the Styrian Provincial Assembly declared that 'the language of the current Linz Party Conference was nothing more than flirtation with Russian Communism'. (*Stenographische Bericht über die Verhandlungen des steiermärkischen Landtages*, Sitting 25 July 1927, p. 82.) The remark was made by Zenz, a Roman Catholic priest.

18. *Arbeiterwille*, 6 February 1927.

shut off the machinery in question, it may safely be assumed that the employers' organisations were not referring to large machines such as blast furnaces, which took days to relight, but to the small machines which could be turned on and off with use.[19] Any saving in time would have been completely outweighed by the possible damage which an unattended machine could inflict upon its operator or even on itself. Some firms, most notably Alpine Montangesellschaft, had a rule that all 'unnecessary' damage or spoilage was the responsibility of the worker. A second and more plausible explanation of the employers' action was given at a meeting of the Confederation of Styrian Industry on 5 February, when the members published a statement saying that they had reached the end of their patience and would resist the Social Democratic tactic of political rather than economic strikes.[20]

The employers' reaction was not evidence of a new hostility towards the strength and activities of the working-class organisations. Such hostility had been manifest since 1918, but employers were becoming aware that they could act upon it. February was only a forewarning of the calamity which was to take place in July.

The trial of the son of the innkeeper Tscharmann and his brother-in-law for the murders began on 5 July and lasted ten days. Each day the *Arbeiter-Zeitung* carried full coverage of the proceedings and alleged that the jury had been packed and that political pressure had been brought to bear on the public prosecutors.[21] The verdict was not given until 10 pm on 14 July, too late for the evening papers. All the accused were acquitted. The defence had argued that the Frontline Soldiers had been terrified by the Schutzbund during the day and had thought that they were being attacked when the Schutzbund had marched past the Tscharmann inn. They pleaded self-defence and the jury accepted the plea.

The verdict became known in Vienna early on 15 July, when

---

19. Closing down a blast furnace is a lengthy business. The walls of the furnace have to be relined before relighting. In 1932, when the Alpine Montangesellschaft management closed down the Donawitz plant for several days, coinciding with a march of all Heimatschutz units in the province, the blast furnace workers remained at work. *Arbeiter-Zeitung*, 19 November 1932.

20. Felix Kreissler, *Von der Revolution zur Annexion* (Vienna, 1970), p. 152.

21. *Arbeiter-Zeitung*, 8 July 1927. Gulick argued that the trial was as fair as possible and that the verdict was part of a wave of acquittals. He acknowledged, however, that the state prosecutor's closing remarks, when he asked for a guilty verdict before the law, but placed moral responsibility on the Schutzbund, 'might have been accountable to some extent for the result'. Gulick, *Austria*, vol. 1, p. 733. G.E.R. Gedye, who was at that time *Daily Express* correspondent for Austria and the Balkans, agreed with the *Arbeiter-Zeitung* that the jury was packed. G.E.R. Gedye, *Fallen Bastions: The Central European Tragedy* (London, 1939), p. 30.

morning papers were sold on the streets and outside factory gates. At 8 am the trams stopped as the electricity workers called a one-hour-long strike, the traditional sign for a general strike in the capital. Shop stewards called meetings outside the factories and places of work. Group after group voted to down tools and protest by marching to the inner city, towards the administrative sector of Vienna. As the *Daily Express* reporter, G.E.R. Geyde pointed out, there was nothing unusual about this. The Social Democrats and Free Trade Union members were following a tradition of protest which had been familiar since the first days of the Republic. The one unusual characteristic was that the Schutzbund were not alerted to act as stewards on the demonstration. Soon after 10 am, when the Ringstraße was crowded with 'thousands of workmen, men and women marching in orderly procession',[22] shots were heard somewhere near the parliament building. The mounted police, who had orders to keep control of the unorganised demonstration, charged the crowd and a riot began. Cobble stones, bricks, wood and iron bars were thrown at the police, who fired into the crowd, in some cases using target ammunition which had the same effect on the victim as expanding dum-dum bullets.[23] As people fell dead or wounded the fury of the crowd deepened; men and women surged forward, forcing the police to seek refuge in the most convenient building, the Palace of Justice. The choice was unfortunate, for the building itself became the target of anger, symbolising as it did a judicial system which had refused to convict anti-socialists who killed party members.[24] The building smouldered and burst into flames as bundles of burning paper were hurled at it. As the blaze raged, the fire brigade was prevented from reaching it by the throng of people. Finally, with the help of mayor Seitz, the firemen got through. By that evening 1,057 people had been injured and 89 were dead: 85 civilians and 4 policemen. Only one policeman was killed during the actual fighting on the Ringstraße. These casualty figures did not support the accusations of the Christian Social and Heimwehr press, that the 'July events' were a premeditated action, part of a Marxist attempt to overthrow the state. A nationalist newspaper even told its readers that a whistle had been blown soon after the crowd gathered as the signal for shots to be fired at the police. The very first shot they claimed was fired by a foreign communist, whom they even named.[25]

22. Gedye, *Fallen Bastions*, p. 31.
23. Ibid., p. 34.
24. The trial had been held at the criminal assize court in the Alserstraße.
25. *Österreichische Grenzwacht*, 24 July 1927.

The *Arbeiter-Zeitung* allotted the blame to the police and to communist agitators.[26] But the paper was not convincing. The party executive had seriously overestimated the powers of its leadership and underestimated the indignation and fury of the Viennese working class. The chaos and slaughter were the result of a different analysis of the situation by the two. The reaction of the workers to the trial verdict was spontaneous; they considered it outrageous and their banners bore slogans denying that socialists and workers would ever gain justice from the state. Had not the Social Democratic Party just won 71 of the 165 seats in the National Parliament and was it not the largest single party in the country? Did it not dominate the Vienna city council? Even here socialists could not obtain justice. Workers decided to demonstrate their anger, as they had done in February, and as they had done many times since the founding of the Republic, but this time the party executive did not support their action.

The decision to march had been taken at factory gates and outside offices on a show of hands. With the exception of the electricity workers, this had not been contrary to the wishes of the executive, for neither the views of the union nor those of the party leadership were known. At 8 am, when the trams stopped, any doubting members took this as the signal for a general strike; there was not a hint of executive disapproval.

But the executives both of the party and the unions did disapprove. The electricity works shop stewards met during the night of 14/15 July and sent a delegation to the labour leaders to ask for instructions, assuming that there would be an organised demonstration. They went away confused and angry. No plans had been made. The police also assumed that there would be some form of protest and forty-eight hours prior to the publication of the verdict the commissioner, Schober, ordered an alert throughout Vienna. Thus, although the demonstration was spontaneous, it was not unexpected. The leadership was not caught unprepared; it was unwilling to act.

At 3 am on the morning of 15 July a meeting of the party executive and union commission was told that the electricity workers had decided to strike, against party wishes. Julius Deutsch, a member of the party's executive, was sent to dissuade them.[27] He failed. The executive had already informed the Vienna police commissioner Schober that there would be no demonstrations and

26. *Arbeiter-Zeitung*, 15 July 1927, evening edition.
27. Deutsch was the leader of the Schutzbund.

the police alert had been called off. Normally there was a force of 150 policemen on duty around parliament, but after the alert this had been reduced to 67.[28] The second and more important consequence of the leadership's inactivity was that the Schutzbund was not mobilised. Since 1923 its members had acted as official stewards at all important, large-scale demonstrations in the capital. The police, moreover, seldom came into contact with crowds and hence they had little experience of crowd control.[29] In his memoirs, Deutsch acknowledged that there had been ample opportunity to mobilise the Schutzbund. The suggestion had been made in the early hours of 15th, when it became obvious that some form of demonstration would take place, but it was rejected: 'It was argued that the appearance of the Schutzbund on the streets would make the spontaneous demonstration appear to be a deliberate intention.'[30] Even later in the day, when the carnage had begun, those members of the executive who were still in the party house issued orders which allowed only a partial mobilisation of the force. The Schutzbund in one district only (Favoriten) was called out, and then only the older men. Arms were not issued although they were available.[31]

Friedrich Austerlitz, the editor of the *Arbeiter-Zeitung*, which that morning had published a severe warning to the 'bourgeois world' that 'from the seeds of injustice nothing can arise but grave disaster', was heard in the evening telling the electricity workers that they should not demonstrate against a jury decision, for they would be questioning a fundamental basis of democracy.[32] Although this was an extreme example, it illustrated the attitude of the party leadership at the time. In the Linz Programme party leaders had confirmed their choice of a democratic and non-violent road to socialism. To challenge the jury decision was to threaten one of the institutions of democracy and, if overplayed, could result in misguided support for the reactionaries' demand for its abolition. But

---

28. Ernst Fischer, *An Opposing Man*, trans. Peter and Betty Ross, with an introduction by John Berger (London, 1974), p. 153. Fischer recorded that Deutsch rang Schober after he had failed to stop the electricity workers' strike, but by that time it was too late to recall the police.

29. The casualties were not the result of police hysteria. Both Gulick and Gedye, whilst agreeing that the police were undermanned, stressed that the initial sabre attack was carried out by mounted police, in formation and under orders. Gulick, *Austria*, vol. 1, p. 737; Gedye, *Fallen Bastions*, p. 32.

30. Julius Deutsch, *Ein Weiter Weg: Lebenserinnerungen* (Vienna, 1960), p. 165.

31. Ilona Duczynska, *Der Demokratische Bolschewik* (Munich, 1975), p. 111.

32. Fischer, *An Opposing Man*, p. 150.

this was not the only reason for hesitation. The April elections had created a state of tension in the country. The anti-socialist front, the Einheitsliste, had won 85 of the seats, whilst the Social Democratic Party had 71. For four weeks after the election, the Landbund, which held the balance of power, hesitated before joining the coalition of Ignaz Seipel, leader of the Christian Social Party. This had exacerbated the tension which had built up during the actual campaign, and in this situation Otto Bauer was reluctant to authorise a general strike for fear of the conflict which could ensue.[33] Once the violence had broken out, the executive strove to prevent it escalating into civil war.

The leadership's decision was another example of deep-rooted inconsistencies in its philosophy. At Linz in one speech Otto Bauer had advocated the peaceful struggle of the workers for the control of the state, whilst at the same time acknowledging that 'the bourgeoisie will not abandon voluntarily its position of power'. When the democratic path was blocked, violence was necessary. For the ordinary party member the Schattendorf verdict was a blatant miscarriage of justice by the jury system, a democratic institution. But the party executive and the Trade Union Commission perceived that any demonstration at that time would lead to violence and could escalate into the very civil war which they were at pains to prevent. They could not have foreseen that the government would order a direct attack on the demonstrators. They had rejected a general strike and a demonstration, but they made a serious error in not sending out instructions to this effect. The electricity workers had refused to accept a policy of inaction and this was an indication of the feelings of other workers. Had they received instructions, it is possible that they, too, would have rejected them, but many workers would undoubtedly have followed the party line. The party had assumed that its members would not act without explicit instructions. They had. One clear point to be drawn from these events was that the party executive had underestimated the fury with which the trial verdicts were greeted. They had hesitated in deciding upon what action to take and the order they finally gave, for the partial mobilisation of the Schutzbund, was too little and too late. The 89 deaths in Vienna not only pointed to an escalation in the conflict between the labour movement and the Christian Social government, with its Landbund and German Nationalist coalition partners, but also to a breakdown in the communications between union and party leaders

33. Ernst Fischer, *Erinnerungen und Reflexionen* (Hamburg, 1969), pp. 184–6.

and the rank-and-file members. It was a further indication of the gulf between the two.

With 85 demonstrators and 4 policemen dead and the Palace of Justice destroyed, some workers were convinced that the party should now issue arms to its members or, at the very least, to the Schutzbund. 'If Seipel and Schober allow shots to be fired at workers, Bauer and Seitz should not withhold weapons from the workers.'[34] The joint decision of the party executive and the Trade Union Commission was to call a 24-hour general strike on 16 July and a strike of railwaymen and post and communications workers which would continue until the government agreed to lift all prosecutions arising from events of the previous day. The Schutzbund was put on permanent alert and there was a ban on street demonstrations in Vienna.

As news of the killings spread throughout the country, so too did news of the strike. In Graz the local Social Democratic leaders met in the party house in the Ungergasse at 11 pm Friday (15th) to organise both the strike and a demonstration in Graz for the following Sunday. In Bruck an der Mur a messenger was sent by car in the middle of the night to bring back the party secretary, Koloman Wallisch, who was on holiday in Eastern Styria.[35] There were 67,074 members of the Free Trade Unions in Styria and 59,787 party members, most of whom were concentrated in Upper Styria and Graz. All were ordered to strike for one day. On Saturday morning the *Arbeiterwille* blazed the motto of the day across its front page: 'Long live discipline. Long live the Social Democratic Party. The battle is not yet over, but it must be carried out with order.'[36]

The railway, post and communications strike was to continue beyond 16 July. The railway union had the largest membership of any single union in the province.[37] It had a long history, dating back to 1898, and, in common with the other industrial unions which were in existence in 1918, its membership dramatically increased after the declaration of the Republic. During the 1920s the larger unions in particular were faced with the problem of retaining the new membership and for this reason the Railway Workers' Union chose to levy a lower rate of union dues than the other

34. Sigmund Kunst, 'Juli 1927', *Der Kampf* (XX) 1927, p. 35.
35. Paula Wallisch, *Ein Held stirbt* (Graz, 1946), p. 157.
36. *Arbeiterwille*, 16 July 1927.
37. *Jb BFG* 1928, pp. 106–7, table 12. Railway Workers' Union 13,313. Metalworkers' Union 9,034; Building Workers' Union 6,493. Figures for 31 December 1928.

unions and held it at a fixed rate for all members. As a result the union's funds were unusually scant, when compared with its membership, but the fall in its membership was relatively low.[38]

Another reason for the importance of the Railway Workers' Union was that a well-organised rail strike was more effective in disrupting the economy than any other industrial action. The general strike had been designed to illustrate the power of the workers. The railway, post and communications strike was designed to win concessions. To quote Otto Bauer: 'One telegram sent out with Tomschik's signature [president of the Railway Workers' Union] – and all the trains between Buchs and Vienna stop. One telegram from Tomschik – and all the trains move again. So it was, so it is. As long as this is the way it remains, no-one in the world can break us.'[39]

There were no important navigable waterways, and road links both internally and with Vienna were tortuous and slow, following the river valleys and crossing the mountains via the Semmering Pass. Railways had been developed in the north of the province to carry goods to and from the iron belt and had spread to the west towards Carinthia and Klagenfurt, and south towards the plains of Yugoslavia. Where the trains went, so too did the railwaymen, and so, again in contrast with the Miners' and Metalworkers' Unions, whose influence was confined to the Graz region and Upper Styria, the Railway Workers' Union had members living throughout the province.

The most zealous response to both strikes came from the workers of Bruck an der Mur, an important railway junction, where the trains from the west and south converged. The town had a population of 12,000. In addition to the railwaymen, the largest groups of workers were the metalworkers from the local wire-drawing works and the employees at the declining wood- and paperworks. In nearby Kapfenberg there was the Böhler steel plant, which concentrated on the production of high-quality steel. There was very little agriculture in the immediate vicinity, as the climate was inhospitable and the soil poor, and as a consequence the people of Bruck had suffered badly during the war and afterwards when food

38. Gulick, *Austria*, pp. 263–5. One reason for the union's decision was that it seldom had to finance long strikes. Railway strikes were devastating to the Austrian economy and therefore tended to be short. In 1924 a railway strike precipitated Seipel's resignation and a general election. The 1933 railway strike led to the suspension of parliament.

39. Fischer, *Erinnerungen und Reflexionen*, p. 182. This quote is not in the English edition, *An Opposing Man*.

was scarce. This was one of the major centres of working-class activity in the province. The local council had been dominated by the Social Democrats since 1919 and the local party had been active in its attempts to educate and improve the position of its members, in addition to fulfilling its role in the council. New roads were built and existing ones repaired, street-lighting was introduced. The party created a strong welfare programme, building and improving old people's homes, improving the pensions paid to widows, and organising the most extensive workers' education programme in the province.[40] But the town was small, increased municipal expenditure meant increases in the rates and local taxes, and by 1927 the relations between the socialist and non-socialist members of the population were very tense.

The town had a reputation for being radical. It had been at the centre of strikes and demonstrations which followed the cut in the flour ration in January 1918.[41] Three years later, in April 1921 the ex-kaiser, Karl, was forced to halt his train journey in Frohnleiten as he returned from Hungary, having failed in his attempt to regain the Hungarian throne. Thousands of people gathered at Bruck station nearby to demonstrate against him. Despite pleas from the provincial leaders, the demonstrators refused to disperse until after midnight, leaving 300 behind to express their feelings to the emperor. More recently there had been accusations of political corruption. The Social Democratic mayor, Anton Pichler, resigned when it was discovered that he had taken funds from the municipal account to help to pay for a new workers' club.[42]

The 1927 general election campaign had been particularly vitriolic in Bruck. Rumours and accusations abounded. On 12 March the *Grazer Tagespost* printed an article accusing the Schutzbund of building up an arsenal in the town.[43] It reported that three consignments of weapon parts had been shipped from Vienna, followed by a weapons expert, who, it alleged, was to show local members of the Schutzbund how to assemble the parts. The article proceeded to refer to the 'open secret' that guns had been hidden in the walls of a workers' hostel in Kapfenberg and concluded by saying: 'we recall that one Sunday in the year 1919 peaceful citizens were pulled out of their homes and beaten half to death'. Reports of weapon hoards

---

40. St AK 1928, p. 92.

41. Ingrun Lafleur, 'Socialists, Communists and Workers in the Austrian Revolution 1918–19' (unpublished PhD thesis, Columbia University, 1972), p. 60.

42. Wallisch, *Ein Held stirbt*, pp. 148–52.

43. This became national news, when the story was published in the *Neue Freie Presse* and the *Reichspost*.

spread: machine-guns were said to have been found in a children's home in Voitsberg and children in Graz were reported to have been trained to use guns.

The reports were interesting for several reasons. The first and most obvious was that there had not been a discovery of armaments in Bruck. A secret report, signed by the governor, Johan Paul, and dated 1 April, informed the police authorities in Vienna that the reports were 'exaggerated'.[44] To be exact, no movement of weapons, nor armed manoeuvres, nor extraordinary activity by the Schutzbund had been detected in either Bruck or Graz, although the report went on, with a Schutzbund membership of 2,700 (Bruck and Kapfenberg combined) there had to be some guns in the area.

The second point of interest was the timing of the reports. The Social Democratic Party had never denied that the Schutzbund had arms. Both it and the other political groups had caches of arms, which had been hidden from the Entente Disarmament Commission in 1918. According to the Social Democrats an arsenal pact had been signed in 1922 whereby the different groups had agreed to respect each other's hiding places and, as a consequence, the whereabouts of the arms dumps were roughly known to many people.[45] On 2 March Chancellor Seipel ordered troops to search one Schutzbund store in Vienna and, with a great deal of publicity, between 6,000 and 8,000 rounds of ammunition and various weapons parts were carried off.[46] The order was well timed. The Christian Social government had known of this particular dump for several years, but chose to 'discover' the weapons two days before parliament was dissolved pending the general election. The election campaign had begun. The stories of new munitions dumps in Bruck and later elsewhere in Styria should be seen in this context for, although the rumours were unfounded, they further raised the tension between the socialist and non-socialist townspeople.

During the debate in the provincial assembly on the general strike and the reaction to it, a Landbund deputy, Hornik, stated that the first signal of alarm was heard in Bruck at 6 am on the morning of the general strike, when the sound of car horns and

---

44. VA Bundeskanzleramt 22/Stmk 1918–28 Box 5131. Der Republikanische Schutzbund in Steiermark. Bewaffnung. Report from Amt der Steierischen Landesregierung Abt.7. 1 April 1927. This is one of the few documents apertaining to 1927 in the Styrian section of the national archive.
45. Duczynska, *Workers in Arms* (New York and London, 1978), pp. 53–9.
46. Ibid., pp. 68–74.

train whistles broke the silence.[47] A meeting of the town council took place three hours later, when councillors were told that the local branch of the Social Democratic Party, under Koloman Wallisch, had appointed a strike committee of eight and had issued a number of orders. All inns were told to close and there was a ban on alcohol. Meetings of three or more people were forbidden and the police were confined to their stations.[48] Thus the town council had, for the time being, been relieved of its duties and the party took over.

During the investigation which the provincial executive of the Social Democratic Party carried out on the conduct of the strikers in Bruck, Wallisch argued that representatives of the 'bourgeois alliance' and the commercial community had suggested similar action should be taken, before they realised that the workers' representatives had issued the orders. This was possible, for with the exception of the confinement of police, there was little controversial in them, if the aim was to preserve law and order and property. Indeed, shopkeepers also closed their shops and in the eyes of the Landbund newspaper, the single laudable action of the 'dictator' Wallisch was that he allowed this to happen. On the other hand, it was an anathema to the bourgeois parties that the Schutzbund, rather than the police, was enforcing the orders. Schutzbund patrols guarded the roads leading in and out of the town and stopped cars to search them for hidden weapons.

By 10 am a crowd of several thousands had gathered in the main square. Two flags were hanging from the town hall; the black flag of mourning and the red flag of socialism. There was talk of avenging those who had died in Vienna by burning the houses of Bruck's rich. Wallisch made a speech in which he promised that 'the instant that workers' blood flows in Bruck, so too will bourgeois blood',[49] and the foundation of the myth, that a dictatorship of the proletariat had been declared in Bruck, was laid. The charge was emotional rather than factual – the means of production had not been seized, nor were the workers organised into workers' councils as they had been in 1919. But the socialist workforce and its leaders had challenged the authority of the state by temporarily

47. *Stenographische Bericht über die Verhandlungen des steiermärkischen Landtages,* 25 July 1927 (Graz, 1928).

48. In his statement to the Landtag, Koloman Wallisch argued that the police made a mistake and were going to ban all patrols from the streets. The Schutzbund in Bruck was called out to prevent the outbreak of violence. *Stenographische Bericht über die Verhandlungen des steiermärkischen Landtages,* 25 July 1927, p. 54.

49. Wallisch, *Ein Held stirbt,* p. 158.

seizing control of the town.

Following the destruction of the socialist labour movement in 1934, the stand which the Bruck workers made in 1927 became almost legendary and was seen as the pinnacle of the Styrian workers' history during the Republic. It was exceptional and transgressed the official policy of the party and Free Trade Union Commission, as the Trade Union Commission was now known. This can be seen most clearly if the events in Bruck are contrasted with what happened in Graz. In the provincial capital, labour leaders met on the evening of 15 July to organise the demonstration and general strike. It was later emphasised by Machold, a senior Social Democratic member, director of a cooperative in Andritz, and a member of the provincial government, that they were intent on restraining their people, on localising the strike, on preventing any disturbances and on easing the situation as far as possible.[50] When the governor complained that he was unable to contact council members and council officials in the outlying districts because the telephonists and telegraph officers were on strike, strike leaders made the arrangement for this. When a deputy, who was also a vet, brought up the plight of the livestock stranded along the railway lines, strike leaders had them moved. In short, everything possible was done to minimise the disruption which the strike caused. There was nothing to suggest that this was not accomplished, for in Graz itself, unlike other towns in Styria, there were no reports of conflict or violence.[51]

Thus, in Graz, the provincial headquarters both of party and unions, the strike was carried out with caution. The leadership of the strike fell quite naturally to the provincial leaders of the labour movement, men who had risen in its administration, such as Vinzenz Muchitsch, the mayor of Graz, Johan Resel, the editor of the *Arbeiterwille*, Reinhard Machold, the director of the Styrian Co-operative Society in Andritz, and Ludwig Oberzaucher, the director of the Alpenländische Volkskreditbank. These men were in close connection with the national leaders in Vienna. The strike leaders in Bruck were very different. The mayor, Franz Gruber, appears to have had no official position in the labour movement and played his role in the strike by leading talks with the representatives of trade and commerce. The actual strike leaders were reported to

50. *Stenographische Bericht über die Verhandlungen des steiermärkischen Landtages*, 25 July 1927, p. 80.
51. Bruce Pauley wrote of a Schutzbund alert in Graz as well as Bruck, but I could not verify this. Bruce F. Pauley, *Hahnenschwanz und Hakenkreuz*, trans. Peter Aschner (Vienna, 1972), p. 48.

be Wallisch and the former mayor, Pichler, who had earlier had to leave Bruck in disgrace. Pichler, according to Wallisch's wife, Paula, had sold newspapers to earn a living and Wallisch himself was a Hungarian exile who had worked in the Hungarian Socialist Party from the age of fifteen, fleeing that country in 1919 when Béla Kun's government was crushed.[52] Wallisch had worked as a Social Democratic Party organiser in Fürstenfeld and had been the party secretary in Bruck since 1921. Thus, whereas the Graz strike was led by respectable members of the provincial administration of the labour movement, in Bruck the leaders were less established.

A second difference between Graz and Bruck was the position which the Social Democrats held in the community. In Bruck the party dominated local politics. Since 1918, the council had had a socialist majority and the mayor was a member of the party. Bruck was a working-class town where a large proportion of the population was employed in industry. The party was not only large, but also well-organised and had an unusually large Schutzbund. The police estimated in 1927 that in Bruck itself there were 1,700 members, whilst in Kapfenberg there were a further 1,000. Equally important, the anti-socialist opposition in the town was weak and ill-organised. Militia forces had been active in Styria since 1919, but the first Burgerwehr was founded in Bruck only on 14 July 1927 – the very day of the Schattendorf verdict.[53] This followed a campaign amongst Heimwehr supporters in the area in which leaflets were circulated alleging that, since the Linz Programme, the Social Democrats had decided that violence was the only path open to them. In a socialist state, the leaflets maintained, children would be taken away from their parents and would be brought up by the state. Despite this, the anti-socialists in Bruck did not mobilise a force to oppose the strike in 1927.

A cursory glance at the size and structure of the Graz party would suggest that it was less vulnerable than the branch in Bruck. The membership figures for 1927 show that 29 per cent of the entire provincial membership was to be found in Graz and the surrounding areas.[54] The party institutions, such as the library, adult education and children's organisation, had long traditions, in

---

52. There was some evidence of Hungarian influence amongst Social Democratic and Communist Parties in Upper Styria. Verwaltungsarchiv Bundeskanzleramt. 22/Stmk. 1918–28 Box 5131. Tätigkeit der kommunistischen Partei in Leoben. Police report from Eisenstadt, July 1926.

53. *Stenographischer Bericht über die Verhandlungen des steiermärkischen Landtages,* 25 July 1927, p. 54.

54. *Jb ö Ab,* 1927, p. 30.

some cases predating the Republic. Graz was the seat of Styrian socialism, but it was not its stronghold, for it was also the centre of the provincial administration, a university town and had a large bourgeoisie, consisting not only of bureaucrats, civil servants, and academics, but also of those employed in the service industries such as banking and insurance. In 1934 31 per cent of the city's population were civil servants' families, 21.24 per cent were involved in trade, and 7.61 per cent in the liberal professions.[55] It has been argued that the large number of bureaucrats and academics in particular was an important factor in the development of the vigorous nationalism, which led to the city's reputation as the 'most German city in the Monarchy'.[56] Nationalism was still very much alive during the Republic, although by then it preached the need for union with Germany. By 1924 'Graz, Innsbruck, Salzburg were the strongholds of reactionary forces in Austria.'[57] Thus, although the Social Democratic Party was numerically strong in the provincial capital, it existed alongside an assertive and well-organised right wing.

A second factor which weakened the Graz party was the size of the city's working class. Only 26.21 per cent of the Graz people were involved in industrial occupations, just some 5 per cent more than those engaged in trade.[58] The heavy industries of Styria, with their large plants and large workforces, were not in Graz, but in the north. The Social Democratic party found the bulk of its support amongst workers who were employed in small firms in the city and the outlying area, for this was a region of light industry.

The situation in Graz was weakened not only by the small working units but also by the housing system. There were few working-class districts in the city itself for workers lived in dwellings known as *Hinterhäuser*, small outhouses which had been built behind the homes of the more affluent members of the community.[59] Thus working-class communities, which might have built up around the areas where workers employed by different firms, would come into contact with each other, were not found within the city itself, but were on its outskirts.

The lack of fervour in Graz during the strike cannot be attributed

---

55. Die Ergebnisse der österreichischen Volkszählung vom 22 März 1934, Table 1a. The 1923 census was not completed and never published.

56. William Hubbard, 'Politics and Society in a Central European City: Graz, Austria, 1861–1918', *Canadian Journal of History*, 1970, p. 41.

57. Gulick, *Austria*, vol. 1, p. 701.

58. Ibid., p. 421.

59. Ibid., pp. 418–19.

to a lack of working-class militancy. It should be pointed out that, had Graz workers rushed into the streets and demanded revenge for the deaths in Vienna, as was done in Bruck, they would have provoked reaction not only from the right-wing paramilitary groups, but also from the legal forces of law and order – the police. There has been much debate as to whether this force would have remained loyal to the state if it had been called out against the strikers and it has been argued that the support which the provincial government gave to Pfrimer and his followers was based on the realisation that they would not have been able to use the police to restore order if workers had attempted to overthrow the state. In a town the size of Bruck, where a large police force with a long chain of command was unnecessary and police officers were part of the community, having been brought up with workers, it was possible that the bonds of friendship were greater than duty. Indeed, this is indicated by the evidence that the police did not move against the strikers. However, Graz was not only the seat of the provincial government, where the influence of Anton Rintelen, thrice governor of Styria and long-standing benefactor of the Heimwehr, prevailed, but it was also the headquarters of the army and police force. Whereas the loyalty of some rank-and-file members of the constabulary was under suspicion, the police hierarchy, under the commissioner Kment, was known to have strong sympathies with the Heimwehr. During the first six months of 1927 the police had twice chosen to ignore the activities of National Socialist students, once in March, when guests were stoned as they arrived at a ball given by the Czechoslovakian consul, and again in May when a performance of *A Midsummer Night's Dream*, which was being staged at the Opera House, was disrupted.[60] Thus the Social Democrats must have been aware that, if there had been any disturbances in Graz, the authorities would not have hesitated to use the police to quash them.

In contrast the general strike in Bruck was a fleeting moment of triumph for the Styrian workers. The nature of the town, a strong cohesive working class, a militant leadership and a weak opposition combined to create the conditions for aggressive execution of the general strike. In Graz the strike call had been heard and followed with caution, precisely as the national executive had directed. If this had been the full story of the Styrian labour movement in 1927, the year might have been considered a success. Instead it marked the decline of the movement, for the strike was broken by the Heim-

60. *Grazer Tagblatt*, 4 March 1927; *Arbeiterwille*, 28 May 1927.

wehr, led by Dr Walter Pfrimer.

To the west of Bruck lay the centre of heavy industry, the Alpine Montangesellschaft empire. In Donawitz, at the very heart of the steel industry, where the pig-iron and rolled steel was produced, the 1925 foundry workers' strike had brought the entire works to a standstill. The apparent success of the strike, which ended with an agreement between the Free Trade Union and company with the government acting as surety, was shortlived. Since then the company had refused to implement the wage increases and had refused to pay the agreed rate for overtime worked. To quote the *Arbeiterwille*, 'they set the hours of work according to their own inclinations', despite the law.[61] By 1927 company schools in Donawitz had become a nest of Heimwehr activity. In February foundry workers organised a meeting to protest at the sackings of spokesmen who had complained to the management about conditions of work and about the company's policy of attempting to prevent shop stewards from carrying out their duties. This was followed in March by elections for the factory council, when National Socialist candidates stood for the first time.[62] The workers were again under attack, and yet they responded immediately to the strike call on 16 July. In Donawitz over 2,600 men and women laid down their tools, making it impossible for the remaining 400 or so workers to carry on.[63] According to the firm, all work stopped both in the iron- and steelworks and in the mines. The main roads joining the Ennstal in the north and the Murtal in the south were patrolled by the Schutzbund, who stopped cars to prevent guns being brought into the area by the Heimwehr.

In the circumstances this was very necessary, for in Judenburg, on the edge of the Styrian coalfield, Heimwehr troops were once more gathering under the command of Walter Pfrimer. Their immediate goal was to break the strike in Upper Styria as they had in Judenburg in 1922, but on a grander scale. The strike took place on Saturday 16 July. That night Heimwehr members from far and wide were arriving in Grünhalle, a village on the outskirts of Judenburg. At 11 am they marched into Judenburg, a company of 15,000 to 20,000 men from all over Styria and Carinthia. They carried arms which were not all remnants of the War, but included machine-guns.[64] Officially, they were there at the request of the

61. *Arbeiterwille*, 6 January 1927.
62. *Arbeiterwille*, 12 March 1927.
63. Fritz Erben, Maja Loehr and Hans Riehl (eds.), *Die Alpine Montangesellschaft* (Vienna, 1931), p. 185.
64. C. Earl Edmondson, 'The Heimwehr and Austrian Politics 1918–34' (PhD

police inspector, Meitzner, whose force was understaffed and who feared that it would not be possible to contain any violence which might arise in the wake of the strike with the men who were available. Under his authority, and without the knowledge of the town council, Heimwehr troops were issued with more guns.[65] They blocked the roads west towards Neumarkt and Scheifling and issued travel passes to those whom they allowed to pass. A socialist deputy was taken into 'protective custody' in Neumarkt by the Heimwehr commander, who had set up his headquarters in the local police station. In Scheifling rumour that seventy railwaymen were about to arrive to organise their strike led to an armed force of sixty men being sent to greet them. Seven railwaymen arrived.[66] The Heimwehr pressed on, this time to break the rail strike.

Support for Pfrimer also came from the Heimwehr movements in southern Styria, notably in Hartberg and Leibnitz. In Hartberg railwaymen took over the station. When a rumour circulated the town that 20 wagonloads of Schutzbund troops were about to arrive, Heimwehr men in the town armed themselves and planned to attack. They were finally dissuaded by the mayor.[67] In Leibnitz a Landbund deputy named Felix Pistor, who was also a member of the Heimwehr, alerted his men and ordered them to gather in the main town square early on 18 July, equipped with two days' provisions. Cars were commandeered to carry weapons from area to area. At midday the Heimwehr was assembled and ready to attack the railway station.[68]

In the meantime a letter was sent from the provincial leadership of the Heimwehr in Judenburg to the leaders of the strike in Knittelfeld and the provincial Schutzbund leadership demanding that the 'declaration of martial law in Bruck' be revoked and an end to what was described as the terrorising of non-socialist townfolk. All roads had to be reopened and the rail strike and telephone strike called off.[69] In the event of a refusal, the Heimwehr threatened to march. It was not clear where they intended to march to; there

---

thesis, Duke University, 1966), p. 68.

65. This was confirmed during the provincial assembly debate on 25 July 1929. The Social Democrats alleged that the gendarmerie had also issued arms to the Heimatschutz in Leibnitz. Stenographischer Bericht über die Verhandlungen des steiermärkischen Landtages, 25 July 1927, p. 58.

66. *Stenographischer Bericht über die Verhandlungen des steiermärkischen Landtages*, July 1927, p. 59.

67. *Arbeiterwille*, 29 July 1927.

68. *Arbeiterwille*, 24 July 1927.

69. Ibid.

were rumours that their destination was Bruck, where they would put down the 'soviet', and other rumours that they were destined for Graz. More recently it has been suggested that Pfrimer wanted negotiations with the Social Democratic Party to fail, to allow him to march on Vienna with some 150,000 men, to surround the city, seize control of the water supply and bring down the socialist council.[70]

The march never began. The provincial leadership of the Social Democratic Party contacted the governor to ask him to arrange negotiations between themselves and Pfrimer. Two separate sessions were organised. The first in Graz was attended by Ludwig Oberzaucher, Reinhard Machold, national deputy Norbert Horvatek, and Hackl for the labour movement, and Pfrimer and the commander of the Graz section of the Association of Frontline Soldiers, with the governor acting as chairman. It took place at 7 pm on 17 July and lasted until the early hours of the morning. The result was a truce which would last until the following midday. The Heimwehr added the proviso that they would only abide by this as long as they were not provoked. On 18 July the second session of the negotiations took place in Knittelfeld and dealt with the immediate problem of the large Heimwehr presence in the area. A problem arose when Heimwehr leaders said that they would order their men to disperse only if the Schutzbund agreed to hand in their uniforms, but when this was firmly rejected it was decided that the dispersal would still take place and would be completed by noon the following day.[71] The Socialist representatives agreed to call off the strike.

The strike was broken in Styria. Local party leaders, Muchitsch, Machold and Oberzaucher telephoned Otto Bauer to tell him of their decision and to urge him to bring the rail and transport strike to an end also, thus avoiding bloodshed. The party directorate saw Chancellor Seipel in Vienna and, having failed to gain any concessions from him for either those arrested on 15 July or the strikers, they issued orders for the strike to be called off at midnight on Monday, 18 July. This decision amounted to a total capitulation for the Social Democratic Party, just months after their partial success in the April election. All hope of extending its political influence in parliament evaporated. It was never again able to pressurise the government by referring to the size and latent strength of its

---

70. Edmondson, 'The Heimwehr and Austrian Politics', (PhD thesis) p. 70.
71. *Arbeiterwille*, 24 July 1927.

support, for that strength had been tried and tested and found to be wanting.

The reasons for the capitulation of the provincial party were exhaustively discussed in the aftermath of the demonstration and strikes. During the provincial assembly debate on the strikes, which took place on 25 July in Graz, socialist deputies frequently asserted that they had to concede defeat because the Heimwehr was armed, whereas the Schutzbund and strikers were not.[72] This was not their principal reason for submitting and nor was it completely correct. Despite the disadvantage of having older weapons, the Schutzbund was relatively well-equipped in 1927 and, although arms were not officially issued during the strikes, some preparations for battle were made. At the same time as Heimwehr troops were gathering in Judenburg, the Schutzbund from Upper Styria was assembling in Bruck, where lorries were standing by to transport them to Judenburg to oust Pfrimer and his men.[73] The Schutzbund may have had the military strength to defeat the Heimwehr, but they could not have withstood an attack by government forces and, although the threats to the party had come from the former, the neutrality of the latter was obviously in doubt. Had the Social Democratic leadership known of the movements in Bruck, and had they contemplated fighting, this factor alone would have deterred them.

Neither of these possibilities was likely. Before reorganisation in 1928 the Schutzbund was relatively autonomous and there was little point in informing the party leadership, when it would very likely forbid any action which was likely to intensify the conflict. Such an attitude may have appeared to be at odds with the more aggressive phrases in the Linz Programme, but it was actually in line with its major points, for at Linz the party had repeated its objective of gaining power through the ballot box and of using 'the power of the state in the forms of democracy and under all the guarantees of democracy'.[74] As in 1918, they rejected the use of violence as self-destructive, leading to the overthrow of democracy, and to death and destruction. The paragraph, which had been misquoted in the right-wing press to suggest that the programme was designed to bring about a dictatorship of the proletariat, had been inserted at the insistence of Max Adler, against the

72. *Stenographischer Bericht über die Verhandlungen des steiermärkischen Landtages*, 25 July 1927, pp. 58–62.
73. Interview with Otto Fischer, 11 October 1976.
74. Gulick, *Austria*, vol. 2, p. 1390.

wishes of Bauer and Renner, and supported the use of violence only as a final resort when all else had failed.[75] Until that time the legitimate methods of demonstrations, meetings and the penultimate use of the general strike were all that the party would sanction. 'Inflammatory' action was rejected and so party leaders refused to continue the strike in July 1927.

The decision which the leadership took was entirely consistent with party policies, but it undermined its political power, which had been based on the latent strength of its membership and on the memories which the bourgeois parties in government still retained of the Revolution. The general strike had been flaunted as a tactical weapon which would demonstrate potential power, but in 1927 it was challenged and seen to be the movement's ultimate weapon. As a result Seipel no longer felt he had to compromise with the opposition, but could openly attack them. Thus 1927 marked a turning-point in national politics, for from that year the Social Democratic Party was forced to defend itself against mounting attacks. Moreover, the control which the leadership thought it had over party members had slipped, for the discipline of the February demonstration emphasised the chaos in July, when no leadership was given. Not only in Vienna but also in Styria, there were sharp differences between the party executive and local officials and members. Strike committees in Bruck and Leoben did not confine their activities to organisation, but also set up road patrols to stop Heimwehr movements. These were the first signs of dissension within the party and were followed by more articulate criticism from younger members, some of whom began to form small opposition groups critical of the central leadership.[76]

The defeat of the Social Democratic Party also polarised politics throughout Austria. Membership both of the socialist party and of the Heimwehr rose immediately and continued to do so over the next few years, along with the level of political violence. The *Arbeiterwille* carried stories of priests calling farmers to Heimwehr meetings after mass.[77] New branches were set up in Rottenmann, Knittelfeld, Hafendorf and Mürzzuschlag weeks after the general strike.[78] Workers in a sanatorium who were in dispute with the management were confronted by an armed Heimwehr unit of

75. Ibid., pp. 1391–2; Peter Kulemann, *Am Beispiel des Austromarxismus*, pp. 385–6.
76. See Chapter 11.
77. *Arbeiterwille*, 28 July 1927.
78. *Arbeiterwille*, 7 August 1927.

thirty in August and told to return to work.[79] In September the Heimwehr defied a three-month ban on marches to make its presence felt in strong Social Democratic areas; one report alleged that members had marched through Bruck at the dead of night, when their enemies were in bed. They avoided confrontation but were able to say that they had 'claimed' the town.[80] At the same time, there were reports of socialists flocking into the Schutzbund and demanding to be armed. Perhaps the most significant result of 1927 was that the national government recognised the usefulness of the Heimwehr in opposing the labour movement, just as the Styrian provincial government had in 1922. By 1930 two leaders of the Heimwehr were in government.

79. *Arbeiterwille*, 23 and 24 August 1927.
80. *Arbeiterwille*, 23 September 1927.

–9–

The Battles, 1927–1929

In the six and a half years between July 1927 and the civil war in February 1934, the Austrian labour movement was faced with greater problems than it had yet experienced. The most immediate consequence of the defeat of the general strike was an increase in class tension and outbreaks of political violence between left-wing groups and their 'anti-Marxist' opponents. In the longer term the most important laws on working conditions, the Eight-Hour Day Act and laws protecting the position of shop stewards and collective contracts fell into general abeyance, as unemployment soared in the wake of the Wall Street Crash and the depression which followed. Between January 1928 and January 1933 the number of people out of work in Austria more than doubled from 230,074 to 478,034, with many more on short time.[1] Trade union membership dropped by one-third. The level of industrial protest fell from the middle of 1929 and this was inversely mirrored by a rise in the incidence of violence, as political parties increased their membership and took to the streets. Between 1926 and 1928, as a direct result of the Schattendorf incident, membership of the Social Democratic Party rose by 20 per cent,[2] whilst the influence and size of the Heimwehr appeared to grow at an even faster rate.[3] Both movements adopted policies of marches and demonstrations which inevitably led to violence. According to national official figures, 46 people were killed and 280 wounded in political clashes between the beginning of 1928 and the end of 1932, in comparison with 12 dead and 53 wounded in the previous six years, excluding the casualties of the 15th July 1927.[4] In addition to this, the socialist movement faced concerted government opposition. By May 1933, nine months before the civil war, the Dollfuß administration had prorogued parliament indefinitely, outlawed the Schutzbund and

---

1. See Table 4, Appendix to this volume, pp. 214–15.
2. See Table 1, Appendix to this volume, p. 211.
3. F.L. Carsten, *Fascist Movements in Austria:From Schönerer to Hitler* (London, 1977), p. 120.
4. Gerhard Botz, *Gewalt in der Politik* (Munich, 1976), pp. 236–7.

banned all strikes and demonstrations. This combination of blatant political aggression and economic depression ultimately resulted in the destruction of the socialist movement and that of the Republic itself.

The inability of the Austrian working class to withstand the growing threat of fascism is a problem which has concerned many historians, especially in recent years. The Social Democratic Party appeared stronger and more resolute than any other working-class party in Europe, with the exception of the Russian's. It was not only the largest single party in Austria, but one in every seven adults in the country was a member.[5] Despite this no Social Democrat had participated in the national government since 1920. Consequentially the party maintained an air of pure and untainted opposition, which was effectively reinforced by the success of the socialist council in Vienna. During the 1920s, as the Austrian economy faltered and wavered, the example of 'Red Vienna', with its extensive public spending programme and balanced budget seemed to justify the socialists' economic policies.[6] The Free Trade Union movement in Austria was also relatively strong, reaching levels which were unrivalled elsewhere in central and western Europe. In this country with a population of only six million, the socialist trade unions boasted a membership of over one million in the early days of the Republic. There were more than 400,000 Free Trade Unionists in Vienna alone in 1929.[7] This spectacle of a large and well-organised socialist movement, which was defeated in the short space of six years, has led many writers to the conclusion that the internal policies of the Social Democratic Party were ultimately responsible for its fate. The reluctance of the party leadership to shed its faith in democracy and call its followers to arms, combined with frequent speeches suggesting that fighting would be necessary, led to despondency and dejection within the Austrian working class. Such writers have dwelt at length on the political philosophy of Austro–Marxism and the internal struggles of the party leadership, which left the ordinary members confused and, more importantly, unarmed in February 1934.[8]

Whilst there is obviously a great deal of truth in these assessments of the political leadership, some very important points about the Austrian socialist movement are often forgotten or are only

5. *Jb ö A* 1928, p. 52.

6. Jill Lewis, 'Red Vienna: Socialism in one city, 1918–27', *European Studies Review*, vol. 13, no. 3, July 1983, pp. 335–54.

7. *Jb ö A* 1929, p. 77. The actual number was 418,055.

8. See Anson Rabinbach, *The Crisis of Austrian Socialism: from Red Vienna to Civil War 1927–34* (Chicago, 1983), pp. 195–215.

briefly mentioned. The machinations of the leadership can only partly explain the vulnerability of the movement, for there is little doubt that, had the order to fight been given in February 1934, it would have led to an even bloodier defeat of the working class than actually took place. This was partly due to the leadership itself, which directed the reorganisation of the Schutzbund under Alexander Eifler and abandoned the guerilla tactics of Theodor Körner in favour of conventional disciplined military training.[9] But it was also a consequence of six years of civil conflict and the hunger and poverty of mass unemployment. It is this point in particular which many writers have overlooked, often because of a preoccupation with the activities of the socialist movement in Vienna. Vienna was the bastion of socialist strength in Austria, and the policies of the Social Democratic council were able to alleviate many of the worst aspects of the depression by providing cheap housing and recreational facilities for workers and the unemployed. The very strength of the socialist movement within the city protected its members against the earlier attacks both by the government and the paramilitary in the immediate aftermath of the Schattendorf incident. It is interesting to note that the Heimwehr chose as its first and greatest gesture of strength to march through the socialist city of Wiener Neustadt in 1928 rather than attempting to impose its presence on the streets of Vienna. In fact, Heimwehr activity in the capital remained relatively slight right up to the civil war itself, for the leadership preferred to attack the socialist movement where it was more vulnerable, in the provinces. As a result of this, the most frequent and bloody fighting between left-wing and right-wing militias from 1928 to 1934 took place outside the boundaries of the capital, in the iron regions of Styria and Lower and Upper Austria, and in the Tyrol, as Gerhard Botz had pointed out.[10] Bearing this in mind, it is easier to understand why the earliest and most sustained resistance to the attack in February 1934 took place not only in Vienna, but also in Linz and Upper Styria.

The level of political violence in Styria in the final years of the Republic is just one puzzle which must be explained in these final chapters. The second is the apparent growth of Heimwehr support amongst the industrial workers of Upper Styria, for as support for socialist trade unions waned here as elsewhere, the Heimwehr appeared to succeed in its aim of not only controlling workers,

---

9. Ilona Duczynska, *Workers in Arms* (New York and London, 1978), pp. 82–139; Rabinbach, *Crisis of Austrian Socialism*, pp. 195–204.
10. Botz, *Gewalt in der Politik*, p. 248.

but actually recruiting them. At the end of 1928, the Heimwehr military commander at Donawitz, Baumgartner, who was also headmaster of the work's school, announced that there were 1,817 Heimwehr members amongst the workforce of almost 5,000.[11] In 1929 the director of the Alpine Montangesellschaft confidently ignored the Free Trade Union majority vote for the factory council and chose instead to negotiate with the newly-founded Independent Union, which had close links with the Heimwehr, because, he said, a majority of the workers were by then members of the Heimwehr.[12] The Alpine Montangesellschaft works in general, and Donawitz in particular, became a centre of fascist activity in Upper Styria. On the face of it, the Styrian workers provided a classic and rare example of working-class fascism, actual shop floor support for a fascist movement, in this case the Heimwehr.

At this point it is necessary to deviate slightly from the main argument and tackle the question of whether or not the term 'fascist' can be applied with any conviction to either the Styrian Heimwehr or more particularly the Independent Unions. In the two-volume study of the First Republic edited by Erika Weinzierl and Kurt Skalnik, the subject of the Heimwehr is confined within an article by Adam Wandruszka entitled the 'Nationalist Camp'.[13] The writer emphasises the nationalist and anti-Marxist tendencies of the movement, but rejects the general title of 'fascism', arguing that although some members accepted the concept of a corporate and authoritarian state, this was by no means general: the Heimwehr leader, Ernst Rüdiger Starhemberg, in particular, may have been impressed by the 'Condottiere Stature of the Duce', but what he really wanted were money and arms.[14]

The wider debate over the fascist tendencies of the Heimwehr movement nationally has been written about at length elsewhere and cannot concern us here.[15] The more specific question of whether or not the Styrian Heimwehr and the Independent Unions were fascist is much clearer. The Styrian Heimwehr was originally

11. *Wiener Neueste Nachrichten*, 18 December 1928.
12. Fritz Erben, Maja Loehr and Hans Riehl (eds.), *Die Alpine Montangesellschaft* (Vienna, 1931), p. 192.
13. Adam Wandruszka, 'Das "nationale Lager"', in Erika Weinzierl and Kurt Skalnik (eds.), *Österreich, 1918–38: Geschichte der Ersten Republik*, 2 vols. (Vienna, 1983), vol. 1, pp. 227–315.
14. Ibid., p. 301.
15. See F.L. Carsten, *Fascist Movements in Austria: From Schönerer to Hitler* (London, 1977); C. Earl Edmondson, *The Heimwehr and Austrian Politics 1918–36* (Athens, Georgia, 1978); Bruce F. Pauley, *Hitler and the Forgotten Nazis: A History of Austrian National Socialism* (London, 1981).

a farmers' organisation which developed a strident, anti-socialist, urban-based wing in the 1920s, as has already been shown. It was this wing which became active in strike breaking in the 1920s and which made headway in recruiting members amongst the white-collar staff and management of the Alpine Montangesellschaft in the aftermath of the 1925 Donawitz strike.[16] From this base the Heimwehr, with the help of the Alpine Montangesellschaft management, established the Independent Union in May 1928.[17] There is no doubt that this wing of the Heimwehr, led by Pfrimer, had accepted fascism by May 1930, when the leaders of the movement adopted the Korneuburg Oath as a statement of their ideology, rejecting parliamentary democracy and advocating a corporate constitution under a strong national leadership. Pfrimer's own reaction to this was given in a speech delivered on the very day that the oath was published: 'On all sides the conviction was evident that here in Austria only fascism could now save us. We must make an attempt to seize power; then the leaders of our movement will be able to take the business of government in hand.'[18] In September 1931 his movement attempted to do just that by organising a putsch attempt. The failure of this persuaded him to strengthen links with the National Socialist Party in Styria in 1931.

The Styrian Heimwehr therefore displayed the necessary criteria of a fascist party: the belief that the economy can be organised above class interests, remaining in private hands, but based on an organisational ethos which is corporate; the belief that the state could and should stand above party politics, representing a common 'national' interest; and the use of organised violence to destroy working-class organisations and so create that political corporatism. The position of the Independent Unions was equally clear. In their first official programme, published in Vienna in 1928, the Unions attacked the role of party politics and emphasised their own political 'independence'.[19] Class conflict, it was argued, led to

16. Erben et al. (eds.), *Die Alpine Montangesellschaft*, pp. 186–7.
17. There is some confusion about the actual date of the founding of the Independent Unions. The *Alpinepost* gave it as 19 May 1928 (*Alpinepost*, 8 February 1929). The executive of the Styrian Free Trade Unions gives the date as November 1929 (*Jb BFG* 1929, p. 257). The Styrian Christian Unions reported a dispute with officials of the Independent Union in June 1928 and 1929 (Graz, 1930) Arbeiterkammer Wien II 6095, p. 68. Julius Deutsch's comment, that the Alpine Montangesellschaft set up the unions in 1919, seems incorrect. Julius Deutsch, *Geschichte der österreichischen Gewerkschaftsbewegung*, 2 vols. (Vienna, 1932), vol. 2, p. 112.
18. Quoted in Ludwig Jedlicka, 'The Austrian Heimwehr', *Journal of Contemporary History*, vol. 1, no. 1, 1966, p. 139.
19. Karl Lohsmann, *Program der Unabhängigen Arbeiter-Bewegung Österreichs*

physical and spiritual exhaustion, and the concept of equality allowed the lazy man to steal from the diligent. Party politics in Austria had encroached on all aspects of life and had to be eradicated, from schools in particular. The programme demanded the private ownership of all property, *Anschluß* with Germany, electoral reform to alter the structure of parliament and a directly-elected president. In 1929 the tone of these demands changed. In October the Unions' official newspaper reiterated the principal aims of economic progress and industrial harmony, but there were two new points. These were justified on the grounds that the activities of rival (i.e. Free) union movements had created deep political divisions within society which could be healed only under a different political system. Consequently the programme had been expanded to include the demand for:

(1) a strong authoritarian state, which stands over all parties and prevents all infringements by individuals or groups and instead represents the welfare of all. For only the welfare of all can really guarantee the welfare of the individual.
(2) The corporate reorganisation of the economy by the planned reconstruction of the hitherto wildly developed corporate, communal and economic organisations and their incorporation into the state.[20]

It was this union body which began to recruit within the Alpine Montangesellschaft plants in 1928 and later expanded into other areas of Styrian industry.

Any explanation of the apparent support for the fascist unions in Styria hinges on timing. If, as Walter Pfrimer argued at the time and Gerhard Pferschy has recently repeated, the Independent Unions appealed to disillusioned socialists who had been alienated from the Free Trade Unions by the 'extremism' of the party leadership in July 1927, there would have been a fall in either Free Trade Union or Social Democratic Party membership which corresponded with the rise in the Heimwehr and Independent Unions.[21] This did not happen. Membership of both wings of the socialist movement increased in Styria between 1926 and 1928, as they did throughout Austria, and, compared with the 1925 figure, party membership was actually 30 per cent higher by 1928.[22]

(Vienna, 1928), Arbeiterkammer Wien II 31439.

20. *Der Unabhängige Gewerkschafter* (Leoben), 15 November 1929.

21. Article by Walter Pfrimer published in the *Heimatschutz-Zeitung*, 19 April 1928. Gerhard Pferschy, 'Steiermark' in Weinzierl and Skalnik (eds.), *Österreich*, pp. 939–60.

22. See Table 1, Appendix to this volume, p. 211.

Moreover, electoral support for the party increased in the two industrial regions of the province, Graz and Upper Styria, from 1919 to 1927 and it continued to rise in Graz, where employer repression was less fierce. In Upper Styria the threat of unemployment was used as a rod with which to drive workers into the Heimwehr.

The actual level of Heimwehr membership in the province is difficult to assess, for no reliable records exist. In 1929 the leadership claimed to have 200,000 members nationally, but Francis Carsten, who quoted this figure, believed that it 'seemed too high'.[23] Bruce Pauley estimated that at its peak the movement had between 300,000 and 400,000 sympathisers with 120,000 trained members and 52,000 armed fighters. In Styria he estimated 120,000 supporters and 20,000 armed activists.[24] However, his figures, which were based on an interview with Walter Pfrimer in 1963, must be treated with some scepticism, for in 1930, when the Heimwehr was at the height of its power and stood as an independent party in the general election, it polled only 63,643 votes in Styria, 28,398 in Upper Styria. The Social Democratic Party lost 7,800 votes in Upper Styria, but the major casualties in this election were the bourgeois parties, the Christian Socials, German Nationalists and the Landbund, which suffered a combined loss of 23,243 votes.[25]

The strength of the Independent Unions is even more difficult to calculate. In 1932 the Free Trade Unions published figures supplied by the Independent Unions, showing a decrease in national membership from 1929 to 1931 of 3,000, from 45,000 to 42,000.[26] However, the lack of corroborating evidence and the round numbers themselves throw some doubt on the verity of this. In the 1929 factory council election at Donawitz the Independent Union polled 1,740 votes, 75 fewer than the Free Metalworkers' Union.[27] But again, electoral support was not proof of union membership. There can, however, be little doubt that by 1930 the majority of the Alpine Montangesellschaft workers were Heimwehr members and therefore probably belonged to the Independent Union as well, producing a membership of 3,500 in that one company.[28]

23. Carsten, *Fascist Movements*, p. 120.
24. Bruce F. Pauley, *Hahnenschwanz und Hakenkreuz*, trans. Peter Aschner (Vienna, 1972), p. 61.
25. *Jb ö Ab* 1930, p. 145.
26. *Jb BFG* 1931, p. 207.
27. *Arbeiterwille*, 10 March 1929.
28. Erben et al. (eds.), *Die Alpine Montangesellschaft*, p. 192.

The explanation for the rise in Heimwehr membership amongst Upper Styrian workers holds one key to the second question, the reasons for the level of political violence in the province, for great pressure was put on workers to join the Heimwehr. There is also evidence that, despite the size of the working-class membership, few workers actually developed an ideological commitment to the movement, whilst most knew that membership was a prerequisite for a job: no membership card, no job. In 1931, some weeks before the Pfrimer Putsch, police commissioner Kment, who was a Heimwehr sympathiser, prepared a confidential report for his superiors on the strength of the Heimwehr in Upper Styria, in which he commented on the difference between the working-class members and the more numerous farming and petty-bourgeois supporters. Whilst the latter wholeheartedly supported the attitude of Walter Pfrimer, the former, he decided, could only be relied upon as long as they remained in work.[29] Just as Heimwehr membership was essential for a job, so, for these workers, a job was essential for Heimwehr membership.

The Independent Unions grew under the protection and patronage of heavy industry in Upper Styria and in particular with the support of the Alpine Montangesellschaft. Political divisions within the company had widened after the 1925 strike and, although the Metalworkers' Union was unable to expand its membership, the small Communist Party increased its activities and almost succeeded in winning a majority in the factory council election at Donawitz in March 1926.[30] This was a 'one-off' success and was not repeated the following year. But it did alert the management to the possibility of a resurgence of shop floor militancy, which was hardly eased by the support which its own workers gave to the general strike in July 1927. The company reacted to this in the summer and autumn of 1927 by actively supporting Heimwehr recruitment at its works and increasing the pressure on its white-collar workers to join the movement, threatening those who refused with demotion.[31] The following February the extent of its opposition to the Free Trade Unions was revealed, when a scandal broke out following publication in the *Arbeiterwille* of letters showing that the company was employing a professional union breaker at Donawitz. His brief was to destroy

29. VA Bundeskanzleramt. 22/Stmk Box 5133. Police report, Heimatschutz in Obersteiermark 188106, 19 August 1931.
30. *Arbeiterwille*, 11 March 1927. Votes cast, Free Trade Union 1,664, Christian Union 400, Communist Party 1,129.
31. *Die Christlichen Gewerkschaften Steiermarks in den Jahren 1928 und 1929*, p. 65.

the remaining vestiges of organised trade unionism in the plant.[32] These activities paled into insignificance in the spring of 1928 as political parties and unions campaigned for local government and factory council elections, both of which brought increased support for the socialists.[33] In March, weeks before election day, the Styrian Heimwehr announced an agreement with the company restricting new recruitment in several mines to Heimwehr members only.[34] At Seegraben 150 experienced miners who had refused to join the Heimwehr were sacked and replaced by less experienced, but more compliant, workers.[35] At the ore mine and foundry at Eisenerz, just before the factory council election, the management intentionally contravened the existing wage contract, by reducing workers' coal allowances without the necessary consultation with the factory council. When shop stewards objected they were sent away empty handed, but the management agreed to meet a delegation of Heimwehr members, led by Fritz Pichler, which emerged victorious. A company circular sent to all workers days before the election congratulated the Heimwehr members on their success in protecting the interests of the workforce, when the Free Trade Union representatives had failed.[36]

In many plants, both within the company and in other enterprises, such obvious political victimisation led to violence between workers. But in one mine, the Hüttenberg mine just over the border in Carinthia, it led to a strike. Miners there had been subject to more intense company campaigning during which membership of the Social Democratic Party became grounds for dismissal. In May the management broke off negotiations with the Metalworkers' Union over paid holidays and wages and tried to reach a settlement with the small Christian Union.[37] Ten of the most experienced face workers, all of them Social Democrats, were demoted and three shop stewards were sacked without notice.[38] The sacking of the shop stewards and the suspension of paid holidays were both violations of the labour laws, but, as few workers at the plant were union members, the company assumed there would be little resistance. The major demands of the strikers were for political freedom, the end of political victimisation and the

---

32. *Arbeiterwille*, 21 February 1928.
33. *Jb ö Ab* 1928, p. 78.
34. *Arbeiterwille*, 20 March 1928.
35. *Die Christlichen Gewerkschaften Steiermarks*, 1928–9, p. 67.
36. *Arbeiterwille*, 21 April 1928.
37. *Arbeiter-Zeitung*, 20 May 1928.
38. *Arbeiter-Zeitung*, 12 May 1928.

proper observances of the labour laws. This made the strike a cause célèbre in union circles. Despite the absence of a strong union base in the plant, the Free Trade Unions donated funds, as they had done in 1925, and several other Alpine Montangesellschaft mines staged short sympathy strikes.[39] At Donawitz, where the Heimwehr was in a minority position on the factory council, the motion to strike was ruled out of order.[40] The Hüttenberg strike became a test case both for workers and the company. The management sacked all those on strike on the third day and brought in strike breaking miners from Upper and Lower Austria. By 15 May, 73 strike breakers were being escorted to and from work by the police and sections of the Heimwehr. A war of words broke out between the unions and the management, as each attempted to prove that the other was distorting the true impact of the strike. After seven days the company issued a statement condemning the strike as a mindless struggle instigated by the chief shop steward, Franz, and warning of the imminent arrival of a hundred more strike breakers.[41] It commended the Heimwehr militia, whose presence, it argued, was in response to a general call to arms by the Schutzbund.

Despite all of this, the company was forced to negotiate with the Metalworkers' Union at the end of the second week and to agree to a compromise, whereby both sides recognised the rights of workers to belong to a political party or union of their choice.[42] The strike was called off on 25 May, amidst general disquiet at Hüttenberg, where the Communist Party accused the national negotiator, Domes, of capitulating and accepting the Independent Union's victory. But it broke out again a few days later when 60 men were sacked for alleged intimidation on the picket line during the strike.[43] In addition the company began what was to become a long-drawn-out court case against the chief shop steward, Franz, for damages which arose from the strike which, it claimed, he had provoked.[44] Finally, on 10 June work resumed, although no further concessions had been made by the management.

39. *Arbeiter-Zeitung*, 16 May 1928.
40. *Arbeiter-Zeitung*, 17 May 1928.
41. *Arbeiter-Zeitung*, 18 May 1928.
42. *Österreichische Metallarbeiter*, no. 24, 16 June 1928.
43. *Arbeiter-Zeitung*, 29 May 1928. The Communists said Domes had conceded the right of the Independent Unions to organise in the plant.
44. The case was finally heard on 23 September 1930 after two years of legal argument. The company accused Franz of provoking the strike. The union argued that he was immune from prosecution because of his position as shop steward, and that he had actually spoken against the call for a strike. The case was important in

As in Donawitz in 1925, the workers of Hüttenberg appeared at first to have won a partial victory. The company admitted to resorting to political intimidation and undertook to refrain from this in future. Moreover, the Alpine Montangesellschaft workers had shown once more that despite their low level of trade unionism, they could and would take industrial action if provoked. However, in the long term the Hüttenberg strike marked a significant downturn in the activities of the Free Trade Unions in the province. Outside strike breakers were brought in for the first time and their use by employers quickly spread, most notably during the Graz tramworkers' strike in September 1928, when they proved to be more effective than they had been at Hüttenberg.[45] More important still, the concession which the unions had made to the management, whereby they agreed to recognise the rights of any union, turned out to be a disaster. At the beginning of the strike the only alternative union bodies were the Christian and German Nationalists, neither of which constituted a significant threat to the Free Trade Unions. But, unbeknown to union officials, the Alpine Montangesellschaft had reached an agreement during the strike with the Heimwehr to establish the Independent Unions.

The founding of the Independent Unions marked a serious change in the company's attitude to industrial relations, for throughout the 1920s it had been content to attack the position of the socialist union by opposing and at times breaking the laws on workers' rights. As long as these rights were enshrined in law and the influence of the Social Democratic Party in opposition prevented their removal, little else was possible. But after Schattendorf the political influence of the Socialists declined and alternative policies to weaken the position of the Free Trade Unions and the Social Democratic Party were feasible. For this reason the company encouraged the growth of the Heimwehr in its plants, expecting that this would also lead to the defeat of the Free Trade Unions on the shop floor. The factory council elections of 1928 showed that this strategy had misfired, for despite some Heimwehr recruitment, the Free Trade Unions retained control of all councils in the

---

that a defeat for the unions would have re-introduced the legal precedent of personal damages for strike action. J. Freundlich, 'Die Haftung für Streikschäden', *Arbeit und Wirtschaft* 1930, vol. 8, no. 1, pp. 837–42.

45. In September Graz tramworkers came out on strike over union recognition and pay. The Christian Union, which had been given negotiating rights by the privately-owned company, refused to support the strike, which was broken with the help of strike breakers. This was the strike in which Strafella came to prominence. *Arbeiter-Zeitung*, 11 October 1928.

company's plants. This meant that, according to the laws on collective bargaining, the socialists remained the legitimate representatives of the workforce in all negotiations with the company over pay and conditions. In addition, both the 1925 and 1928 strikes had shown that weak union membership did not necessarily ensure an acquiescent workforce. In order to break the hold of the Free Trade Unions the management was forced to find an alternative union body, one which could be more amenable to or more aware of the interest of the company.

The most obvious solution would have been to set up a company union, under the direct control of the management. By 1928 this was hardly possible, for the company had earlier chosen to support the Heimwehr both financially and morally and could scarcely try to establish yet another area of anti-socialist support among its workers. Nor was it necessary, for the Heimwehr had already set up employment exchanges in some towns to provide employers with 'loyal' workers.[46] In addition, the Heimwehr could bridge the gap between union and political party, providing opposition to the socialists on both fronts, which a company union could not. As many of the management of the Alpine Montangesellschaft were Heimwehr members and as the ideology of the DINTA was closely in line with that of the more militant wing of the Styrian Heimwehr, there appeared to be little conflict of interest between the company and the Independent Unions. Both shared the same goal, the destruction of the socialist movement, the resurgence of national economic power by integration with Germany and the defeat of bourgeois democracy which restricted that growth. As the Styrian Heimwehr moved into a closer alliance with the National Socialist Party in 1932, so too did the management of the Alpine Montangesellschaft.[47]

It would be a mistake to dismiss the Independent Unions as straightforward yellow or company unions. Their actual independence was to some extent a facade, for, as the Christian Unions pointed out, they could not have expanded without the protection and financial support of the employers; one feature which attracted some workers was the low level of union dues which were supplemented by contributions from the employers.[48] However, both

---

46. The first one was set up in Bruck in September 1927. *Arbeiterwille,* 6 September 1927.

47. In 1933 the police reported that the company was only taking on miners who belonged to the National Socialist Party. VA Bundeskanzleramt. 22/Stmk. Box 5135. Police report 206.155 GD/33.

48. *Die Christlichen Gewerkschaften Steiermarks,* 1928–9, p. 69.

their ideology and the scope of their recruitment excludes them from the strict definition of yellow unionism, for they drew members from different firms and industries, whilst still maintaining a central base in the Alpine Montangesellschaft heartland in Leoben. The Unions' founders, Lichtenegger and Lengauer, were not only company employees, but also prominent members of the Heimwehr.[49] As a result, the objectives of the Unions were not confined to furthering the interests of the management by maintaining industrial harmony at any cost, but included the wider political ambitions of the Styrian Heimwehr, its anti-socialist and anti-democratic ideology, producing a trade union which was fundamentally fascist in outlook, rather than generally subservient. There were times, though these were rare, when Independent Union shop stewards even came into conflict with the management.[50]

Despite its assurances at the time, the company did not abandon its policy of political intimidation of its employees after the Hüttenberg strike. In the autumn of 1928 it extended the earlier agreement with the Heimwehr over recruitment to the mines to cover all its plants, including Donawitz. New workers were told to provide evidence of at least three months' membership of the Heimwehr.[51] The socialist press published more accusations of experienced workers being sacked for refusing to leave the Free Trade Union. High structural unemployment in the area provided a ready pool of willing workers and as a result support for the Independent Unions increased. In the 1929 factory council elections at Donawitz the Free Metalworkers' Union polled only 75 more votes than the new union, creating a tied council, with each side having ten seats.[52] Seven weeks later the management announced a new wage contract, which had been negotiated with the Independent Union and which increased piece rates, but not basic rates, introduced compulsory overtime, which was still officially illegal, and restricted the allocation of coal allowances to married men only.[53] At the same time, tenants in company housing were issued with new regulations banning socialist newspapers, flags and

---

49. Lengauer joined the NSDAP in 1935, whilst Lichtenegger remained with the Starhemberg section of the Heimwehr when the movement split in 1932. Edmondson, 'The Heimwehr and Austrian Politics, 1918–1934' (PhD thesis, Duke University, 1966), p. 82.
50. One example was the ending of collective contracts in 1931.
51. *Arbeiterwille*, 27 November 1928.
52. *Arbeiterwille*, 10 March 1929. Votes cast, Free Trade Unions 1,815, Independent Union 1,740, Christian Union 168, Communist Party 96.
53. *Arbeiter-Zeitung*, 24 June 1929.

insignia from their homes and even red paint and red curtains at the windows.[54]

The defeat of the Free Trade Unions at Donawitz was crucial for all the Alpine Montangesellschaft plants, for all the company's manual workers were covered by the same wage contract, negotiated between the management and the Donawitz factory council. By defeating the Free Trade Unions in this one factory council the Independent Unions controlled negotiations for all other works within the company. Although it was never able to eradicate the presence of the Free Trade Unions from its plants, by the spring of 1929, before the crisis of the depression, the company had virtually emasculated the movement. This success was based on a series of linked factors beginning with the low level of trade union membership in its plants in the 1920s, which effectively prevented any organised campaign by the workers in their own defence. The legal status of the factory councils had been whittled away by the employers to a point where shop stewards themselves could find no protection in the law and were sacked without notice. If the law could not protect these men and even allowed them to be prosecuted for damages arising from a strike, there was nothing it could offer ordinary workers. The only weapon which the workforce retained was the right to strike, but even this was limited, for although a strike could force concessions from the employer in the short term, there was no guarantee that these would then be observed. Solid strike action in an unorganised plant was also a volatile element and could not be relied upon. The second factor which ensured victory for the management was yet again the relatively low level of skill required in heavy industry which enabled them to replace unskilled and semi-skilled Social Democratic workers with workers drawn from the Heimwehr; in a more skilled industry the Heimwehr's role as an employment agency would have been impractical. A third factor was the high level of unemployment, even before 1930, which, combined with a severe housing shortage, gave the unemployed two major incentives for agreeing to join the Heimwehr – a job and a company roof over their heads. Finally, the crucial factor was the determination both of the Alpine Montangesellschaft and of the Heimwehr to attack the labour movement at its weakest point, on the shop floor, thus combining the economic motives of the employer with the political motives of the Heimwehr leadership.

---

54. *Arbeiterwille*, 11 April 1929. In 1930 the company sacked a shop steward for painting the windows of his house red. St AK 1930, p. 179.

This defeat also had wider implications, both for the rest of the labour movement in Styria and in Austria as a whole. Styria had been the weak link in the chain of Austrian trade unionism, having a large but relatively unorganised workforce. The trade union movement had been unable to build up a solid base of support in this area, and this reflected not only the internal economic structure of the province, but a deep-seated problem within the policy of the trade union leadership. There had been little attempt to combat decreasing union membership in the 1920s when the problem first appeared, for the union leaders were more concerned with central reorganisation and their successes in Vienna. Although the movement provided financial assistance for non-unionists during both the 1925 and 1928 strikes, it failed to take advantage of this afterwards. Even within the province, union organisation was blinkered, concentrating its activities in and around its own head-quarters in Graz, rather than spreading out into the industrial regions beyond. By 1929, when the provincial executive became acutely aware of the problem and sought to rectify it, the battle for Free Trade Unionism in Upper Styria had already been lost.[55] Other employers, particularly in heavy industry, tried to follow the example of the Alpine Montangesellschaft, but met greater resistance. In May 1929 a strike broke out at the Wasendorf rolling-mill over the sacking of a shop steward, in the middle of protracted pay negotiations.[56] The same month a national convention of shop stewards from the Felten and Guilleaume Steel Company met at Bruck and warned their own employer of the dangers of continuing to infringe the right of workers to organise freely.[57] In March a delegation of shop stewards from companies throughout Graz and Upper Styria met representatives of the provincial government to protest against Heimwehr violence, following an attack on a union meeting at the Andritz paper mill.[58]

In addition to these formal protests, frequent fights broke out between socialist and Heimwehr members in the street, in pubs and clubs and on the shop floor, creating an atmosphere of violence throughout the industrial regions of the province. Heimwehr workers from several plants complained to the police in 1928 about intimidation by other workers. Paper workers at Pöls went on strike for a few hours to demand the removal of all Heimwehr

55. *Jb BFG*, 1929, p. 262.
56. *Arbeiterwille*, 11 May 1929.
57. *Österreichische Metallarbeiter*, no. 21, June 1928.
58. *Arbeiterwille*, 26 March 1929.

members from their factory.[59] At the Böhler steelworks in Kapfenberg 500 people took part in a brawl during counting for the factory council election in October 1928.[60] Fights were reported between workers at Donawitz, Seegraben, Trofaiach and Leoben, where the local Social Democratic Party organised a boycott of Heimwehr pubs and shops.[61] In a province where firearms were readily available, fights also led to gunshot wounds. In July 1928 a young Heimwehr worker from the Böhler works shot and wounded two women during a socialist rally. He pleaded self-defence at his trial.[62] So did a Heimwehr man who assaulted and then shot dead a socialist youth in Langenwang in 1929; he was acquitted on the grounds that the youth had lunged at him with a penknife during the fight.[63] In Knittelfeld shots were fired when socialists hurled stones at a Heimwehr march in April 1929. Four socialists were badly wounded and a Heimwehr man was arrested. The next day a crowd of a hundred Heimwehr supporters gathered in the town square to demand his release, only to be met by over five hundred socialists, who were there to ensure that he remained in custody. There was no fighting, but both sides refused to be the first to leave the square and they remained there until well past midnight.[64]

Each incident added to the general hostility. Industrial disputes merged into political battles between Left and Right; neighbourhood squabbles exploded into brawls. Marches and demonstrations were held each weekend as both the socialists and the Heimwehr strove to prove themselves masters of the streets, particularly working-class streets. If one side announced a march, the other countered with their own, on the same day, in the same place. If violence was avoided during the march itself, it often occurred just after, as one group ambushed the other on the way home. There were some attempts by the police to control the situation, but these were generally unsuccessful, either by design or incompetence. On 18 August 1929 one of the most violent battles took place in St Lorenzen, a small town between Knittelfeld and Bruck, when

---

59. *Arbeiterwille*, 15 February 1928.

60. VA Bundeskanzleramt. 22/Stmk. Box 5131. Police report 174/249, 3 November 1928.

61. VA Bundeskanzleramt. 22.Stmk/ Box 5131. Police report, 'Ausschreitungen anläßlich der Fahnenenthüllung der Ortsgruppe Zeltweg des Republikanischen Schutzbundes in Zeltweg an 10 Juni 1928' (28 August 1928).

62. *Neue Freie Presse*, 24 July 1928. *Arbeiterwille*, 24 July 1928.

63. *Arbeiterwille*, 22 October 1929.

64. *Neue Freie Presse*, 15 April 1929.

the Social Democratic Party held a rally to celebrate the tenth anniversary of the local party.[65] No less than five other rallies were also scheduled for that day, the Social Democrats holding them in Bruck and St Marein and the Heimwehr in Kindberg, Stubalpe and Thörl.[66] Koloman Wallisch, the Bruck socialist leader, was due to speak at one of the socialist rallies, but the party refused to disclose which one, following a previous Heimwehr attempt to prevent him from speaking: since 1927 Wallisch had become the Heimwehr's prime target. A police contingent of 23 was dispersed throughout the area, leaving only three men on duty in St Lorenzen, when it was announced that Wallisch was about to arrive there. About lunchtime Heimwehr members arrived also, having abandoned the Thörl meeting and travelled by foot from Kindberg to St Lorenzen along forest paths to avoid being seen. They arrived apparently unarmed, but in the town picked up weapons which had mysteriously arrived from St Marein. Apart from handguns and rifles they also had a machine-gun and threatened to break up the meeting if Wallisch spoke. A battle broke out during which the machine-gun was set up in the main square. Three socialists were killed and many wounded, although the machine-gun itself was not used. The police were hopelessly outnumbered and could do little but watch. Reinforcements were not called in, even though there was a police training school nearby. It was later argued that a storm had brought down the telephone wires, cutting off communication.[67]

The battle in St Lorenzen was particularly serious. The Social Democratic Party accused the police of collusion and of deliberately leaving St Lorenzen unprotected. The police replied that in the circumstances they could not have foreseen what was going to take place, nor where the violence was most likely to occur. They also pointed out that some members of the Heimwehr had suffered gunshot wounds, suggesting that members of the Schutzbund had also been armed. However they conceded that no weapons were found on the Schutzbund and that the main weapons the Left had used to defend themselves were iron bars and wooden staves.[68] The

65. *Jb BFG* 1929, p. 260.

66. VA Bundeskanzleramt. 22/Stmk. Box 5132. Ministerial report by Friedrich d'Elvert on the disturbances at St. Lorenzen, 27 August 1929. Z.Z. 159 399–8/1929.

67. *Jb BFG* 1929, p. 261.

68. The Heimwehr denied having machine-guns. In July 1929 a Social Democratic member of parliament, Horvatek, produced a photograph of Heimwehr men training with five machine-guns, taken in November 1928. He complained that although the police had been aware of the incident, no action was taken against those

more serious question, of how the Heimwehr were able to transport so many weapons without being detected, remained unanswered, as did the question of why the police failed to confiscate any arms when government reinforcements finally arrived. The presence of the machine-gun was also disputed, for the only witnesses who would testify to this were Social Democratic Party members. However, the scale of the attack in St Lorenzen and the later us of machine-guns by the Heimwehr do suggest that something more serious than yet another party fight had taken place. C. Earl Edmondson has gone as far as to suggest that this was the first putsch attempt by the Heimwehr in Styria, which was foiled by the unexpected strength of the socialist resistance.[69] The strange behaviour of the police during the incident gives added weight to this view.

In the autumn of 1929 the international depression began to affect the Styrian economy, which had already suffered a ten-year structural decline. Civil conflict increased as unemployment soared, but it is important to realise that the source of that conflict lay in the 1920s, not in the 1930s. Serious political violence was already endemic in the industrial communities in 1929, fuelled by the employers' repression of industrial workers. Trade union membership had not embedded itself within the metal industry, but the presence of the Free Trade Unions continued for some time through the factory council elections. This came under attack after 1927 as the employers strove to break the remaining bonds between the Styrian industrial workers and the socialist movement, by forcing workers to abandon their membership of the Social Democratic Party and join the Heimwehr. On the one hand there was violence on the shop floor as some workers resisted this growing pressure and on the other there was a battle for the streets, which erupted into bloody and often fatal confrontation as the socialists fought to retain their hold on the working-class areas and the Heimwehr fought to break it. The blood which was spilled was not, as both Bruce Pauley and Gerhard Botz have implied, the culmination of hostile rivalry between the agricultural block of the south and the industrial areas of the north, but the more direct consequence of an earlier alliance between industrial capital and fascism to crush the socialist enclaves at their very centres.[70] As a

---

involved, most of whom were Alpine Montangesellschaft employees. VA Bundeskanzleramt. 22/Stmk. Box 5132. Police report, Heimatschutz Gau Aichfeld 1 January 1930, 100 39/9.

69. Edmondson, *The Heimwehr and Austrian Politics*, pp. 78–9.
70. Pauley, *Hahnenschwanz*, p. 22. Botz, *Gewalt in der Politik*, p. 248.

result the basically economic protests of the industrial workers became entwined in a political battle against the increasing strength and activity of the Pfrimer section of the Heimwehr and later the Nazi Party. Over the next four years, as unemployment rose and the last threads of the socialist labour legislation were discarded, economic protest became almost impossible. But when strikes did break out they were more fierce and more political than hitherto. One consequence of mass unemployment as opposed to high unemployment was that fighting in the streets intensified.

−10−

The Depression

In the 1920s the Styrian labour movement was characterised by indiscipline which prevented the development of a strong trade union movement and rendered the province's workers particularly vulnerable to employer aggression. The weak economic position of the miners and metalworkers led to low trade union commitment and a lack of organisational strength. As a result Styrian workers were unable to protect themselves either by recourse to the law or by flexing union muscle. In the 1930s this very lack of organisational discipline led to an aggressive defence of political rights in the province and support for oppositional groups within the socialist movement which challenged the tactics of the central leadership. The catalyst for this support was the depression.

Styrian industry had been faced with crisis for almost ten years by 1930 when the depression began to accelerate the rate of unemployment, more than doubling it in four years. In some ways the problems which the international crisis created in the province were merely extensions of the earlier lack of capital and demise of foreign markets. In other ways the crisis was a new phenomenon, for it threatened the very existence of entire industries, including heavy industry, glass and wood. Whereas in the 1920s companies had responded to a downturn in the economy by reducing their labour forces and then increasing the pressure on those in work to maintain productivity, in the the 1930s entire industries shut down for months at a time, laying off all their workers or retaining just skeleton staffs. This gave the employers a fresh opportunity to intensify their attacks on the labour movement and to abandon the legal protection for workers on the shop floor. A second aspect of the depression was that the anti-socialist policies of the employers and the government, which had been functioning in Styria for some time, spread throughout the rest of the country. By 1934, when the Social Democratic Party was finally defeated, its main opponent was neither the Heimwehr nor even the National Socialist Party, but the Austrian government itself, which rejected democracy and adopted the principles of authoritarianism and fascist corporatism as the only solution to the crisis.

The psychological impact of unemployment on Styrian workers appears to have been less severe in the 1930s than it had been in the previous decade, when the first waves of high unemployment sapped the strength of the recently expanded trade union movement. Membership of both the socialist party and its unions fell from 1929 to 1933, but both avoided the mass exodus which the province's labour movement had experienced in 1925 and 1926: party membership was actually 10 per cent higher in 1932, the last year for which figures are available, than it had been in 1925. To some extent this was a direct result of the political polarisation which characterised the province: not only the Social Democrats, but also the Communist Party and the Heimwehr expanded in the early years of the depression, whilst the most spectacular rise in membership was that of the National Socialist Party. In this region where German nationalism had a long tradition, the anti-socialist camp, including the steel companies, swung towards the Nazi Party at an early stage in its development. This had two major consequences in the province. The first was that the nature of political violence changed. Although demonstrations and marches continued to be held until banned in April 1933, the possibility of an outright civil war became more overt after the Heimwehr putsch attempt of 1931. Bombings, shootings and political murders increased as military training became a central feature of all political life, both socialist and anti-socialist. Whilst the socialist party leadership, both in Vienna and in Graz, continued to pursue a policy of disciplined, legal and, whenever possible, non-violent opposition to the growing influence of fascism and state authoritarianism, support for a more militant stance gathered ground in Styria. The second consequence was that the apparent fascist base among the miners and metalworkers was shaken. Workers who had joined the Heimwehr in order to preserve their jobs found that the security they had been promised evaporated as companies announced more redundancies, lowered wages and switched their preference to members of the National Socialist Party. When the civil war finally broke out in February 1934 there was no great rising of working-class fascists in Upper Styria, but instead one of the most intense battles against the government forces and Heimwehr reserves by workers in Bruck, Kapfenberg, and even Leoben and Donawitz. Although unemployment had provided the initial spurt to the growth of working-class membership of the Heimwehr in Upper Styria, its continuation had dissipated that mechanical support.

The official figures for registered unemployment in Styria show a rise of 75 per cent, or 25,434, between January 1929 and January 1933.[1] As devastating as these figures are, they still underestimate the full extent of the economic crisis in the province, for they continue to exclude many who, for some reason or another, did not register with the authorities, including those groups who were unlikely to receive benefits, such as young people, women, land-based workers and those who had already exhausted their entitlement to social welfare allowances, having been out of work for over a year. Figures for insured workers give a more accurate indication of the size of the problem, if the existing high rate of structural unemployment is also borne in mind: these show a fall of 39,820, or 45 per cent, over the same four years, but even so, they omit reductions in labour which arose from the widespread introduction of short-time working.[2] By January 1933 approximately 10 per cent of the entire adult population of Styria was receiving unemployment benefit, despite the time restrictions on eligibility. Of all the industrial provinces of Austria, only Vienna had a higher rate of unemployment during this time.[3]

The collapse of world trade had a catastrophic effect on export industries such as iron and steel and glass. Production of crude steel fell by 80 per cent between 1929 and 1933, whilst the manufacture of pig-iron ceased altogether for several months in 1931. Lignite production dropped in 1930 by 25 per cent, but revived a little in 1931 after government intervention. Nevertheless the number of lignite miners fell by 1,000. Production of iron ore fell by 73 per cent between 1929 and 1932 and the number of ore miners dropped from 2,200 to 547.[4] Employment in the foundries was also reduced by 67 per cent, with 60 per cent of the remaining workforce of 3,867 on short time.[5] The situation in the machine industry was equally bad: the number of workers was reduced from 9,661 to 3,474, with 1,673 on short time. Production in the wood industry dropped by 46 per cent in twelve months. By 1931 even those industries which relied on the local market were feeling the spin-off effect of the depression. The famous brewing industry cut its

1. See Table 4, Appendix to this volume, pp. 214–15.
2. *WsJ* 1931–3, p. 350.
3. The percentage increase over 3 years was 55.8 per cent in Lower Austria, 41.2 per cent in Upper Austria and 96.6 per cent in Vienna. The proportion of the adult population which was registered as unemployed in January 1933 was 15.3 per cent in Vienna, 10.5 per cent in Lower Austria, 9.5 per cent in Upper Austria and 10 per cent in Styria.
4. *Stat Hdb Österreich* 1930, p. 70; 1931, p. 72; 1935, p. 79.
5. *St AK* 1932, p. 23.

workforce from 1,629 in 1929 to 780 in 1932, producing 40 per cent less beer. Butchers could no longer sell meat and laid off assistants. Bakers found that the demand for white bread and cakes dried up and they were forced to concentrate on the less profitable trade in maize loaves. The building industry ground to a virtual standstill as all major projects stopped and employment was slashed. In the foundries and rolling-mills, which had traditionally employed considerable numbers of building workers, most were laid off by 1931. What little work there was involved maintenance of existing buildings and seldom provided more than six to eight weeks employment. January figures for unemployment in this industry trebled between 1928 and 1932, but the July figures, taken at a time when building activity was normally at its height, were even more disturbing: in July 1932 10,250 building workers were on the dole in Styria, compared with 472 in July 1928. This was just 2,000 fewer than in the depths of the previous winter.

The regulations for unemployment benefit also adversely affected this group, for a recipient had to provide evidence of twenty weeks work during the previous year to be eligible. In a seasonal industry such as building, this stipulation was a serious setback. The tradition of supplementing income by doing odd jobs was also out of the question, for, after twenty weeks unemployment, benefit was issued at the discretion of the local authorities and was automatically withdrawn at the hint of any misdemeanour. It ceased altogether after fifty-two weeks. The average level of unemployment benefit in 1931 was just over 17 schillings a week or 891 schillings p.a., approximately one quarter of the average worker's income. In 1932, it fell to 870 schillings p.a. and in 1933 to 769 schillings. A kilo of maize flour cost 70 groschen in February 1932, lard was 3 schillings a kilo and pine kernel oil, a local product, 4 schillings a litre. The price of these basic foodstuffs was relatively high in comparison with meat: pork was 3 schillings a kilo, smoked sausage between 2.40 schillings and 4 schillings.[6] However, a kilo of flour went much further than a kilo of meat, which virtually became an unobtainable luxury for many. The staple diet of the unemployed consisted of an unvarying combination of potatoes, flour, black bread and dripping, which could be supplemented by home-grown vegetables in the summer months, if land was available.

The plight of the unemployed in the northern regions tended to

6. Karin Schmidlechner, 'Die Situation der steierischen Industriearbeiter zwischen 1918–1934', pp. 53, 68.

be worse than in the south or around Graz, for in many of the industrial towns the majority of workers were out of work and everyone was scavenging for food and fuel, the more so as unemployment persisted. By December 1931 12,000 people had already exhausted their unemployment benefit and a further 9,000 had been refused benefit because they were over the age limit.[7] As all plans to introduce a national system of old age pension had been postponed indefinitely, these older people were forced to seek local assistance. The young also suffered. In 1930 the lower age limit was raised from seventeen to eighteen and as many young people still lived with their parents, they were ineligible for emergency benefit from the community. Those under twenty-five could receive unemployment benefit only for twenty-two weeks, rather than the full fifty-two weeks. Apart from these legal restrictions, administrative problems also arose. In order to claim benefit a worker had to register with the health insurance office and obtain a certificate vouching for his fitness and proving that he was covered by the terms of the employment act.[8] The processing of an application often took up to two months, during which time workers had to feed and clothe both themselves and their families. The extent of the misery caused by this delay forced the Chamber of Labour to provide emergency funds for the newly unemployed. This organisation also dealt with cases which had been rejected by the unemployment office and in 1928, in its last full-scale annual report, it showed that the majority of the workers who had been refused benefit had either fallen foul of the stipulation that they must have worked for at least twenty weeks the previous year, or had not been considered in physical danger from lack of subsistence.[9] In addition, workers from the argicultural regions were still excluded from unemployment benefit, as were all those who had been employed by small firms with a staff of less than five people. There were minor consolations: the category of workers who were turned down on the grounds that they had made themselves redundant voluntarily all but disappeared in 1930.

The unemployed were also faced with acute housing problems in most industrial communities. The postwar housing crisis had not been eased during the 1920s, despite piece-meal attempts by several socialist councils to follow the Viennese example and create both

7. Dieter Stiefel, *Arbeitslosigkeit, soziale, politische und wirtschaftliche Auswirkungen am Beispiel Österreichs, 1918–1933* (Berlin, 1978), p. 147.
8. St AK 1928, pp. 65–7.
9. Ibid.

jobs and homes by increasing capital expenditure on building projects. In Graz the whole issue of rented accommodation became a political battleground as landlords organised themselves into an association under the leadership of the Christian Social deputy, Felix Pistor, in order to oppose rent restrictions and state intervention in the housing market.[10] The city's council did initiate some building projects after 1926, providing employment for over 1,000 workers, but its contribution to the housing market was minimal, for the major projects included a new bridge, improvements to the slaughterhouse and a cable railway. Only fifty-three workers were allocated to housing projects, less than twice the number engaged in maintaining the parks and gardens.[11] The situation in Bruck was slightly better, for the council there had a socialist majority and attempted to use this to increase expenditure on housing and social welfare. But its resources were minimal. When it tried to increase revenue by imposing local taxes and raising the price of local services, it faced serious opposition from the town's bourgeoisie, which revived a five hundred-year-old legal battle over ownership of the surrounding forests. Subsequent attempts to raise funds by selling off unrented municipal property were also challenged. This led to the aforementioned scandal involving a projected old people's home, which cost Pichler, the Social Democratic mayor, his position and reputation. By 1924 the Bruck council had built a few houses on the Mur Insel and run out of funds. As an alternative it urged employers, in particular the Felten and Guilleaume steel company, to provide more company housing for its workers and to replace wooden barracks which were still in use and which were barely suitable for single workers let alone whole families.[12] By 1930 the high level of company housing was itself causing problems, as firms sought to maximise the return on all their assets and increased rents, or introduced them on property which had previously been let rent-free as a worker's benefit. Many unemployed workers were evicted and they once more turned to the shacks and barracks, which quickly became overcrowded. In 1930 Leoben and Donawitz had the worst figures

10. *Arbeiterwille*, 6 January 1929; 15 January 1929. In March 1928 Walter Pfrimer set up a branch of the Haus- und Grundbesitzer Organization in Judenburg. *Arbeiterwille*, 6 March 1928.

11. *Arbeiterwille*, 1 January 1929.

12. *Bericht des Gemeinderates der Stadt Bruck an der Mur über seine Tätigkeit in den Funktionsperioden 1919 bis 1922 und 1922 bis 1924. Erstattet vom Bürgermeister Anton Pichler*, pp. 19–35.

for housing in Austria, followed by Knittelfeld.[13] The Chamber of Labour found that its own efforts to improve standards in these overcrowded and privately-owned workers' colonies could back-fire: in 1928 it tried to force the owner of sixteen homes in Graz, which had been built on unsteady ground, to repair his property. When he refused the council threatened to clear the entire site without rehousing the existing tenants.[14]

There is no doubt that poverty and overcrowding took their toll amongst the Styrian unemployed, as they did throughout Austria, increasing hunger, idleness and lethargy. But it also increased militancy amongst some groups, most notably in Graz and Bruck. From 1930 the Communist Party attempted to increase its local support by adopting the plight of the unemployed as a major platform and by exploiting the differences between those on the dole and those in work. The Heimwehr also adopted this policy, but with less success. In May 1929 a group of thirty Heimwehr members went into a former prison camp at Knittelfeld, which had been taken over by the town's poor and unemployed, most of whom (according to the police) were socialists. The Heimwehr men were attacked and shots were fired, although no one was killed. Twelve people ended up in hospital, eight Heimwehr and four socialists. The local police inspector urged the provincial government to increase his force over fivefold, from six to thirty-three, to prevent further disturbances.[15]

Life for the unemployed grew steadily worse as the depression deepened. In the first two years of the depression 9,000 firms went out of business in Styria, most of them small family concerns.[16] However, in terms of employment, the larger firms, employing over 500 workers, were the main casualties. In 1928 38 per cent of insured workers were employed in nine plants of this size, but in 1933 only five remained, employing 23 per cent of insured workers. Conversely, small firms employing fewer than 50 workers expanded their proportion of the total labour market from 29 per cent to 38 per cent as the contraction in the labour force reduced the size of existing firms.[17] In Upper Styria alone 22 factories shut down for good in 1930, whilst another 29 were closed for a full 12

13. Charles A. Gulick, *Austria from Habsburg to Hitler*, 2 vols. (Berkeley, California, 1948), vol. 1, p. 419.

14. St AK 1928, p. 86.

15. VA Bundeskanzleramt. 22/Stmk. Box 5132. Police report 113 831/8, 14 April 1929.

16. *WsJ* 1930–1, p. 109.

17. *WsJ* 1928, pp. 80–1; 1933–5, pp. 326–7.

months. The number of working hours for those still employed fell by between 35 per cent and 54 per cent in the iron and steel industry, 34 per cent in mining, 24 per cent in the saw mills and 64 per cent in the paper industry.[18] So that although the greatest hardship was experienced by the unemployed, hourly paid workers also saw a drastic fall in their living standards. In the vain hope of avoiding more redundancies, many workers were at first willing to accept a reduction in hourly rates, in addition to cuts in the working day. These amounted to between 5 and 20 per cent by 1932 in all sectors of heavy industry, including lignite and iron ore mines, foundries and rolling-mills. In the magnesium mines, where unemployment had fallen by 68 per cent since June 1929, the reductions were less: 5 per cent of the hourly wage, but almost 10 per cent of piece rates, so increasing the daily pressure on the workers to step up productivity.[19] In 1932 there was a 5 per cent reduction of woodworkers' pay, whilst the glass industry closed almost completely, having reduced pay by 3 per cent the previous year.[20] Although comparative figures for the cost of living in Styria are unavailable, figures for Vienna show that the price of food and clothing did not fall until 1933. This suggests that, if a similar pattern was followed throughout the country, real wages fell by between 20 and 30 per cent in the four years from 1929 to 1933.[21]

The depression also gave employers even greater opportunities to attack the remaining labour legislation. In January 1931 the Alpine Montangesellschaft director, Dr Apold, announced the immediate redundancy of all 1,300 miners at the Seegraben pit. The mine was not closed. Instead miners were offered re-employment, providing that they accepted new individual contracts and abandoned the practice of collective bargaining.[22] There was some opposition to this in the mine, which still had a Free Trade Union majority on the factory council, but it failed to stop the plan from succeeding. The tactic was then repeated in other plants and other companies. A few weeks after the Alpine Montangesellschaft announcement, the Böhler Steel Company issued a similar ultimatum to its workforce and by 1932 the entire iron and steel industry had followed suit.[23] By 1932 the only industries in Upper Styria in which collective contracts still operated were paper, brewing,

18. Schmidlechner, 'Die Situation', p. 24.
19. St AK, 1931, pp. 22–8.
20. St AK, 1932, pp. 25–8.
21. *WsJ* 1931–2, p. 342; 1933–5, pp. 292–3.
22. *Arbeiterwille*, 18 January 1931; *Arbeiter-Zeitung*, 31 January 1931.
23. *Arbeiterwille*, 2 March 1931.

building, flour milling and saw mills.[24] All other industrial employers had successfully broken the most basic measure of labour protection, for without collective contracts the battle for employment became a free-for-all, in which workers could undercut each other for work. This was less serious in Upper Styria than it might have been elsewhere, for the Free Trade Unions had already lost the right to negotiate on behalf of workers in many plants and, to some extent, a free-for-all had already emerged as a result of political bias in recruitment. Nevertheless, the blatant rejection of collective contracts still amounted to a serious defeat for the labour movement.

The depression also led to changes in the pattern of the labour force and an increase in industrial accidents. In the early years of recession many employers had turned to youths and women, employing them in unskilled jobs at rates which were far lower than those for adult males. Female employment was traditionally low in Styria, precisely because of the dominance of heavy industry, which provided few jobs for women.[25] By 1931 these workers were once again out of work, as wage rates for men fell to a level which made them once again competitive. The number of industrial accidents also increased as new recruitment was based on political suitability, as well as, or even in preference to, manual skills. In January 1930 a crane went out of control in the rolling-mill at Donawitz. One man was killed and another seriously injured. Workers blamed the management for the accident, for the crane driver was a new man, a Heimwehr member, and had replaced an older, more experienced worker who had refused to join the Heimwehr and had been sacked. The accident occurred when the new crane driver went berserk at the controls. According to his colleagues, this was due to his lack of experience and was, therefore, indirectly the fault of those who had employed him in the first place.[26]

Neither the fresh attacks on the rights of workers nor deteriorating working conditions passed entirely without protest. When the changes in contracts were announced in 1931 they were accompanied at the Alpine Montangesellschaft works by a general reduction in wages. Both Free Trade Union shop stewards and their Christian Union counterparts urged a total boycott of the new system.[27] This

---

24. Schmidlechner, 'Die Situation', p. 38, quoting from Die Amtstätigkeit der Gewerbe-Inspectorate im Jahre 1932 (Vienna, 1933), p. 95.
25. Ibid., p. 14.
26. Steyer Tagblatt, 29 January 1930.
27. Arbeiter-Zeitung, 31 January 1931.

failed, mainly because at least half of the miners in the district were already out of work. Strike action was out of the question: not only was it economically unviable, but, in addition, miners employed by the company had been officially laid off. The company's announcement amounted to a lock-out. The Free Trade Unions tried to force a debate in parliament through the Social Democratic Party, to persuade the government to intervene. That also proved to be futile, for by this time the government was in no mood to compromise with the opposition and backed the employers. In fact government action had given the employers the green light in the first place. Under the terms of the 1930 Anti-Terror Act the legal status of collective contracts had been altered, invalidating all closed shop agreements and halting the practice of deducting union dues at source.[28] One clause of the act outlawed intimidation of workers on the shop floor and so, although collective contracts remained legally binding where they still existed, the unions could do little to resist an employer's decision to abandon a contract, with the 'support' of the workers. There was little hope of convicting an employer of intimidation within his own factory.

Despite the virtual defeat of collective bargaining in Upper Styria, the Free Trade Unions maintained a hard core of support in the industrial region of the province, based around the railways, machine industry and chemical industry, which had suffered less from the depression than most other industries. In December 1932, despite the dramatic rise in unemployment, the Free Trade Unions had 41,855 members, a fall of only 36 per cent in four years.[29] However, the threat to these members was growing. In 1930 the government announced the appointment of the former Christian Social deputy major of Graz, Franz Strafella, to the post of director of the national railways.[30] His appointment was vigorously opposed by the Social Democrats. The party still had vivid memories of the role which Strafella had played in defeating the socialist tramworkers' union when he had been director of the Graz Tramways and the reputation he had for dishonesty and ruthlessness.[31] In addition Strafella was a prominent member of the Heimwehr and there were fears that his appointment would trigger off a campaign against the relatively strong Railway Workers' Union and enable Heimwehr members to control the critical rail links between Austria and Italy and Hungary, allowing the free passage

---

28. Gulick, *Austria*, vol. 2, pp. 889–91.
29. See Table 2, Appendix to this volume, p. 212.
30. Lajos Kerekes, *Abenddämmerung einer Demokratie: Mussolini, Gömbös und die Heimwehr* (Vienna, 1966), pp. 73, 81.
31. *Arbeiter-Zeitung*, 13 May 1930.

of arms from the fascist governments in these countries to the Heimwehr.[32] The *Arbeiter-Zeitung* mounted a strongly-worded campaign against Strafella, which led to a libel action being brought against the paper for describing him as 'unclean and incorrect'. The court judged in the paper's favour, saying that the evidence presented to it appeared to justify the description, but Strafella was appointed nevertheless.[33]

By this action and by the introduction of the Anti-Terror Act the government had shown that the attack on the Free Trade Unions, which had hitherto been led by private employers, was to be extended to the public sector and intensified. The terms of the new law effectively outlawed socialist or communist political activity on the shop floor, laying it open to the accusation of political intimidation. Real political intimidation, as practised by the employers, was allowed to continue. As a result of this and increased unemployment, political conflict between the socialists and the Heimwehr was transferred from the factories to the streets. Both movements increased their activities, parading up and down, often in military formation wearing military-style uniforms. The theft of weapons increased, as did their use in the streets. Rumours of arms dumps ran rampant, leading to official and unofficial house searches. These were not always successful in tracking down weapons: in January 1931 there was a serious explosion in Hafendorf, when a domestic fire in a worker's house ignited ammunition which was hidden there.[34]

To some extent the increase in violence in the early 1930s was little more than an extension of the conflict which had characterised Upper and Middle Styria since 1927, but it was taking place in the streets rather than in the factories. There were also other differences, which the police, in particular, were quick to note. By 1930 both the National Socialist Party and the Communist Party were expanding their activities, at first amongst the unemployed, but later within the unions and farming communities. The actual extent of this is difficult to assess, for in the case of the Communist Party, police surveillance was unusually intense and the number of reports on this relatively small group was far greater than for the Christian Social Party, the Social Democratic Party or the Heimwehr, the last of which had a special relationship with the Graz police force.[35]

32. Kerekes, *Abenddämmerung*, p. 73.
33. Gulick, *Austria*, vol. 2, pp. 900–5.
34. VA Bundeskanzleramt. 22/Stmk. Box 5133. Police report 104 688/30. 10 January 1931.
35. In May 1931 police director Kment sent a detailed report to the Chancellor's

Nevertheless, these reports do indicate that many new Communist and Nazi groups were established at this time. The National Socialists began recruiting vigorously within the Independent Union in Upper Styria in 1930, whilst also expanding membership in Graz. In December 1930 50 uniformed storm-troopers took part in a meeting in Graz which was chaired by an Independent Union official.[36]

Reports on the Communist Party are entirely different, but should be approached with caution, for their frequency and length may have resulted from the level of police interest in the party rather than its level of activity. Membership figures, for instance, were often exaggerated. Nevertheless, they do provide some useful information on the growth of the Communist influence in the area. From 1926, when Communists made significant headway amongst the Alpine workers at Donawitz, the party fell into a period of decline in the province, maintaining a few enclaves of support in Leoben and Graz. In 1925 members had attempted to establish youth branches in Upper Styria and set up a Committee of Unemployed in Graz, but this came to an abrupt end when the police arrested the entire committee. For some years, and with obvious satisfaction, the police noted dwindling Communist activity.[37]

The explosion of unemployment in 1930 was followed by renewed campaigning which went beyond the boundaries of Leoben and Donawitz. In January 1930 a Committee of Unemployed was resurrected in Graz and Communists won control of this over the heads of Social Democrats.[38] Public open-air meetings were held in Leoben, Donawitz and Bruck in early 1930 in the run-up to the national elections, but these rarely attracted more than 50 people.[39] By February 1931 the size of meetings at Leoben was estimated at 1,500, despite police efforts to ban them as a threat to public safety. Similar estimates for party membership in the town increased from

office in Vienna giving details of the reorganisation of the Heimatschutz in Graz. In June he followed this with a letter from the new Heimatschutz area leader, which regretted any misunderstanding between the police and the former leadership and hoped that good relations between the two would be restored. VA Bundeskanzleramt. 22/Stmk. Box 5133. ZL 187 539 Pos. 164 483, 17 June 1931.

36. VA Bundeskanzleramt. 22/Stmk. Box 5133. Police report 255 766. 3 May 1931; 4 October 1931.

37. VA Bundeskanzleramt. 22/Stmk. Box 5133. 1931. Police report. Tätigkeit der Kommunistischen Partei in Leoben, Pr. ZL.IV. 1406/26. 2 March 1926.

38. VA Bundeskanzleramt. 22/Stmk. Box 5132. Police report 113 37 3 January 1930.

39. VA Bundeskanzleramt. 22/Stmk. Box 5132. Police report 114 047/30, 4 February 1930.

20 to 500 and the organisation expanded in other areas.[40] In Graz 15 meetings were held in a single month, May 1930, attended by up to 600 people. New groups were established in Knittelfeld, Fohnsdorf and Judenburg with over 100 members, most of whom were unemployed workers who had lost their jobs to members of the Heimwehr, or so the police thought.[41]

The unemployed were not the only group to show some interest in the Communist Party. In 1931 the police reported intense activity amongst smallholders in the Judenburg area, where their estimate of Communist Party membership was incredibly high, at 800.[42] Later that year similar reports came in from other agricultural regions, reflecting the success of a political campaign against the decline in the wood industry and the uneven allocation of taxes amongst the agricultural communities.[43] The emergence of this unfamiliar area of support, amongst farmers who had been described as diametrically opposed to all forms of socialism, was not as surprising as it at first seemed. Despite obvious support for the Heimwehr in some of these communities, the Communist Party seems to have been the first party actively to campaign on the specific issue of the plight of the small farmer and the agricultural worker. In 1932 the Heimwehr tried to take over the cause and organised a tax strike in the southern and western districts.[44]

The Communists also made inroads into the remaining sections of the Free Trade Unions. In October 1929 a recruitment campaign began in Graz, based at the Weitzer Waggonfabrik.[45] Little more was heard until March 1931 when a group called the Revolutionary Trade Union Opposition published leaflets criticising the socialist leadership of the Metalworkers' Union for weakness, and calling for a new union body.[46] Response to this was at first limited – only

40. VA Bundeskanzleramt. 22/Stmk. Box 5133. Police reports 121 000 31, 26 February 1931; 122 632, 25 February 1931.

41. VA Bundeskanzleramt. 22/Stmk. Box 5133. Police report 188 105, 19 August 1931.

42. VA Bundeskanzleramt. 22/Stmk. Box 5133. Police report 173 237, 7 July 1931.

43. VA Bundeskanzleramt. 22/Stmk. Box 5133. 'Kampfprogramm der Bauernaktionskomitees Österreichs', 1931. 129 726/31. This attacked the government's agricultural policy and the role of the Heimwehr and Social Democratic Party. It called for lower agricultural taxes and a trade agreement with Russia.

44. VA Bundeskanzleramt. 22/Stmk. Box 5133. Police report 112 670. 22 January 1932. The Heimwehr did not replace the Communists in this campaign. Indeed the Heimwehr leader Arbesser joined the Communist Farmers' Action Committee.

45. VA Bundeskanzleramt. 22/Stmk. Box 5132. Police report. 76 090, 10 October 1929.

46. VA Bundeskanzleramt. 22/Stmk. Box 5133. Police report. 127 758, 7 March 1931.

47 people turned up to the first meeting. But the following summer shop stewards from this group opposed the terms of a new collective contract for the machine industry, which included cuts in family allowances and which the Free Trade Union's provincial leadership had accepted. This led to a leadership contest in the Graz branch of the union between the Social Democratic area secretary and a Communist Party rival, Weiss. Weiss won.[47]

The size and importance of the Communist Party can easily be over-emphasised if police reports are taken at their face value. Whilst its influence certainly increased in the early years of the depression, especially amongst the unemployed, its overall role in the industrial regions was dwarfed by the Social Democratic Party. Central police reports comparing the strength of armed paramilitary units in the province show a much smaller membership than do the local police reports. In Graz in 1932 local authorities estimated that there were 350 members of the Communist paramilitary Arbeiterwehr, including in this almost all party members, irrespective of age or sex.[48] This compared with a Schutzbund force of over 2,500 in the city, and a Social Democratic membership of 19,509.[49] However, the importance of the Communist presence cannot be gauged just by numbers, nor even in total isolation from the Social Democratic Party itself. Its members were organised into small and vociferous groups within the industrial communities and acted as hostile critics of the Social Democratic leadership, but seldom came to blows with a larger socialist movement.

Although a great deal of energy was expended on the unemployed, it was the influence of the party within the unions which produced greater though still limited results in Styria. Outside the formal structure of the trade unions the Communists lacked strength because they lacked numbers. But within the local branches of trade unions they worked as a radical influence, constantly urging resistance to further reductions in the living standards of workers, even when these were quite obviously hopeless, and attacking the Social Democratic Party for reformism and 'social fascism'. At the national level there was little love lost between the Social Democratic Party and the Communist Party. However, locally, especially amongst the young Social Democrats,

---

47. VA Bundeskanzleramt. 22/Stmk. Box 5133. Police reports 180 568, 27 July 1931; 190 937, 25 August 1931.
48. VA Bundeskanzleramt. 22/Stmk. Box 5134. Wehrformationen in Steiermark, 9 March 1932. 128 462/32.
49. *Jb ö Ab* 1932, p. 93.

who were becoming fierce critics of the national leadership, things were slightly different. From 1932 onwards some Styrian members of the Social Democratic Jungfront began to work with individual Communists from time to time, though they remained aware of the fundamental differences between the two movements.[50]

50. Officially there was no working agreement between the Communist Party and the Left opposition. In his memoirs Ernst Fischer accused the Communist Party of being 'isolated from the mass of the working class and made up of unemployed and intellectuals' (*An Opposing Man* trans. Peter and Betty Ross, with an introduction by John Berger (London, 1974), p. 219). At the local level Communists and Styrian Jungfront members did work together, most obviously during the 1933 strikes at the Seegraben mine and the Niklasdorf paper factory. (Interview with Willi Scholz and Ditto Pölzl, 13 October 1976.)

The Pfrimer Putsch and its Aftermath

The origins of the informal and ad hoc relationship between the local Communist Party and members of the Jungfront lay in a putsch attempt. In September 1931 the Styrian Heimwehr and sections of the Lower Austrian Heimwehr took part in an ill-planned exercise to overthrow the democratic constitution. As the background to this strange and potentially disastrous event has been covered by many writers, only a brief outline of the incident will be given here.[1] The putsch began during the night of 12/13 September, when, after several months of preparation, members of Pfrimer's Heimwehr began to assemble fully armed at specified points through Middle and Upper Styria. Once again, the main target of the attack was the town of Bruck, where Heimwehr members were told that the Schutzbund was mobilising.[2] One section, under the command of Hans Reuter, surrounded Graz with the intention of seizing the city. Other units moved into Bruck itself, Leoben, Fohnsdorf and other towns along the industrial belt, stopping and searching cars and pedestrians and arresting Social Democratic leaders and mayors. Two socialist workers were shot and killed when the Heimwehr tried to occupy Social Democratic offices in Kapfenberg.[3]

Neither the police nor the army made any move to prevent the rising, despite rumours which had been circulating in the area for months. Just a few weeks earlier, the director of police, Kment, had reported to his superiors in Vienna that all was quiet within the Heimwehr camp in Upper Styria.[4] The complicity of the local

---

1. See: C. Earl Edmondson, *The Heimwehr and Austrian Politics, 1918–36* (Athens, Georgia, 1978) and the thesis of the same name (Duke University, 1966); Josef Hofmann, *Der Pfrimer Putsch: der steirische Heimwehrprozeß des Jahres 1931* (Vienna, 1965): Charles A. Gulick, *Austria from Habsburg to Hitler* 2 vols. (Berkeley, California, 1948), vol. 2, pp. 951–8.

2. Gulick, *Austria*, vol. 2, p. 952. Stenographische Berichte über die Verhandlungen des steiermärkischen Landtages. Sitting 20 November 1931, pp. 300–20.

3. *Jb ö Ab* 1931, p. 50.

4. VA Bundeskanzleramt. 22/Stmk. Box 5133. Police report 'Heimatschutz in Obersteiermark', 188 106, 19 August 1931.

authorities in the province was also borne out by their failure to alert the national government to the movement of paramilitary troops during the night. Unlike St Lorenzen, just two years earlier, there was no excuse that the telephones were not working: for some inexplicable reason, the Heimwehr had not cut the telephone lines during their manoeuvres. The Minister of the Interior, Franz Winkler, first heard about what was happening in Styria when he received a telephone call from the Social Democratic executive from Vienna. Kolomann Wallisch had telephoned party head-quarters in Bruck at 2 am on the 13th. No government action was taken. Finally the Social Democratic leadership put the entire Schutzbund on alert and threatened to confront the Heimwehr if the government did not intervene first. Government troops in Graz were ordered to Bruck, some thirty miles away, but without speed. The journey took them three hours, allowing the Heimwehr ample time to withdraw.[5]

The farcical nature of this putsch was deceptive. Fourteen-thousand men, equipped with modern weapons, including machine-guns, had assembled in a deliberate attempt to overthrow the democratic structure of the Republic. Placards were posted in towns proclaiming that 'In the highest emergency the patriotic people of Austria had named me the supreme guardian of their rights', and signed by Walter Pfrimer.[6] According to the plan, the Heimwehr would first seize Styria and Lower Austria and then march on Vienna, drawing support from other provinces in the meantime. It would force the capital into submission. The consti-tution would be abandoned, replaced by dictatorship and ulti-mately a corporate state.

The plan failed for two main reasons. In the first place, internal divisions within the Heimatblock scuppered support from Heim-wehr groups outside Styria. Secondly, the government was suf-ficiently worried by the threat of a direct conflict between the Schutzbund and the Heimwehr to withdraw any tacit support which it might have given to the putschists. Even so, no action was taken when the first news of the rising reached Vienna and very little was taken subsequently. Pfrimer fled to Hungary, returned and was acquitted at his trial. Some arms were confiscated, but very few in relation to the number the Heimwehr were known to have. Rintelen, the Governor of Styria who had apparently known

5. Gulick, *Austria*, vol. 2, pp. 952, 957.
6. Proclamations reprinted in *Wiener Sonn- und Montagszeitung*, 14 September 1931.

of the putsch plans for some time beforehand, tried to dismiss the entire event as 'tipsy twaddle'.[7] But the Pfrimer Putsch provided clear proof, if it was needed, that the authorities, including the government, police and army, had all but abrogated the responsibility of defending the Republic. Within Styria it also raised fresh doubts in the minds of some young members of the Social Democratic Party about the policies of their own movement's national leadership.[8]

Throughout the 1920s the main battleground between the Styrian working class and the joint forces of the employers and the Heimwehr had been the factory floor, as both sides engaged in what was primarily an economic conflict over the laws, collective bargaining, working conditions and wages. The Free Trade Unions had borne the brunt of the attack, for they represented both the economic power of the workers and the weakest link in the socialist chain. In Styria, in particular, the absence of a strong trade union tradition, the nature of the labour market, employer oppression and high unemployment had debilitated trade union organisation rendering the trade unions incapable of mounting a concerted defence of the working class. Despite the lack of organisation workers were not entirely subdued, as the Alpine Montangesellschaft strikes illustrate. Support for the Social Democratic Party had continued as the party weathered the onslaught of the depression. The 1930 national election increased the number of Social Democratic members of parliament and local elections returned many Social Democratic mayors in the province's industrial regions.[9] Party membership did fall from 1929 to 1932, but even so it remained higher than it had been in the middle of the 1920s. Morale was not high, for many were out of work and had little or no prospect of employment in the future, but party rallies and celebrations continued to draw crowds even when these were likely to be the scene of Heimwehr attacks. In these circumstances, the Social Democratic Party appeared to be more capable of protecting

7. Ernst Fischer, *An Opposing Man* trans. Peter and Betty Ross, with an introduction by John Berger (London, 1974), p. 185.

8. Interview with Willi Scholz, 2 June 1977, Liverpool.

9. *Jb ö Ab* 1932, pp. 113–14. Results of local government elections (1932). In Upper Styria the Social Democratic Party lost eight council seats, which the Communist Party gained. The greatest gains were made by the National Socialists in Bruck, Fohnsdorf and Judenburg. The number of Nazi councillors rose from one to twenty-one. Nevertheless the Social Democrats held control of most councils in the area, including Bruck, Kapfenberg, Eisenerz, Fohnsdorf and Donawitz, where the Social Democrats lost four seats but retained their majority. This is further evidence that membership of the Heimwehr did not necessarily mean electoral support for it.

the political rights of its members than the Free Trade Unions had been in protecting their economic rights.

The Pfrimer Putsch threw some doubt on this. Styrian workers had never been the most disciplined members of the Austrian socialist movement. In both the Revolution and during the 1920s workers in the province had taken part in risings and fights, some of which were spontaneous and radical and few of which were supported by the Social Democratic leadership. Local socialists had engaged in frequent and scurried scuffles with the Heimwehr. The St Lorenzen incident in 1929 had shown that local workers would defend themselves against attack when they felt the need arose. However, during the Pfrimer Putsch, orders were given by the central leadership of the party that no action should be taken against the putschists without prior approval from Vienna. The Schutz-bund would intervene only if the government failed to take any action.[10] Whilst their local leaders were locked up and their towns occupied, Styrian workers were told to remain calm and alert and to await events. It is perhaps surprising, considering the political tension in the province at the time, that they did just that. With the exception of the casualties at Kapfenberg, local socialists did not oppose the Heimwehr troops in September 1931.

The tactics of the Social Democratic executive worked that time, but they involved a dangerous risk, relying on government forces to protect the Republic. The decision not to fight was entirely consistent with the leadership's overall policy, which still main-tained that victory for socialism would only be achieved through the electoral system and that non-violent parliamentary procedure was the only way to preserve parliamentary democracy. In Vienna, where the Social Democrats still controlled the city council, such a policy seemed feasible, but in Styria, where the political rights of workers were already under attack, there was some hesitation. Kolomann Wallisch, who had been elected to parliament in 1930, made an indirect attack on the leadership at the party conference in October 1931. He pointed out that the defeat of the putsch in Styria had not stopped official support for the Heimwehr.[11] Other, younger members were more openly critical. In January 1932 an article by Ernst Fischer appeared in the journal *Die Weltbühne*, in which he argued that victory for socialism was not the point at issue. Defence was now the main problem. He wrote of his own province: 'Styria is a fascist country; in this eastern part of the Republic, the Consti-

10. Martin Kitchen, *The Coming of Austrian Fascism* (London, 1980), pp. 133–4.
11. Gulick, *Austria*, vol. 2, p. 967.

tution is a scrap of paper, fascism is a reality.'[12] Others accused the leadership of pessimism, over-caution and even conservatism, having ordered moderation in the 1920s, because capitalism was strong, and again in the 1930s, because capitalism was in crisis.[13] When, if ever, would capitalism be ripe and the leadership order action?

Within Styria the fiercest criticism came from young party members in their twenties who had recently established their own groups within the party, opposed to the strict discipline which was imposed upon them. Their chief spokesman was the same Ernst Fischer, a journalist from Graz who had moved to Vienna in 1927 to work as an editor in the *Arbeiter-Zeitung*. In 1929 he published his first book, *The Crisis of Youth*, in which he expressed the frustrations of his generation both with the capitalist system and with the ideas of an older socialist leadership, who, he argued, 'would prefer to change people into small well-tempered party machines'.[14] Fischer was not alone in his condemnation. In 1930 the whole question of generational conflict became a major issue within the party, as fears were raised that the youth movement was failing to attract members and even losing control of those groups which remained.

One part of the problem was behavioural, a legacy of the party's paternalism. Young members were expelled for offences such as frequent drunkenness or loose sexual morals. There were also political differences. Apart from basic disagreement over tactics, many young party members felt they had been used during the 1932 local elections, when the youth vote became a major issue, drawing the attention of not only the Social Democrats, but also the Communists and National Socialists. All three parties canvassed heavily amongst the young and the socialists broke with their traditional view, that the youth were political apprentices to be schooled and tutored, to set up youth committees designed to attract both new members and new votes. After the election older members at district and national level tried to dismantle what they had seen as purely a temporary structure. The youth committees fought back, demanding greater independence, a voice in decision-making and the right to extend their activities into all areas of political propaganda. In May 1932 they set up a separate organisation,

12. Anson Rabinbach *The Crisis of Austrian Socialism: from Red Vienna to Civil War 1927-34* (Chicago, 1983), p. 85.

13. Gulick, *Austria*, vol. 2, p. 967.

14. Rabinbach *The Crisis of Austrian Socialism*, p. 71.

the Jung Sozialistische Front (Jungfront), which worked alongside the party, but was independent of it. This created a furore and led to head-on conflict between the executive and leaders of the youth movement. By November 1932 a compromise was reached whereby the Jungfront accepted the general supervision of the party but was allowed some degree of internal autonomy.[15]

The emergence of the Jungfront revealed growing dissension within the party. This was particularly true of Styria, where support for it was strong amongst party activists, including Otto Fischer (Ernst's younger brother), Willi Scholz, Ditto Pölz and Heribert Hütter.[16] The first three were youth leaders. Otto Fischer was a student, commander of the Student Battalion in Graz. Hütter was a shop steward in the Niklasdorf paper factory, opposed to the cautious attitude of the Free Trade Union leaders and thought by the police to be a member of the Communist Party.[17] From this base Jungfront members in Styria built up a network of fellow thinkers opposed to the defensive stance of the Social Democratic Party and in favour of an aggressive policy, of fighting to preserve the Republic using any support which was available, even if this came from the Communists.[18]

Jungfront members played an important role in the final attempts to stem fascism in Styria. Before discussing this, some comment should be made about the reasons for the relative strength of the Left opposition, the Jungfront, in the province. One contributory factor was the personal contact which Ernst Fischer maintained with the province through his brother and a small group of friends, including Scholz and Pölzl. This group provided a central focus for what might otherwise have been dispersed and ineffective dissension amongst some young party members. A second reason was the existing level of violence in the province, for, unlike their colleagues in the capital, these party activists already knew what it was like to live in an area where fascists had built up support with the tacit approval of the state authorities. The third reason, and one which is closely connected to the second, was the fiasco of the Pfrimer Putsch itself. Many Jungfront supporters were also members of the Schutzbund and, as such, in September 1931 they had

15. Ibid., pp. 72–5.
16. Ibid., p. 76.
17. Hütter appeared on a police list of Communist Party members drawn up in January 1933. It is unlikely that this was correct. See Rabinbach *The Crisis of Austrian Socialism*, p. 146. VA Bundeskanzleramt 22/Stmk, Box 5135. Police report, 'Kommunisten-evidenz für Steiermark Ergänzung und Berichtigung' 101 340, 12 January 1933.
18. Interview with Willi Scholz and Ditto Pölzl, 13 October 1976.

been ordered by the party to stand by whilst an armed force took control of their province. Few believed (or at least said out loud) that they could have defeated the Heimwehr, for the fascist forces were far better equipped and could rely to some extent on government protection, as they had earlier. But there were those who felt that the humiliation of 1931 was a lesson which the national executive should have taken to heart by strengthening the Schutzbund and making provisions to arm workers.[19]

This did not happen. In the autumn of 1931 Alexander Eifler, the national commander of the Schutzbund, issued a twelve-page plan outlining the action which the Upper Styrian Schutzbund would take in the event of another putsch.[20] He gave details of the estimated strength of the Schutzbund, the arms which were available, and the rival strengths of the Heimwehr. In Leoben, the centrepoint of the plan, 1,068 Schutzbündler were told to assemble in hills outside the town and observe the Heimwehr. If the fascists left the town for Bruck, the Schutzbündler were to attack them en route and try to cut them off. The Heimwehr force in Leoben was estimated at 2,220 men, armed with 50 machine-guns and almost 2,000 guns and rifles. Between them the Schutzbündler could muster 290 guns and six machine-guns. This pattern of ill-equipped socialists attacking and even defeating numerically superior and heavily-armed Heimwehr troops was to be repeated in each of the 12 districts of Upper Styria and, in areas where even Eifler realised there was no chance of success, the Schutzbündler were told to resort to hit-and-run tactics of guerilla warfare which Eifler's predecessor, Theodor Körner, had developed. Körner's own reaction to this plan was one of undisguised anger. In a fifty-page critique, which he sent to the party executive, he listed its most ludicrous assumptions, accused Eifler of deliberately exaggerating the size of the Heimwehr and pointed out that the only result which the plan could achieve was outright defeat and a possible blood bath. If civil war did break out, he argued, there was no point in ordering the cream of the socialist movement to march out in regular military formation against Heimwehr units, who, it was hoped, would adopt the same line of attack, only shoot badly. Women, children and older workers would be left behind without protection. At the

---

19. Ibid.
20. The Eifler Plan and Körner's response are discussed at length in Ilona Duczynska, *Workers in Arms* (New York and London, 1978), pp. 107–55. Copies of both documents are contained in Christian Vlcek, 'Der Republikanische Schutzbund in Österreich: Geschichte, Aufbau und Organisation' (unpublished PhD thesis, Vienna, 1971), pp. 512–47.

same time, he drew a more accurate picture of the political strength of the Social Democratic Party in the region, based on party membership and election returns, rather than the size of the para-military. He urged the party to build its defence on this base, involving the entire movement rather than just a selected few thousand and using guerilla warfare rather than traditional military tactics. He was particularly outraged by Eifler's suggestion that the police and army could be persuaded to remain neutral in a battle between the Schutzbund and Heimwehr, if socialist officials re-minded them of their constitutional duty.[21]

Körner's critique was a direct attack on basic party policy, one of several which emerged in 1931 and 1932. It was completely rejected by the party executive, which accepted Eifler's plan in the autumn of 1931 and ordered Schutzbund members to be trained accord-ingly.[22] This decision was one direct cause of the growth of the Jungfront in the region. Rather than abandon their political role, as ordered, Jungfront members began to build up links with the remaining socialist shop stewards. Their attitude incurred the wrath of older party members, who accused them of inciting political conflict at a time when the official party policy was to avoid violence and work for a political solution to their problems. One major bone of contention was the role of strikes in political cam-paigning. The attitude of the party establishment on this matter was straightforward. It considered strikes to be economic protests which had little political potential, with the exception of the general strike, and which remained the prerogative of the trade unions. The Styrian Jungfront had other ideas. They believed that strikes pro-vided opportunities to extend basic economic grievances against wage cuts into political protest against the government. This difference of opinion and the refusal of the Jungfront to remain aloof from strikes led to open conflict with party leaders. During a strike in Fohnsdorf in the autumn of 1933 the socialist mayor, Horvatek, threatened to arrest a Jungfront worker, Willi Scholz, who had arrived in the town to help to organise the strike.[23] Heribert Hütter was threatened with expulsion from the party in 1933 for defying policy and opposing his union's attempts to end a strike in the paper factory in which he worked.[24] Antagonism between the old guard and the new generation of party activists

21. Ibid.
22. *Jb ö Ab* 1931, p. 98.
23. Interview with Willi Scholz and Ditto Pölzl, 13 October 1976, Graz.
24. Rabinbach *The Crisis of Austrian Socialism*, p. 146.

mounted. Pölzl and Scholz took part in talks with the Communists to try to build a common anti-fascist alliance in the province. These came to nothing. Members of the Jungfront worked with the Communist Revolutionary Trade Union Opposition in the strikes at Niklasdorf and Seegraben, although they rejected suggestions of a formal alliance.[25] Finally, in the winter of 1933–4 the police received reports that a group of young socialists led by Otto Fischer, Willi Scholz and Ditto Pölzl were trying to oust the old guard from the leadership of the provincial party.[26]

These divisions within the Social Democratic Party developed as political tension in the province increased and the depression deepened. The failure of the Pfrimer Putsch had led to disarray within the Heimwehr camp and pushed sections nearer to the National Socialists. In the middle of 1932 entire groups disbanded and moved over to the National Socialists.[27] Other groups maintained their formal independence, but held joint meetings and manoeuvres. There was some dissension and fights between the National Socialists and Heimwehr stalwarts did occasionally break out, but these were rare. Within Upper Styria the major centre for Nazi activity was the Alpine Montangesellschaft headquarters at Donawitz, where many of the management and technical staff switched their allegiance from the Heimwehr to the National Socialists.[28] The remaining Alpine Montangesellschaft workers, numbering fewer than 7,000 by 1932, soon found that the security which the Heimwehr membership and wage reductions had appeared to offer them disappeared. In July 1931 the entire company was shut down for several months and most of the workers laid off. Ten months later miners at Seegraben were laid off and a further wage reduction of 8 per cent was introduced in other mines and plants. When the notices were put up Heimwehr workers threw their caps into the dust as a sign of frustration and anger.[29] In November, when production at Donawitz was halted for a few days, the *Arbeiter-Zeitung* accused the company of blatant political

25. Ibid., p. 160.
26. VA Bundeskanzleramt, 22/Stmk, Box 5136. Police report 227 443/33, 13 October 1933.
27. In February 1932 a new provincial leader of the Styrian Heimatschutz was appointed, August Polten, who was also a member of the National Socialist Party. VA Bundeskanzleramt, 22/Stmk, Box 5134. Police report. 120 681, 3 February 1932.
28. F.L. Carsten, *Fascist Movements in Austria: From Schönerer to Hitler* (London, 1977), pp. 205–6.
29. VA Bundeskanzleramt, 22/Stmk, Box 5134. Police reports, Obersteirisches Industriegebiet: Situationsbericht. 171 010, 8 July 1932; 170 389 3 June 1932.

manipulation, laying off workers to enable them to take part in a large provincial Heimwehr rally in Graz.[30] True to previous form, the management used the lay-offs to put political pressure on workers, only this time there was a significant change in the political climate: instead of re-employing Heimwehr members the company gave preference to National Socialists. The Christian Union representative complained of political intimidation of his members.[31] The Alpine works magazine began to carry National Socialist propaganda reflecting the views of the management and technical staff, and one senior manager chose to wear his Nazi uniform whilst on duty.[32] Support for the Nazis was not confined to Donawitz; in 1933 a local priest wrote to the Chancellor complaining that this type of intimidation was also openly practised by the Böhler management in Kapfenberg and at the Blech- und Eisenwerke plant at Wasendorf.[33]

In Leoben and Donawitz the political situation became critical. Four parties, the Social Democrats, Communists, Heimwehr and National Socialists built up paramilitary units which were armed and trained. Throughout the northern half of the province people appeared to be preparing for war. Political demonstrations and rallies continued, but they were overshadowed by paramilitary parades and illegal manoeuvres. The traditional May Day rally in Graz in 1932 included a parade of 6,000 socialist workers and 1,000 Schutzbündler marching in civilian clothes, but in military formation.[34] Even gymnastics displays assumed a military air, ending with drill exhibitions.[35] In the meantime paramilitary groups trained in earnest in the hills around the towns, under the unconvincing guise of rambling associations or nature groups. Police arms searches uncovered illegal dumps in the Donawitz works in August 1932, in private houses, railway stations and even in the military depot at Rottenmann.[36] Some belonged to the National Socialists, some to the Heimwehr, but the police were

30. *Arbeiter-Zeitung*, 19 November 1932.

31. VA Bundeskanzleramt, 22/Stmk, Box 5135. Police report. 'Die Christliche Arbeitsgemeinschaft in Fohnsdorf' 206 155 G.D./33, 21 September 1933.

32. Carsten, *Fascist Movements*, p. 206.

33. VA Bundeskanzleramt, 22/Stmk, Box 5135. Police report. 194 768 G.D./33, 11 July 1933.

34. VA Bundeskanzleramt, 22/Stmk, Box 5134. Police report 156 716, 1 May 1932.

35. VA Bundeskanzleramt, 22/Stmk, Box 5134. Police report. 'Arbeiterkammerfeier in Eggenberg', 21 September 1932 (no number).

36. VA Bundeskanzleramt, 22/Stmk, Box 5134. Police report, Rottenmann. 235 035, 1 October 1932.

particularly diligent in their search for weapons belonging to the socialists, who, unlike the other two groups, had no access to new weapons, supplied by friendly neighbouring governments. The number of robberies increased, as all sides tried to discover each other's hiding places and remove weapons. In 1932 one Heimwehr member stooped to selling his company's rifles to the Schutzbund before he disappeared.[37]

Inevitably the build up of paramilitary units and increased National Socialist activity in the region heightened the level of violence. Street battles between fascists and socialists became more common, with young socialists playing an increasingly more active role, turning up at rival meetings and demonstrations and attacking Nazis in the street. Anyone who died in a fight was hailed a hero and such incidents were exploited for their full propaganda value. This was particularly true of the Nazi Party. In September 1932 a National Socialist was killed during a fight in the Griesplatz in Graz. His coffin was escorted to the grave by a column of 1,000 uniformed Nazis.[38] Six months later Nazi members came upon a group of young socialists who were ripping down posters in the city centre and one more Nazi was stabbed to death. This incident led to the temporary arrest of Otto Fischer, who was accused of the murder.[39] Paramilitary night patrols started to appear in the early months of 1933 in Kapfenberg, Bruck and Bad Aussee.[40] Pedestrians were stopped, questioned and searched, houses entered and weapons taken away. The police seldom intervened, unless a fight broke out.

Intense Schutzbund activity took place in February 1933 in response to Hitler's appointment as German chancellor and the campaign which the Styrian National Socialists mounted to capitalise on this. Schutzbund parades were held weekly in many industrial towns, sometimes twice weekly, culminating in three major rallies in Graz.[41] Jungfront members leafleted the city centre and some were arrested, accused of disturbing the peace.[42] But by

37. St LA Präs. E.91. Report by provincial government, Graz, 10 September 1932. E.Nr.365.

38. VA Bundeskanzleramt, 22/Stmk, Box 5134. Police report, 209 194, 12 September 1932.

39. VA Bundeskanzleramt, 22/Stmk, Box 5134. Police report 125 551/33, 12 September 1932.

40. VA Bundeskanzleramt, 22/Stmk, Box 5135. Police report, 132 651/33, 16 March 1933.

41. VA Bundeskanzleramt, 22/Stmk, Box 5135. Police report, 'Schutzbund Tätigkeit', February 1933; 130 485/33.

42. VA Bundeskanzleramt, 22/Stmk, Box 5135. Police report, 120 438/33,

this time the internal conflict within Styria was overshadowed by national events, as the government abandoned its democratic facade and began to attack the fundamental structure of the constitution. In March 1933 the Dollfuß administration exploited a technical loophole in the constitution to prorogue parliament. With it went all pretence of democratic government.[43] The opportunity arose from a procedural argument in the national assembly during a debate over a national railway strike, which had broken out some days earlier. The railway board had announced in February, only twelve months after a major cut in railwaymen's wages, that it did not have enough funds to pay pensions the following month. Wage payments were to be staggered over four weeks with the final payment of 40 per cent being dependent on the availability of additional funds. All three railway unions, the Socialist, Christian and Nationalist, objected to the terms of the wage cut and to the way in which it had been announced, without any prior consultation, so abandoning collective bargaining within this large state industry. The unions, including the Nazi-dominated Nationalist Union, threatened to call their members out on strike, whereupon the employers issued a counter threat, invoking a First World War imperial decree which outlawed railway strikes and carried a penalty of six weeks' imprisonment.[44]

To repeat a point made earlier, the Railway Workers' Union was of particular importance to the whole socialist labour movement in Austria. It was not only the second largest trade union in the country, but its members had successfully fought off attempts by the employers to reduce its strength and foster the Nationalist Union. Railway workers had acted as watchdogs for the movement, checking freight-trains for consignments of arms from Italy and Hungary and carrying news and information throughout the country. Whereas most unions drew their membership from specific geographical areas, the railway union had branches throughout the country and its members were in regular contact with each other. The defeat of this union would cut off one of the remaining strengths of the working-class movement, for were a general strike to be called, it would die a sad death if the trains kept running.

The debate in the national assembly on 4 March hinged on two main factors: the probability that the railway board intended to take draconian action against the striking railway workers, and the duty

---

20 February 1933.
  43. Gulick, *Austria*, vol. 2, p. 1018.
  44. *Arbeiter-Zeitung*, 2 March 1933.

of the state, as the owners of the railway, to provide funds to pay wages and pensions.[45] In the end the arguments deteriorated into a procedural row over voting and two of the three assembly presidents, Renner, a Social Democrat, and Ramek, a Christian Social, both resigned. Finally the last remaining president, the German Nationalist Straffner, followed suit, leaving the Chamber without any apparent authority. The seriousness of these events did not dawn on those who had taken part, for it was assumed that the outgoing presidents would remain in office until their successors were appointed. This did not happen. Instead the government decided to rule 'in an authoritarian fashion until, through negotiations with the opposition, an alteration to the constitution as well as the rules of procedure of the Nationalrat [national assembly] are secured so that the functioning of the administration and the legislative organs of the state appear assured'.[46] Press censorship was introduced to 'ease' the transfer of power.

The suspension of parliament opened up the final phase of the conflict in Styria. On 5 March the Schutzbund in Bruck was put on alert and members formed a guard around the police barracks.[47] Rumours of a general strike spread alongside tales of a general arming of the workers, but these were without foundation. On 18 March Schutzbündler throughout the region were again put on alert. Night patrols were stepped up and fighting increased. On the streets of Leoben on 27 March 600 people appeared and occupied the local school.[48] The police reported that every Schutzbund member had been issued with two hand-grenades in preparation for a general rising.[49] Telegraph poles and trees were pulled down during socialist demonstrations in Bruck and Kapfenberg on 18 March. Reports of these and similar actions poured in from police throughout Austria, giving the government the thin excuse it needed to ban the Schutzbund on 31 March. Three weeks later the right to strike was removed and then the right to demonstrate. The *Arbeiter-Zeitung* carried the headline 'Marching is forbidden – walking is allowed.'[50]

45. Gulick, *Austria*, vol. 2, pp. 1016–17.
46. Ibid., p. 1023, quoting a speech which Dollfuß made at Villach on 5 March 1933.
47. VA Bundeskanzleramt, 22/Stmk, Box 5135. Police report, 132 651/33, 16 March 1933.
48. VA Bundeskanzleramt, 22/Stmk, Box 5135. Police report. Leoben 28 March 1933 (no number).
49. VA Bundeskanzleramt, 22/Stmk, Box 5135. Police report, Langenwang. 134 307, 15 May 1933.
50. *Arbeiter-Zeitung*, 24 April 1933.

The destruction of parliamentary government and the removal of constitutional rights to demonstrate and to strike amounted to the very attack of which the Social Democratic Party had warned in its Linz Programme of 1926. At that time the party had declared itself ready to fight to defend the Republic, but in 1933 its leaders procrastinated, beguiled to some extent by the government's promise of consultation over constitutional changes. At the Vienna Party congress held in May 1933 Bauer fought against calls for a general strike and ignored criticism that the party had missed its chance by not taking action on 15 March, the final date on which parliament could have reassembled.[51] He emphasised once more the horrors of civil war and accused his critics, most of whom were young, of an immature faith in confrontation and the powers of a general strike. Without directly abandoning the Linz Programme, he re-interpreted its general arguments and produced a four-point analysis of events which would necessitate an armed rising.[52] These were the abolition of the Vienna council, an attack on the rights and independence of the trade unions, a permanent end to direct franchise or a direct attack on the party itself. Once again the party's executive was concentrating its attention on Vienna and ignoring the provinces. Trade union rights had already been removed in much of Upper Styria.

The initial aim of the young socialists at this last party conference was to confront the executive and demand a vote in favour of increased mobilisation of party members. The Jungfront had increased its support in the provinces and within Styria it won the elections for party delegates in Graz, Leoben and Bruck. However, for some reason which has never been fully explained, the leader of the Left opposition, Ernst Fischer, withdrew from the conference at the last minute, leaving the task of leading the debate against Otto Bauer to a less experienced and less gifted orator, Karl Scharmer.[53] The result was a compromise, whereby the conference accepted Bauer's four points, but added six tactical amendments, which it hoped would placate the young socialists.

The banning of the Schutzbund did not halt its activities, it merely drove them underground. Jungfront members continued to hold clandestine demonstrations and meetings, out of sight of both the police and party officials.[54] So, too, did the Nazi Party which

51. Kitchen, *The Coming of Austrian Fascism*, p. 186.
52. Rabinbach, *The Crisis of Austrian Socialism*, p. 112.
53. Ibid., p. 130.
54. Interview with Willi Scholz and Ditto Pölzl, 13 October 1976, Graz.

was banned in June 1933, but swiftly found an alternative way of operating. Its members rejoined the Heimwehr and continued their military training without interruption. Police investigations into Nazi activity in the Alpine and Böhler works in July 1933 revealed that the majority of former Nazi members had enrolled in the Austrian Heimatschutz (as opposed to the Styrian Heimatschutz of Walter Pfrimer which had also been banned), but had retained their allegiance to the National Socialist Party.[55] As a result, they were immune from prosecution, unlike the Schutzbündler.

In June 1933 the police reported that the dissolution of the Schutzbund had resulted in increased activity amongst the young socialists and a growth in their numbers.[56] Kolomann Wallisch addressed a large number of meetings throughout the province in May and June and urged those present to maintain the discipline of the movement, despite the ban. Alexander Eifler spoke at Kapfenberg on 10 May and drew a crowd of 700.[57] The police concluded that the apparent lack of activity amongst Social Democratic members was a deliberate camouflage for increased mobilisation and, despite warnings from the party leadership, the young socialists were still preparing for a general strike.

In the autumn of 1933 police fears seemed to be confirmed. A strike broke out in the West Styrian coalfield in September. It spread to Fohnsdorf, Seegraben and Köflach and within days most of the miners in Styria had stopped work.[58] The cause of the strike was an announcement by the Alpine Montangesellschaft management that wages were to be paid monthly, rather than fortnightly. Although workers had been told of this in July, it was only when the system was actually introduced on 1 September that work stopped. In Fohnsdorf, where the Free Trade Unions had held their majority, the Jungfront played some part in the organisation of the strike, against the orders of the Social Democratic Party leadership.[59] In Voitsberg, Hans Steiner, a member of the Left opposition and a miners' shop steward, led the strike committee. But the strikes were not confined to socialist miners. The Independent Union which controlled the factory council in Seegraben initially supported the action, although all participants took great care to

---

55. VA Bundeskanzleramt, 22/Stmk, Box 5135. Police report, 'Nationalsozialistische Bewegung', June 1933. 187 701/33.

56. Ibid., 'Sozialdemokratische Partei Tätigkeitsbericht', April 1933, 160 847/33.

57. Ibid., May 1933, 173 542/33.

58. *Arbeiterwille*, 10 September 1933; 11 September 1933.

59. Interview with Willi Scholz and Ditto Pölzl, 13 October 1976, Graz.

point out that the strike had been spontaneous.[60] The perils of being held responsible for such actions were even greater now that strikes were illegal. However, the nature of the strike did suggest that no preparations had been made, for rather than refusing to go into work and face prosecution, the strikers chose instead to remain down the mine in one of the first sit-in strikes to take place in a mine in Europe. This had the added effect of preventing the use of strike breakers, for even those miners who were theoretically willing to work refused to enter the pithead whilst the sit-ins continued, for fear of accidents. It also created serious problems for the protesting miners, all of whom had gone into the shafts without taking food or water. At the Piberstein pithead miners' families tried to persuade the management to allow them to send down refreshments. When this failed and the first shift refused to come out, the second shift went in, concealing water flasks and loaves about their bodies and they, too, joined in the protest. At the Rosenthal pit a crowd of 300 men, women and children surged past the police, who had cordoned off the mine, and sent in packages of food.[61] At Seegraben, 160 miners joined the strike on the fourth day and 700 miners at Fohnsdorf, half the total workforce, joined on the fifth day. Conditions in Fohnsdorf were particularly dangerous, for the mine was deep, damp and prone to gas blasts. The police intervened, overruling the management's decision to ignore the strikes, and ordered the company to allow food and water to be sent down the shaft.[62] Doctors were sent in at Piberstein, and a number of miners left the sit-in in a state of collapse. When a Heimwehr provincial deputy went into the mine at Fohnsdorf, strikers refused to let him out again.[63]

The strike created havoc in the area. Donawitz closed down because of lack of coal. Electricity workers cut off power to the one mine which remained in operation, and paper mills closed.[64] On 17 September, the eighth day of the strike, the Alpine Montangesellschaft was forced, under government pressure, to negotiate with a strike committee, including four members of the Free Trade Union, and to accept the re-introduction of fortnightly payments and two weeks notice of redundancy for any worker who had been employed by the company for more than ten years. On 19 Septem-

---

60. *Arbeiter-Zeitung*, 13 September 1933; 15 September 1933.
61. *Arbeiterwille*, 10 September 1933.
62. *Arbeiterwille*, 13 September 1933.
63. *Arbeiterwille*, 14 September 1933.
64. *Arbeiterwille*, 15 September 1933.

ber the strike was called off with an assurance that those who had taken part would not be prosecuted.[65]

The story does not end there. On the 19th, members of the Independent Union at Fohnsdorf called a meeting at which they proposed to reject the terms of the agreement as too modest.[66] The next day the strike began again, but it lasted only one day and was confined to this one pit. However, the apparent new-found militancy within the Independent Union did raise some eyebrows. The union was, by this time, controlled by the Nazi Party, thinly disguised as the Heimwehr. The company management was of the same persuasion and it seemed hardly possible that the strike had broken Nazi ranks within the company. The police certainly did not believe this and referred the government to a Christian Union complaint that a number of Fohnsdorf miners, some of whom had worked at the mine for over ten years, had lost their jobs the previous summer and been replaced by Nazi sympathisers.[67] The police conclusion was that the management had deliberately provoked the strike in the hope that it would spark off serious civil conflict in the area.[68] Left to their own devices the management would have allowed the strike to escalate, resulting in deaths in the mine. When the government refused to allow this, the company sought, instead, to create a fresh protest through the Independent Union.

Irrespective of the role of the company, the miners' strike was the last major protest in Styria before the civil war, although a series of smaller strikes broke out in the paper industry in October and January. The character of the strike was moulded by the legal changes of 1933, in particular the laws which made most forms of protest illegal, whether they were political or economic. Because of this and the censorship of the press few details of the organisation of the strike exist, but those which are available suggest that the action had not been pre-planned, although it must certainly have been discussed beforehand. The mines were not occupied on the same day, but when news of the first protest at the Graz-Köflach pit at Rosenthal reached other mining communities it was decided, sometimes immediately, sometimes over a number of days, to

65. *Arbeiterwille*, 17 September 1933.

66. *Arbeiter-Zeitung*, 20 September 1933.

67. VA Bundeskanzleramt, 22/Stmk, Box 5135. Police reports, 'Christliche Arbeitsgemeinschaft in Fohnsdorf', 21 September 1933; reports on Nazi activity in the mine 17 August 1933, 206 155 GD/33.

68. VA Bundeskanzleramt, 22/Stmk, Box 5135. Police report, Pr. ZL.IV–7416/33. 28 September 1933.

follow suit. Organisation would have been dangerous. Managements in working pits were watching for miners carrying provisions into the mines, for this was a clear sign that a strike was on its way. As a result, no preparations were possible. So the absence of food and water alone does not prove the spontaneity of the action. The pattern of the protest provides clearer evidence of this. The scale of the strike was also significant, for after the fourth day over four thousand miners had stopped work and several hundred of these were down the pits. There were no reports of violence between workers and support for the strike was almost unanimous, with the exception of one small mine in West Styria. Wives and families were directly involved, bringing in food and water by whatever means they could. But most important of all, many of these workers who had been or still were members of the Heimwehr took part. In the Seegraben mine 90 per cent of miners had been in the Styrian Heimatschutz at the time of its dissolution in June.[69] Despite this, they went on strike. It could be argued that the protest itself was inspired by the fascists, as part of a campaign to disrupt Styria and so create a situation in which the German government could intervene in Austrian affairs. The role of the miners on strike would not necessarily have been in conflict with their membership of the Heimwehr. There is little doubt that initially this was the case. But the attempt to extend the strike failed everywhere except Fohnsdorf, one of the few pits in which miners had resisted the Independent Union and retained Free Trade Union representation. At Seegraben, which had been a veritable Heimatschutz nest in June 1933, the strikers turned on their Independent Union shop stewards and refused to allow them to negotiate with the management.[70] Whatever the company may have hoped to achieve from the strike, it was finally faced with defeat.

The miners' strike was yet another example of the pattern of workers' protest which had dominated Styrian heavy industry for almost ten years. The socialist trade union movement had failed to retain the support of workers in the mines and factories, but this had not prevented spontaneous and large-scale strikes from breaking out. Styrian workers remained basically unpredictable. The Eifler plan of 1931 had pointed this out, when it said that in the mining areas any Schutzbund response to a Heimwehr putsch would have to be based on the attitude of the miners themselves at the time: no-one could be sure whom they would support or

69. *Arbeiterwille*, 15 September 1933.
70. Ibid.

how.[71] The Alpine Montangesellschaft workers were notorious within the socialist movement for their lack of organisation and inability to protect themselves and yet it was in this company that the major illegal strike wave had broken out. In the eyes of the Jungfront members this was additional proof that their own policy of sharpening resistance to the authoritarianism of the state and mounting a winter offensive through the general strike had a chance of success, a greater chance than the executive's policy of 'wait and see'. Throughout the winter of 1933–4 the young socialists continued their campaign of leafleting and arguing in favour of a general strike, which they knew could not succeed without the support of the party executive.[72] The argument within the party was still going on when, on 12 February 1934, government troops attacked its buildings, arrested its leaders and banned its activities.

The civil war of 1934 is a broad enough topic to warrant its own study. The most obvious questions it raises concern the behaviour of the party executive, who, having warned of the possibilities of a concerted attack upon the party, appear to have been unprepared when that attack actually took place. According to the Eifler plan, the prime function of the Schutzbund was to defend the working class should just such a situation arise. Despite this, orders to mobilise this highly centralised machine were given too late. The police were able to arrest many of the most important leaders before battle commenced. Others went into hiding or fled. The entire military structure of the Schutzbund had been based on discipline and hierarchy, in which orders came from Vienna and were carried out in the provinces as well as the city. But in the chaos the movement had been figuratively decapitated, leaving each region to fend for itself. As a result the most serious fighting took place not only in Vienna, where the strength of the socialist movement lay, but also in Linz and Styria, where the Left opposition had been active amongst the rank-and-file members.

The attack in Styria began at midday on 12 February when police cordoned off main roads in the north of the province and began searching the houses of all Social Democratic activists and former Schutzbund members.[73] A few hours later they reported heavy

71. Vlcek, 'Der Republikanische Schutzbund', p. 520.
72. VA Bundeskanzleramt, 22/Stmk, Box 5135. Police report, 237 397/33. 11 November 1933.
73. The archives on the fighting were unavailable when I completed my research. Footnotes refer to a photocopy held in the Styrian Arbeiterkammer of the *Chronik des Landesgendarmerie Kommandos für Steiermark*. These are dated, but have no reference numbers. References refer to this copy. *Chronik*, pp. 7–8.

fighting in Graz, Bruck and Gösting and strikes in the paper factories, electricity works and machine rooms.[74] The call for a general strike went out, but only in Styria. Even here, the trains kept running, because railway workers refused to heed the call. Without the railway workers, no general strike could succeed. Without a national general strike the provincial protest had no chance of success. Fighting was concentrated in Graz where Otto Fischer led an attack on the central police station on the Hackhergasse, firing from the school opposite and killing six policemen, before being forced to flee when troop reinforcements arrived.[75] His group of Schutzbündler made their way along the railway tracks to Gösting where in the early hours of the morning they opened attack from two sides on the local police station, forcing those inside to put up barricades. The battle at Gösting lasted for over an hour, as forty or fifty Schutzbündler surrounded the building. One of them was killed and seven others wounded. At about 7 am a company of Alpine Jäger arrived in the town, followed by a company from the Graz Heimwehr. The Schutzbündler dispersed through the houses of glassworkers nearby, but twenty of them were arrested. The rest made for the hills.[76]

In Köflach all work in the mines and glass factories stopped at midday on 12 February. A hundred armed Schutzbündler seized the railway station and held off police. Army troops were mobilised. An infantry company arrived in the town on 14 February armed with seven machine-guns and a mortar thrower. By this time the Schutzbündler had moved from the station to one of the local glass factories. The police estimated that 1,000 armed men were inside the building and threatened to use mortar fire if they did not come out. Whilst shouted negotiations were taking place, the Schutzbündler left by a backdoor. The police found the building empty, except for one light machine-gun, six rifles, a hand-grenade and several empty boxes of ammunition.[77]

The most intense fighting took place in Bruck an der Mur where a strike broke out at the Felten and Guilleaume works at midday on the 12th. Soldiers went into the steel mill and three workers were killed. As the troops tried to withdraw, a group of thirty or forty

74. Ibid., p. 8.

75. Duczynska, *Workers in Arms*, pp. 174–5. Otto Fischer was badly wounded and captured during the fighting. One of his legs was amputated in prison hospital. He managed to escape by feigning madness and, having procured an artifical limb, travelled across Europe to Russia, where he remained until after the war.

76. *Chronik*, pp. 16–18.

77. Ibid., p. 25.

Schutzbündler opened fire from outside, pinning them back. Another group attacked the police station, whilst 600 men in Kapfenberg prevented reinforcements being sent from there. The main Schutzbund force took over the Schloßberg, where they fired down on troops with rifles, machine-guns and hand-grenades. The army brought in mortar throwers and bombarded the hilltop, but they made little headway.[78] As night fell the town was left in darkness and without water as electricity and water workers cut off supplies. Fighting continued until the early hours of the morning when troops stormed the Schloßberg. The Schutzbündler withdrew into the woods towards Oberaich, where they remained for three days before dispersing. Kolomann Wallisch, who had led the Schutzbund attack, was arrested in Frohnleiten on the 18th, court-martialled and hanged in Leoben before midnight on the same day.[79] Josef Stanek, secretary of the Styrian Social Democratic Party, was hanged a day earlier.

The fighting in Styria was the most bitter and widespread of the civil war. Not only in Bruck and Graz, but also in Leoben, Donawitz, Mürzzuschlag and many other towns along the industrial belt, workers resisted the government offensive. If the police reports are to be believed, the number of people who took part was greater than estimates of Schutzbund strength. In the end 1,600 people were arrested, an untold number killed and wounded and two men, Stanek and Wallisch, hanged. The Styrian labour movement was finally crushed in February 1934, but not without a violent struggle.

78. Ibid., pp. 28–33.
79. Duczynska, *Workers in Arms*, p. 174. The police said that they realised the propaganda value of capturing Wallisch and broadcast the news of his arrest in all areas where fighting took place on 14 February, three days before they actually captured him. *Chronik*, pp. 38–42.

Conclusion

Two years before the outbreak of the Spanish Civil War workers in Austria fought an armed battle against fascism. In contrast with those later events in Spain, the Austrian Civil War was short, lasting for only four days. During the fighting many Social Democratic leaders fled abroad and the remainder were either killed, arrested or went into hiding. The party was outlawed and its newspapers and organisations closed. In May 1934 the government introduced a corporate constitution which announced a 'Social, Christian, German State, Austria, founded upon estates under a strong authoritarian leadership'.[1] The parliamentary democracy of the First Republic was displaced by 'Austro-fascism'.

The Austrian labour movement ultimately suffered a similar fate to labour movements across Europe. It was smashed by fascism, in this case fascism in Catholic garb.[2] Its failure was part of a wider political battle. But there had been reason in the 1920s to hope that workers in this country would have been more prepared to face the onslaught of a right-wing attack. Since 1919 the Social Democratic Party had followed a policy which many believed to be the salvation for socialism, a midway path between the limitations of social reformism and the excesses of bolshevism. It had accepted the principles of parliamentary democracy, rejecting Lenin's dictatorship of the proletariat, and, abiding by the rules, had withdrawn into opposition when faced with electoral defeat. Unlike the German Social Democratic Party, it did not subsequently compromise its position by re-entering coalition government. In this way, party leaders retained the mantle of radicalism they had somewhat unjus-

1. Charles A. Gulick, *Austria from Habsburg to Hitler*, 2 vols. (Berkeley, California, 1948), vol. 2, p. 1404.
2. The nature of the *Ständestaat*, the corporate state which existed in Austria from 1934 until *Anschluß* in 1938, is a matter of heated debate. It is often described as a conservative dictatorship which adopted the trappings of fascism. My own view is that it was a distinct form of Austro-fascism which developed within Christian Social and Heimwehr circles. See Jill Lewis 'Conservatives and Fascists in Austria, 1918–34', in Martin Blinkhorn (ed.), *Fascists and Conservatives. The Radical Right and the Establishment in Twentieth-Century Europe* (London, 1990), pp. 97–117.

tifiably assumed at the end of the war.[3] They continued to campaign for radical policies. In parliament socialist deputies fought to protect tenants' rights and welfare reforms, untinged by the stigmas of retreat and political collaboration which fell upon their German comrades. By 1927 the party headed one of the strongest socialist movements in Europe in terms of membership per capita of the population. It had not only the largest representation in parliament but boasted a membership of over 10 per cent of all Austrians. Its organisations were broad-based and disciplined. Again in contrast to Germany, it never faced serious competition from rival left-wing groups: the Austrian Communist Party remained weak throughout the First Republic, unable to challenge the political authority of Otto Bauer and the SDAP leadership. The failure of Austrian socialism cannot be attributed to factionalism or internal division.

Nor was the party inactive. It strove to exploit its political power in opposition, rejecting the conventional impotence of parties which are outside of government. Its greatest glory was Vienna. Within the confines of the capital a socialist council harnessed the many talents of party intellectuals to reorganise the city's budget, introducing progressive taxation and accumulating revenue which it invested in bricks and mortar. Homes, hospitals and schools were built, clinics and day-centres were opened. The city council declared new holidays in celebration of left-wing causes. For a time Vienna appeared to be a living example of socialism in action. It seemed to prove that in any economy, even one as shaky as that of Austria, government could administer effectively to provide for the needs of workers and their families. In the 1920s Austro–Marxism became synonymous with municipal socialism, backed by a large and active membership. From its base in Vienna the party campaigned to win a national election and extend its policies across Austria.

But the transition from government to opposition had involved an implicit change in the party's concept of socialism. In 1919 Otto Bauer had argued that socialist revolution came in two stages. The first, the political stage, would bring the working class to power.

---

3. Christian Fleck has argued that many young intellectuals were influenced by Friedrich Adler's decision to remain within the SDAP rather than join the new Communist Party in 1919. Adler's assassination of the prime minister in 1916 was the symbol of the revolutionary spirit for many. Christian Fleck, 'Zur Einführung', in Maria Jahoda, *Arbeitslose bei der Arbeit. Die Nachfolgestudie zu 'Marienthal' aus dem Jahr 1938*, trans. Hans Georg Zilian, ed. Christian Fleck (Frankfurt am Main, 1989), pp. ix–x.

The second, the social and economic stage, would allow the economic reorganisation of capital and the education of workers which led to socialism itself. The socialisation of industry and banking and worker participation in management, leading to worker control, were all pre-requisites of the ultimate goal. In the chaos of 1919 it appeared that the first stage was complete. But, after defeat in the election of 1920, this was obviously not the case. The short-term goal became political or rather electoral victory. This was a dubious quest for a party which professed Marxism and had earlier argued that the state represented the interests of the dominant economic class. Bauer's explanation was the 'Balance of Class Forces', a theory which allowed for the independence of the state from class domination in specific circumstances: when the strength of the working class balanced that of the bourgeoisie. At such times a socialist party could take power through the electoral process and put through economic and social reforms, in the knowledge that the state could enact them. But the class balance could not be taken for granted. Working-class strength needed protection, which the party's paramilitary organisation, the Schutzbund, was designed to provide. Young socialist men trained weekly and prepared to defend the Republic and the movement against any right-wing attacks. In 1926 Bauer warned the party conference that this would be most likely to occur after the SDAP had won power through the ballot box.[4]

The theoretical basis for this early development of 'Bonapartism' may be debatable, but, without a doubt, the theory itself was completely inappropriate as a class analysis of the First Austrian Republic. The power of the workers was great after the war and was represented by the party and the Free Trade Unions. Conversely, the bourgeois parties were in disarray, divided and weak. The employers' position had been undermined by economic dislocation, triggered by the break-up of the Empire, and by the militancy of the workforce. But this situation changed rapidly. By 1923 the bourgeoisie had re-grouped, or at least re-aligned. The SDAP was the largest party in the Republic, but opposition to it was united. Anti-socialist parties blocked its path to government and even fought one election on a single anti-socialist ticket. When the socialists continued to make electoral gains, successive right-wing governments stripped away democratic rights and finally destroyed the party and the Republic.

SDAP leaders were faced with a dilemma which arose from their

4. Anson Rabinbach, *The Crisis of Austrian Socialism* (Chicago, 1983), pp. 46–6.

attempts to reconcile the party's philosophy of class conflict with its new faith in constitutional government. The Schutzbund represented the former, municipal socialism the latter. The Schutzbund had been set up to provide worker protection shortly after the army had reverted to bourgeois control. Its very existence amounted to a tacit acceptance of a shift in class forces away from the working class, but this was never acknowledged. It also raised difficulties for the party's democratic goals. As long as the SDAP maintained a paramilitary wing and a revolutionary vocabulary, it could be accused of undermining democracy and increasing political polarisation. Without their own paramilitary, party members, marches and organisations were physically vulnerable to outside aggression. This contradiction fostered conflicting views on the role of the Schutzbund within the party which reached a peak after 1927. As civil violence increased party leaders became more reluctant to call out the force and increasingly afraid of any action its members might take on their own initiative. They placed it under tighter executive control and reduced its political role, creating dissatisfaction amongst younger members and inciting a row between the Schutzbund's former commander, Körner, and his successor, Eifler. Körner believed that in any forthcoming civil war the Schutzbund should be based in working-class communities and should employ guerilla tactics, including political propaganda. He recognised that the battle would be political, not just military. Eifler, backed by the party executive, rejected this, arguing that 'it is absolutely wrong to despair of training the Schutzbund to be equal to a regular conventional fight'.[5] His view did not reflect misplaced optimism, as his own figures for military personnel on both sides showed. It arose from a deep-seated reluctance to accept that civil war was a likely possibility and a decreasing faith in the ability of the socialists to win. Civil war, party leaders correctly believed, would destroy the party as well as the Republic. Class conflict was only acceptable as long as it did not escalate into class war.

Conversely the leadership's faith in the constitutional road to power remained firm up to and including the last few years of democracy. After the prorogation of parliament in March 1933, attempts were made to find a compromise with the authoritarian government which would maintain the legal framework of democracy, even if that meant accepting its temporary suspension. Otto Bauer published a series of articles in January 1934 in which he

5. Ilona Duczynska, *Workers in Arms*, p. 101.

sought to moderate the differences between aspects of the corporate state and socialist principles.[6] It was a desperate last-minute attempt to preserve the party's political existence and was spurred by the belief that Nazism was a greater threat than Catholic Corporatism. By this time the notion of the 'Balance of Class Forces' was obviously dead, or at least held in abeyance. But the concept itself had been fundamental to Austrian socialist thinking for the previous fifteen years and had underpinned the party's belief in parliamentary democracy. It had nurtured the policy of Red Vienna and municipal socialism. More important, it had allowed party leaders to confuse their tactics for achieving socialism with the goal itself. They overestimated the strengths of the movement and were blind to its increasing weakness outside the capital. In Vienna the party was able to create an all-embracing political and social welfare system which proclaimed the unity and strength of the working class. But it was protected by numbers and by a tight-knit organisation which did not and could not exist outside the capital. The SDAP in Vienna was a mass party which advocated political participation and action, but maintained a rigid and intransigent hierarchy. Even for most Viennese members, participation was limited to cultural and social activities. Policy decisions were made by the leadership. Debate at the lower level was sometimes stifled and seldom encouraged. This was a problem in a party which was undergoing drastic changes in both philosophy and strategy. The leadership's solution was to advocate education and instruction, to seek progress through direction. But the policies it pursued stemmed from a complex and, at times, ambiguous theory in which it tried to reconcile its philosophy with its practice. It was perplexing for rank-and-file members, particularly for those who lived outside the capital, and became increasingly so after 1927.

The growth of support for the SDAP in the Republic was not due to its theory, but the practical benefits the socialist Viennese council brought to its members. In the 1920s the gap between socialism in Vienna and socialism in the provinces actually widened. Working-class membership of the party rose in the capital, but fell elsewhere and even the increase in electoral support displayed disturbing regional variations. Party leaders were aware of this, but as long as they continued to follow party policy, there was little that they could do to alter it. Their political power was limited. The 'middle road to socialism' was based on municipal socialism and the development of a socially and politically educated working

6. Rabinbach, *Crisis of Austrian Socialism*, p. 169.

class, areas over which the party had some control. It had no power to carry out radical economic policies, nor even to ensure the enforcement of existing labour legislation. The 'Propaganda der Tat', or 'Living Propaganda', set the limits of its policy to those areas over which it did have control. The Viennese experiment was, therefore, based on fiscal and social welfare reforms. The party could offer little protection to supporters outside the capital, to whom it rarely listened and whom it seldom understood. It could not offer solutions to the problems of high unemployment and employer harassment. In defeat it abandoned the economic basis of its theory in favour of reformism.

It was in these circumstances that working-class fascism seemed to evolve in the late 1920s. In 1928 the Free Trade Unions were replaced as the main representatives of organised labour in the Upper Styrian metal industry by a fascist union, the Independent Union. In the 1930 general election this area returned a Heimwehr member to parliament, allowing his party to take up other parliamentary seats on the strength of his overall majority. In 1931 a fascist putsch attempt began and ended in Upper Styria. Fascist leaders argued that the workers had become disillusioned by socialism and had turned to fascism instead.

The events of 1931 and February 1934 proved conclusively that this was not the case. The growth of the Heimwehr in the area indicated the weakness of the labour movement in the province and the failure of the SDAP to address the problems of its members. Styria was not a province in which the mass of working people became ideologically committed to fascism. Despite the growth of the Independent Union and its links with fascism through the Heimwehr and the National Socialist Party, the majority of working-class people in the province continued to support the Social Democratic Party up to and including the civil war. But the party did not produce policies which were directed at these members. Political membership in the province was qualitatively different from Vienna. Party organisation was weaker and the wide variety of extra-mural activities which the Social Democrats set up in the capital was largely missing in the provinces. Clubs and societies did exist, but their role in working-class life was more limited. More important, the economic influence which the party had in Vienna, through its control of the metropolitan council, was a unique phenomenon. Elsewhere in Austria, Social Democratic councils had to content themselves with minor public welfare and expenditure schemes, which did little to alter the lives of the majority of their supporters. In many ways, the provinces in general and Styria in particular suffered from the party executive's dominance, its preoccupation with Vienna and its failure to develop a political strategy which could maintain and even extend support in the countryside. The whole emphasis of the leadership was to succeed in Vienna and build up support in the rest of the country, based on that success.

Such a policy was politically naive. There was no area outside of Vienna where the working class formed a large enough proportion of the population to challenge the political control of the bourgeois parties. In Styria the party would have had to increase its share of the vote in local elections by roughly 50 per cent to have taken over the provincial government. In a province where the working class accounted for at most 40 per cent of the population such a goal was impossible. The success which the provincial party did have in maintaining its share of the vote despite fierce and active opposition by the bourgeois parties and the industrial employers, was, in the circumstances, notable. But it was not enough to introduce municipal socialism locally, nor to help the party to win power nationally.

The failure of the Styrian labour movement was, therefore, not essentially political, although the policies of the national executive were in many ways unsuited to a province in which the working class was in a minority and had been subjected to a long campaign of anti-socialist tactics. There was little point in constant warnings that protection would come only from the law, for in Styria both the local government and the police had long shown themselves unwilling to provide such protection. For this reason, the Left opposition, which was primarily a movement of the younger generation of more militant party activists, drew support from outside this group in Styria. It set up a network of trade union activists who were committed to an armed defence of the socialist movement, at a time when the party executive was preaching caution. It was the influence of this group which was largely responsible for the level of resistance which took place in Styria in February 1934.

The labour movement was a failure in the economic sphere. The unions could not protect their members. Despite the size of the total industrial workforce in the province, unions in the most important sector, the iron and steel industry, were unable to establish themselves. As a result, trade unions in many other sectors of the economy were also vulnerable to attack. The example of the Alpine Montangesellschaft, which managed to contravene many of the provisions of the postwar industrial legislation, proved very attractive to other steel companies and eventually to employers in the building trade and wood industry. The first concerted attacks on the status of trade unions and on the eight-hour day were mounted in Styria by the Alpine Montangesellschaft. The Independent Union was sponsored by the company and drew most of its members from the iron and steel industry of Upper Styria. This defeat of the Free Trade Union movement in Styria had a profound effect on the entire Austrian labour movement.

The reasons for the weakness of the trade unions in Styria were partly a consequence of the structure of industry and partly a consequence of the economic crises of the interwar years. The workers were geographically fragmented, making united action more difficult. Most jobs were found in only a handful of industries, of which the metal industry was by far the most important. In contrast to the division of working-class strength, the scale of these industries was such that one company, the Alpine Montangesellschaft, had an over-riding influence on employer policy in the province. The low level of skill required by the dominant industries, including not only the metal industry, but also the wood industry, meant that unsatisfactory workers could be replaced by new recruits when the labour market was balanced in the employers' favour. In the nineteenth century this had enabled employers to repress the development of trade unions and in the twentieth century it allowed them to exert pressure on workers not only to abandon the Free Trade Unions, but also to join the fascist-based Independent Union.

The Revolution and the legislation of the first democratically elected government had not altered class relations in the province. Although extensive social legislation was passed on working conditions, pay and workers' rights, these had only limited effects in Styria. The Revolution, which had led to the introduction of parliamentary democracy and thus, indirectly, to the social welfare legislation, marked the high point of working-class politics in the country. The legislation itself reflected this strength. But without a strong trade union movement many of these laws could not be enforced. In Styria the Free Trade Unions were only briefly in a position to ensure such implementation. By 1925 their influence had waned as unemployment increased. This led to intense competition for jobs and provided the employers with an opportunity to pick and choose. By 1929 a job applicant had to prove his suitability by producing a Heimwehr membership card. From then on the economic battle between the unions and employers escalated into a political battle between fascism and socialism.

The structure of industry also affected the impact of unemployment in the province. The collapse of the Empire and the disruption of trade with eastern Europe led to a decline in the metal industry. As a result unemployment in Styria was particularly high in the 1920s even before the international depression of the 1930s. Wages were low, whilst competition for jobs was high. It was during this period, at least five years before the national attack on the labour movement, that working-class organisation in the province began to crumble. Whilst the political commitment to the Social Democratic Party continued, membership of the Free Trade Unions fell drastically and once this had happened there was room for an alternative employer-orientated movement to grow.

There is no doubt that the Independent Unions and thus the apparent working-class support for fascism would have failed without the active support of the Alpine Montangesellschaft. Workers were cajoled rather than wooed into the fascist camp and their commitment lasted in most cases only as long as their jobs. The anti-socialist forces were unable to rely on workers who were notionally members of the Heimwehr either in 1931 or in 1934. At the same time, the company's support for both the fascism of the Pfrimer section of the Heimwehr and later for the National Socialist Party was constant. In the early years of the Republic the partnership between the Alpine Montangesellschaft and the Heimwehr was based on a common antipathy to strikes and trade unionism. By 1929 this had escalated into mutual opposition to socialism and eventually to the Republic itself. For the management the cost of the social welfare legislation was the main catalyst for its persecution of Social Democratic workers, for it rightly identified the socialist party as the main obstacle to the removal of the legislation on collective bargaining and the eight-hour day. At the personal level there is strong evidence to suggest that many senior members of the management were ideologically committed to fascism even before Hitler's rise to power in Germany. The role of the Alpine Montangesellschaft suggests that the relationship between big business and fascism was somewhat closer than some writers would have one believe. Although the Alpine Montangesellschaft was based in Austria, it was a subsidiary of the German Vereinigte Stahlwerk and imported many of its ideas on labour relations from the mother company. The founding of the DINTA in 1927, with its philosophy of corporatist industrial relations, was the first step towards industrial fascism in the country. It was part of a policy to reassert control over workers, to divert political aggression away from the workplace and direct it against the Social Democratic Party.

Appendix

Table 1 Membership of the Social Democratic Party, 1919–1932

Year		Austria	Styria	Vienna
June	1919	332,391	56,396	105,431
	1920	335,863	53,562	123,684
	1921	491,150	73,853	188,379
	1922	553,022	78,697	204,698
	1923	514,273	68,738	199,115
	1924	565,124	59,804	266,415
	1925	566,124	49,849	301,744
	1926	592,346	53,242	324,525
December	1926	595,417	53,977	330,184
	1927	669,586	59,787	387,677
	1928	713,834	62,552	417,347
	1929	718,056	63,673	418,055
	1930	698,181	60,561	415,170
	1931	653,605	56,510	398,753
	1932	648,497	55,572	400,484

Sources: Protokoll des sozialdemokratischen Parteitages, 1923–6.
   Jb ö Ab 1927, p. 20; 1927, p. 23; 1928, p. 47; 1929, p. 77; 1930, p. 111; 1931,
   p. 83; 1932, p. 85.

Table 2 Trade union membership, 1919–1932

Year	Free Trade Unions		Christian Trade Unions		German Nationalist Trade Unions[2]	
	Austria	Styria	Austria	Styria	Austria	Styria
Jan. 1919	295,147	31,363	20,626	793	26,165	3,400
Jan. 1920	772,146	81,854	29,276	1,848	30,098	7,384
Dec. 1920[1]	900,820	110,141	64,149	3,806	–	–
1921	1,079,777	128,547	78,737	4,084	–	–
1922	1,049,949	128,222	78,105	3,764	–	–
1923	896,763	94,128	79,377	3,969	45,364	–
1924	828,088	73,015	80,128	4,169	46,882	–
1925	807,515	67,569	77,200	4,588	47,019	6,329
1926	756,392	64,589	76,122	4,653	50,858	6,037
1927	772,762	67,074	78,906	5,181	47,877	6,165
1928	766,168	65,610	100,087	8,181	51,247	6,815
1929	737,277	62,216	107,657	9,789	51,250	5,968
1930	655,204	55,570	111,939	10,621	48,899	5,838
1931	582,687	48,104	108,420	10,613	49,645	5,872
1932	520,162	41,855	100,606	10,704	53,376	6,650

[1] All figures after January 1920 are for December.
[2] No figures available between January 1920 and December 1924.

Sources: Stat Hdb Österreich 1921, p. 115; 1923, p. 103; 1924, vol. 4, p. 105; 1924, vol. 5, p. 106; 1925, p. 130; 1926, p. 127; 1927, p. 149; 1928, p. 155; 1929, p. 158; 1930, p. 161; 1931, pp. 162–3; 1932, p. 169; 1933, p. 172.

Table 3 Strikes 1919–1933

Year	Austria			Styria		
	Number of strikes	Number of strikers	Total workforce affected	Number of strikes	Number of strikers	Total workforce affected
1919	151	63,703	69,728	28	20,432	23,878 [1]
1920	329	179,352	198,749	–	–	–
1921	435	207,974	302,259	26	11,039	12,113
1922	381	211,429	306,545	47	13,949	15,202
1923	268	116,669	133,447	24	22,497	23,369
1924	401	268,696	286,287	25	4,147	6,118
1925	287	46,743	56,764	24	5,012	7,619
1926	186	18,624	24,714	13	1,979	2,804
1927	195	28,769	37,454	18	3,145	4,361
1928	242	32,948	44,046	21	4,721	8,230
1929	202	23,799	37,502	10	702	2,788
1930	83	6,170	10,269	3	352	370
1931	56	8,502	11,695	1	130	130
1932	30	5,429	6,622	1	41	41
1933	23	5,034	5,774	2	2,702	2,794

[1] Figures unavailable

Source: *Stat Hdb Österreich* 1921, p. 112; 1923, p. 99; 1924, vol. 4, p. 101; 1924, vol. 5, p. 103; 1925, p. 127; 1926, p. 124; 1927, p. 146; 1928, p. 152; 1929, p. 155; 1930, p. 158; 1931, p. 160; 1932, p. 167; 1933, p. 170; 1935, p. 186.

Table 4 Insured unemployment, 1919–1933

Year	Austria		Vienna		Wiener Neustadt		Linz		Graz[2] (inc. Leoben)	
	i.	r.	i.	r.	i.	r.	i.	r.	i.	r.
1919 June	170,682		127,556		8,100		11,200		8,300	
1920 Jan.	69,427		56,511		947		5,666		1,477	
June	22,403		17,758		399		2,065		705	
1921 Jan.	16,217		12,617		392		1,256		338	
June	11,035		9,726		57		419		104	
1922 Jan.	53,554		16,489		1,157		5,996		1,834	
June	33,355		25,473		1,769		1,629		985	
1923 Jan.	161,227		85,037		12,342		17,482		14,534	
June[1]	92,789		58,218		9,143		7,366		8,129	
1924 Jan.	119,766	150,915	52,142		11,425		17,451		10,827	
June	63,556	91,725	36,587		6,816		6,450		7,731	
1925 Jan.	187,099	219,332	78,013	100,317	16,831	17,347	23,895	25,879	23,750	26,941
June	118,366	149,415	66,720	88,995	12,909	13,482	11,796	13,287	11,088	14,271
1926 Jan.	231,361	253,819	104,434	114,915	19,882	20,337	6,851	31,216	4,609	24,089
June	150,981	173,165	83,643	95,173	16,638	17,110	1,548	17,392	2,069	17,373

1927 Jan.	235,464	269,633	99,453	117,316	22,859	23,390	28,743	31,146	24,380	29,226
June	145,136	168,997	77,754	90,990	14,544	15,270	14,907	16,627	17,129	20,968
1928 Jan.	230,754	260,018	89,247	103,786	20,390	21,020	29,816	32,088	27,976	32,371
June	118,737	140,931	60,757	72,829	12,836	13,450	10,874	12,358	16,897	20,712
1929 Jan.	245,606	275,407	89,264	102,878	21,120	21,968	31,334	34,290	28,667	33,503
June	110,266	133,106	54,620	68,559	14,214	14,872	9,697	11,012	14,687	17,860
1930 Jan.	273,195	308,238	97,638	114,893	25,657	26,645	36,191	38,635	31,311	36,596
June	150,075	179,610	72,762	90,370	16,788	17,619	14,245	16,396	18,288	22,187
1931 Jan.	331,239	374,926	116,905	141,667	27,659	28,823	41,305	44,185	41,793	47,209
June	191,150	230,766	85,250	111,253	19,215	20,024	19,365	21,516	24,120	28,069
1932 Jan.	422,684	358,114	125,458	167,679	30,126	30,286	44,185	46,252	45,323	53,657
June	265,040	327,531	106,990	150,985	25,192	26,064	28,064	30,175	36,617	43,249
1933 Jan.	397,920	478,034	146,547	202,333	31,950	32,656	45,753	48,428	50,414	58,937
June	307,873	380,785	126,682	177,493	25,422	26,299	32,965	35,290	39,463	46,812

r. registered unemployed (figures for 1925 onwards)
i. unemployed receiving benefit.

[1] Figures up to 1922 exclude Burgenland.
[2] Leoben was a separate industrial area before 1924.

Sources: Stat Hdb Österreich 1921, p. 110; 1923, p. 95; 1924, vol. 4, p. 97; 1924, vol. 5, p. 99; 1925, p. 123; 1926, p. 120; 1927, p. 142; 1928, p. 146; 1929, p. 149; 1930, p. 152; 1931, p. 155; 1932, p. 162; 1933, p. 165; 1935, p. 181.

Appendix

Table 5 Comparison of employment and unionisation in the metal industries of Austria and Styria, 1928

	Austria	Styria
Total employment in iron production and processing (including lignite and ore mining)	169,140[1]	34,764[1]
Employment in iron production	37,653[1]	21,278[1]
Employment in iron processing	131,487[1]	13,486[1]
Employment in iron production and processing excluding mining	153,637	24,358[2]
Total employment in mining	15,503[2]	10,406[2]
Employment in iron mining	3,791[2]	3,548[2]
Employment in lignite mining	10,487[2]	6,858[2]
Membership of Metal Workers' union	123,836[3]	9,034[3]
Membership of Miners' Union	8,505[3]	2,925[3]
% total metal workers workforce in union (excluding mines)	80.6	37
% total miners in union	54.86	28
% total iron production and processing workers in union – miners and metal workers	78.24	34.4[3]

[1] Insured workers. *Wirtschaftsstatistisches Handbuch* 1931–2, p. 136, Table 73. *Anzahl der unfallversicherten Arbeiter Österreichs in den Jahren 1926–31*.

[2] Verband der Bergarbeiter Deutschösterreich in Leoben *Bericht des Vorstandes für die Berichtsjahre* 1926/1927/1928 pp. 27–8. Im österreichischen Braun- und Steinkohlen bergbauBeschäftigte, Zahl der Betriebe und Anteil der Arbeiter an der Jahresleistung in Tonnen.

[3] *Jahrbuch des Bundes der Freien Gewerkschaften* 1928, p. 100, Table 10. Gesamtübersicht der Freien Gewerkschaften; p. 107, Table 12. Ortsgruppen und Mitglieder in den Ländern.

Bibliography

UNPUBLISHED SOURCES

Steiermärkisches Landesarchiv, Graz

Präsidialakten, E.91, 21–25, Polizeiberichte
Landesamtsdirektion 1928, Abschnitt 384
Bezirkshauptmannschaft Judenburg 1932
Bezirkshauptmannschaft Donawitz-Leoben 1932

Allgemeines Verwaltungsarchiv, Vienna

Bundeskanzleramt, Staatsamt des Innern und der Justiz
22/Stmk. 1918–1928 Box 5131
        1929–1930 Box 5132
        1931 Box 5133
        1932 Box 5134
        1933 Box 5135
        1934 Box 5136

Documents on the First Republic are now held in Das Archiv der Republik.

Kammer für Arbeiter und Angestellte, Graz

Photocopies of:
Chronik des Gendarmeriepostens Kapfenberg 1933–4
Chronik des Gendarmeriepostens Mürzzuschlag 1933–4
Chronik des Landesgendarmeriekommandos für Steiermark 1933–4

International Institute for Social History, Amsterdam

Kautsky Archiv:
Letters from Kautsky to Friedrich Adler, 1–2 AF
Letters from Kautsky to Otto Bauer, 67
Letters to Kautsky from Otto Bauer 1904–31, KD II 463–534

Bibliography

Interviews

Otto Fischer, 11 October 1976, Vienna
Willi Scholz and Ditto Pölzl, 13 October 1976, Graz
Willi Scholz, 2 June 1977, Liverpool

PUBLISHED SOURCES

Bericht des Gemeinderates der Stadt Bruck an der Mur über seine Tätigkeit in den Funktionsperioden 1919 bis 1922 und 1922 bis 1924. Erstattet vom Bürgermeister Anton Pichler (Im Selbstverlag der Stadtgemeinde Bruck an der Mur. Druck 'Typographia', Graz)

Die Christlichen Gewerkschaften Steiermarks in den Jahren 1928 und 1929, Verantwortlich: Landeskommission der Christlichen Gewerkschaften Steiermarks

Die Ergebnisse der österreichischen Volkszählung vom 22 März 1934, Hrsg. vom Bundesamt für Statistik, Wien, Verlag der österreichischen Staatsdruckerei

Jahrbuch der österreichischen Arbeiterbewegung, Hrsg. von der Parteivertretung der Sozialdemokratischen Partei Deutschösterreichs, Wien: Wiener Volksbuchhandlung, 1927–1932

Jahrbuch des Bundes der Freien Gewerkschaften Österreichs, Hrsg. die Freien Gewerkschaften, Verlag Arbeit und Wirtschaft, Wien, 1928, 1929, 1931, 1932

Jahresbericht der Kammer für Arbeiter und Angestellte Steiermark 1928, 1930, 1931, 1932

Kammer für Arbeiter und Angestellte, Graz, *Rechenschaftsbericht für die Zeit des Bestandes, (Mai 1921 bis Mai 1926),* Verlag für Arbeiter und Angestellte Druck 'Typographia' (Graz, 1926)

Lebensnot, Wohnungselend und Hilfsbedürfigkeit in Graz. Bericht verfaßt über Aufforderung eines Schweizer Hilfsausschusses von Gemeinderat Engelbert Rückl (Graz, 1920) International Institute for Social History, Amsterdam

Lohsmann, Karl, *Programm der Unabhängigen Arbeiterbewegung Österreichs* (Vienna, 1928)

Statistisches Handbuch für die Republik Österreich 1919–1934 (1922 was not published), Hrsg. vom Bundesamt für Statistik, Wien, Verlag der österreichischen Staatsdruckerei

Stenographischer Bericht über die Verhandlungen des steiermärkischen Landtages 1927–34

Verband der Bergarbeiter Deutschösterreichs in Leoben. Bericht des Vorstandes für die Berichtsjahre 1926, 1927, 1928

Wirtschaftsstatistisches Jahrbuch 1925–35, Verlag der Kammer für Arbeiter und Angestellte, Wien

Bibliography

Newspapers and Periodicals

Arbeiterwille: Organ des arbeitenden Volkes für Steiermark und Kärnten, 1920–33

Arbeiter-Zeitung: Zentralorgan der österreichischen Sozialdemokratie

Arbeit und Wirtschaft: Organ der Freien Gewerkschaften (Vienna), 1928–33

Der Kampf: Sozialdemokratische Monatsschrift (Vienna), 1918–33

Neue Freie Presse

Österreichische Metallarbeiter: Zentral Organ der österreichischen Metallarbeiter (in 1930 this became the *Österreichische Berg- und Metallarbeiter*)

Österreichische Grenzwacht

Steyer Tagblatt

Wiener Neueste Nachrichten

Wiener Sonn- und Montagszeitung

Selections of the following from the Newspaper Archive, Kammer für Arbeiter und Angestellte, Vienna, covering the years 1920–1934

Alpinepost

Der Tag

Der Unabhängige Gewerkschafter, Leoben

Grazer Tagblatt

Neues Montagblatt

Neues Wiener Tagblatt

Tagespost

Secondary Sources

Adler, Alois, *Die Christlichsoziale Bewegung in der Steiermark von den ständischen Anfängen zur Volkspartei* (Graz, 1956)

Aggermann, Franz, 'Die Arbeitsverhältnisse im Bergbau', in Ferdinand Hanusch and Emmanuel Adler et al. (eds.), *Die Regelung der Arbeitesverhältnisse im Kriege* (Vienna, 1927), pp. 171–221

Ahrer, Jakob, *Erlebte Zeitgeschichte* (Vienna, 1930)

Ausch, Karl, *Als die Banken fielen* (Frankfurt am Main, 1968)

Austria: Facts and Figures (Federal Press Service, Vienna, 1955)

Basch, A. and J. Dvoracek, *Austria and its Economic Existence* (Prague, 1925)

Bauböck, Rainer, *Wohnungspolitik im sozialdemokratischen Wien, 1919–34* (Vienna, 1980)

Bauer, Otto (alias Heinrich Weber), *Die russische Revolution und das europäische Proletariat* (Vienna, 1917)

——, 'Die Bolschewiki und wir' *Der Kampf*, March 1918, pp. 137ff.

Bauer, Otto, *Der Weg zum Sozialismus* (Berlin, 1919) (originally published in the *Arbeiter-Zeitung* in January 1919)

——, *Bolschewismus oder Sozialdemokratie?* (Vienna, 1920)

——, *The Austrian Revolution*, trans. J.H. Stenning, (abridged New York, 1970)

Beller, Stephen, *Vienna and the Jews* (Cambridge, 1989)

Benedikt, Heinrich (ed.), *Die Geschichte der Republik Österreich* (Vienna, 1954)

Blinkhorn, Martin (ed.), *Fascists and Conservatives. The Radical Right and the Establishment in Twentieth-Century Europe* (London, 1990)

Bottomore, T. and P. Good, *Austro–Marxism* (Oxford, 1978)

Botz, Gerhard, 'Gewalt und politisch-gesellschaftlicher Konflikt in der Ersten Republik (1918 bis 1933)', *Österreichische Zeitschrift für Politikwissenschaft*, 1975, pp. 511–34

——, 'Austro–Marxist Interpretation of Fascism', *Journal of Contemporary History*, vol. 11, no. 4 (October 1976), pp. 129–56

——, *Gewalt in der Politik* (Munich, 1976)

Boyer, John W., *Political Radicalism in Late Imperial Vienna. Origins of the Christian Social Movement, 1848–1897* (Chicago, 1981)

Braunthal, Julius, 'Auf dem Weg zur Macht', *Der Kampf* (XVI) 1923, pp. 345–8

——, *The Tragedy of Austria* (London, 1948)

Braverman, Harry, *Labor and Monopoly Capital* (New York and London, 1974)

Brusatti, Alois (ed.), 'Die wirtschaftliche Entwicklung', vol. 1 of A. Wandruszka, and P. Urbanitsch (eds.), *Die Habsburg Monarchie 1848–1918* (Vienna, 1973)

Bunzel, Julius, *Die Anfänge der Grazer Arbeiterbewegung in der Steiermark* (Leipzig, 1914)

Buttinger, Josef, *In the Twilight of Socialism* (New York, 1953)

Carsten, F.L., *Revolution in Central Europe* (London, 1972)

——, *Fascist Movements in Austria: From Schönerer to Hitler* (London, 1977)

Childers, Thomas, *The Nazi Voter: The Social Foundations of Fascism in Germany 1919–1933* (Chapel Hill, 1983)

Chladek, P.P., 'Geschichte und Probleme der Eisenindustrie in der Steiermark' (unpublished PhD thesis, Vienna, 1955)

Danneberg, R., *Das Neue Wien* (Vienna, 1926)

——, *New Vienna*, trans. H.J. Stenning (London, 1931)

Deutsch, Julius, *Ein Weiter Weg: Lebenserinnerungen* (Vienna, 1960)

——, *Geschichte der österreichischen Gewerkschaftsbewegung*, 2 vols. (Vienna, 1932: reprinted Glashutten/Ts. 1975)

Diamant, Alfred, *Austrian Catholics and the First Republic: Democracy, Capitalism and the Social Order, 1918–34* (Princeton, 1960)

Docherty, Charles, *Steel and Steelworks: the sons of Vulcan* (London, 1983)

Duczynska, Ilona, *Der demokratische Bolschewik* (Munich, 1975)

——, *Workers in Arms* (New York and London, 1978) (this is an abridged version of the German original, *Der demokratische Bolschewik*)

Edmondson, C. Earl, 'The Heimwehr and Austrian Politics, 1918–1934', PhD thesis, Duke University, 1966

——, *The Heimwehr and Austrian Politics, 1918–36* (Athens, Georgia, 1978)

Engels, Friedrich, 'The Origins of the Family, Private Property and the State', in *Karl Marx and Friedrich Engels: Selected Works*, with an introduction by V.I. Lenin (London, 1968: original edn, Progress Publishers, Moscow), pp. 455–593

Erben, Fritz, Maja Loehr, and Hans Riehl (eds.), *Die Alpine Montangesellschaft* (Vienna, 1931) (the book was written by members of the Alpine management to commemmorate the firm's fiftieth birthday)

Feldman, G., *Iron and Steel in the German Inflation 1916–1923* (Princeton, 1977)

Fischer, Ernst, *Erinnerungen und Reflexionen* (Hamburg, 1969)

——, *An Opposing Man*, trans. Peter and Betty Ross, with an introduction by John Berger (London, 1974) (This English edition of Fischer's autobiography is a slightly revised version of the German original, *Erinnerungen und Reflexionen*)

Fyrth, H.J. and H. Collins, *The Foundry Workers* (Manchester, 1958)

Garamvölgyi, Judit, *Betriebsräte und sozialer Wandel in Österreich 1919/20* (Vienna, 1983)

Geary, Dick, *European Labour Protest, 1848–1939* (London, 1981)

——, 'Identifying Militancy: the Assessment of Working-class Attitudes towards State and Society', in R.J. Evans (ed.), *The German Working Class, 1888–1933* (London, 1982), pp. 220–46

Gedye, G.E.R., *Fallen Bastions: The Central European Tragedy* (London, 1939)

Gerlich, Rudolf, *Die gescheiterte Alternative: Sozialisierung in Österreich nach dem ersten Weltkrieg* (Vienna, 1980)

Goode, Patrick, *Karl Korsch: a Study in Western Marxism* (London, 1979)

Gross, N.T., 'Industrialisation in Austria in the nineteenth century', (unpublished PhD thesis, University of California, 1966)

——, 'The Habsburg Monarchy 1750–1914', in C.M. Cipolla (ed.), *The Fontana Economic History of Europe. Vol. 4. The Emergence of Industrial Societies, No. 1* (London, 1973), pp. 228–78

Gruber, Helmut, 'Socialist Party Culture and the Realities of Working-Class Life in Red Vienna', in Anson Rabinbach (ed.), *The Austrian Socialist Experiment: Social Democracy and Austromarxism, 1918–1934* (Boulder and London, 1985), pp. 223–46

Gulick, Charles, A., *Austria from Habsburg to Hitler*, 2 vols. (Berkeley, California, 1948)

Haas, Hans, 'Otto Bauer und der Anschluß 1918–1919', in Helmut Konrad (ed.), *Sozialdemokratie und Anschluß, Historische Wurzeln Anschluß 1918 und 1938 Nachwirkungen* (Vienna, 1978), pp. 36–44

Hamilton, Richard F., *Who Voted for Hitler?* (Princeton, 1982)

Hannak, Jacques, *Johannes Schober: Mittelweg in die Katastrophe* (Vienna, 1966)

Hanusch, Ferdinand and Adler, Emmanuel (eds.), *Die Regelung der*

Bibliography

Arbeitsverhältnisse während des Krieges. Carnegie-Stiftung fur Internationalen Frieden. Wirtschafts- und Sozialgeschichte des Weltkrieges Österreichische und Ungarische Serie (Vienna, 1927)

Hautmann, Hans, *Die Anfänge der Linksradikalen Bewegung und der Kommunistischen Partei Deutschösterreichs* (Vienna, 1970)

Hautmann, Hans and Rudolf Hautmann, *Die Gemeindebauten des Roten Wien, 1919–1934* (Vienna, 1980)

Hautmann, Hans and Rudolf Kropf, *Die österreichische Arbeiterbewegung vom Vormärz bis 1945* (Vienna, 1974)

Hinteregger, Robert, 'Die Steiermark 1918/19' (unpublished PhD thesis, Graz, 1971)

——, 'Graz zwischen Wohlfahrtausschuss und Räteherrschaft', *Historisches Jahrbuch der Stadt Graz*, 7–8 (1975), pp. 213–39

——, 'Abwehrmaßnahmen an der untersteirischen Grenze 1918–19', *Zeitschrift des Historischen Vereines für Steiermark*, 66, 1976, pp. 213–48

Hinteregger, Robert, K. Müller, E. Staudinger, *Auf dem Weg in die Freiheit. Anstöße zu einer steirischen Zeitgeschichte* (Graz, 1984)

Hofmann, Josef, *Der Pfrimer Putsch: der steierische Heimwehrprozeß des Jahres 1931* (Vienna, 1965)

Hubbard, William, 'Politics and Society in a Central European City: Graz, Austria, 1861–1918', *Canadian Journal of History*, 1970, pp. 25–45

Huber, Edmund, 'Die Geschichte der österreichischen Metallarbeiterschaft, 1914–34' (unpublished PhD thesis, Vienna, 1951)

Hufton, Olwen, 'Women in Revolution', *Past and Present*, no. 53, 1973, p. 93

Hwaletz Otto et al., *Bergmann oder Werkssoldat. Eisenerz als Fallbeispiel industrieller Politik* (Graz, 1984)

Hyman, Richard, *Strikes* (London, 1972)

International Labour Office, *The Social Aspects of Rationalisation. Introductory Study* (Geneva, 1931)

Jahoda, Maria, Paul F. Lazarsfeld and Hans Zeisel, *Marienthal: The Sociography of an Unemployed Community* (London, 1972)

Jahoda, Maria, *Arbeitslose bei der Arbeit. Die Nachfolgestudie zu 'Marienthal' aus dem Jahr 1938*, trans. Hans Georg Zilian, ed. Christian Fleck (Frankfurt am Main, 1989)

Jedlicka, Ludwig, 'The Austrian Heimwehr', *Journal of Contemporary History*, vol. 1, no. 1, 1966, pp. 127–44

Jelavich, Barbara, *Modern Austria. Empire and Republic 1800–1980* (Cambridge, 1987)

Joyce, Patrick, *Work, Society and Politics. The Culture of the Factory in Late Victorian England* (London, 1980)

Kele, Max H., *Nazis and Workers: National Socialist Appeal to German Labour 1919–1933* (Chapel Hill, 1972)

Kerekes, Lajos, *Abenddämmerung einer Demokratie: Mussolini, Gömbös und die Heimwehr* (Vienna, 1966)

Kitchen, Martin, *Fascism* (London, 1976)

——, *The Coming of Austrian Fascism* (London, 1980)

Klemperer, Klement von, *Ignaz Seipel* (Princeton, 1972)

Klenner, Fritz, *Die österreichischen Gewerkschaften* 2 vols. (Vienna, 1953)

Knapp, Vincent J., *Austrian Social Democracy, 1889–1914* (Washington, 1980)

Knowles, K.C.J.C., *Strikes: a Study in Industrial Conflict* (London, 1952)

Kreisky, Bruno, *Zwischen den Zeiten. Erinnerungen aus fünf Jahrzehnten* (Berlin, 1986)

Kreissler, Felix, *Von der Revolution zur Annexion* (Vienna, 1970)

Kulemann, Peter, *Am Beispiel des Austromarxismus* (Hamburg, 1979)

Lafleur, Ingrun, 'Socialists, Communists and Workers in the Austrian Revolution 1918–19' (unpublished PhD thesis, Columbia University, 1972)

Lackenbacher, Ernst, *Die österreichischen Angestelltengewerkschaften* (Vienna, 1967)

Langewiesche, Dieter, *Zur Freizeit des Arbeiters: Bildungsbestrebungen und Freizeitgestaltungen österreichischer Arbeiter im Kaiserreich und in der Ersten Republik* (Stuttgart, 1979)

Layton, W.T. and Charles Rist, *The Economic Situation of Austria. Report to the League of Nations* (Geneva, 1925)

Lazarsfeld, Paul, 'Dinta', *Arbeit und Wirtschaft*, 1927, p. 438.

Lederer, Max, 'Social Legislation in the Republic of Austria', *International Labour Review*, vol. II, nos. 2–3, May–June 1921, pp. 133–59

Leichter, Käthe, *So Leben Wir. 1320 Industriearbeiterinnen berichten über ihr Leben* (Vienna, 1932)

Leichter, Otto, *Otto Bauer: Tragödie oder Triumph?* (Vienna, 1970)

Leser, Norbert, *Zwischen Reformismus und Bolschewismus: Der Austromarxismus als Theorie und Praxis* (Vienna, 1968: 2nd edn, Vienna, 1985)

Lewis, Jill, 'Red Vienna: Socialism in one city, 1918–27', *European Studies Review*, vol. 13, no. 3, July 1983, pp. 335–54

——, 'Conservatives and Fascists in Austria, 1918–1934', in Martin Blinkhorn (ed.), *Fascists and Conservatives* (London, 1990), pp. 98–117

Löw, Raimund, *Otto Bauer und die russische Revolution* (Vienna, 1980)

Luschin-Ebengreuth, Arnold, *Styria Cut into Pieces* (Graz, 1921)

Macartney, C.A., *The Social Revolution in Austria* (Cambridge, 1926)

Marx, Karl, 'Critique of the Gotha Programme', in *Karl Marx and Friedrich Engels: Selected Works* with an introduction by V.I. Lenin (London, 1968: original edn, Progress Publishers, Moscow), pp. 317–35

März, Eduard, *Austrian Banking and Financial Policy* (New York, 1984)

Mason, Tim, 'National Socialism and the Working Class, 1925–May 1933', *New German Critique*, 11, Spring 1977, pp. 49–93

Massey, Doreen and Richard Meegan, *The Anatomy of Job Losses* (London, 1982)

Mayer, (ed.), *Hundert Jahre österreichische Wirtschaftsentwicklung* (Vienna, 1949)

Messerer, Ingeborg, 'Die Frontkämpfervereiningung Deutsch-Österreich' (unpublished PhD thesis, University of Vienna, 1963)

Mühlberger, Detlev, 'The Sociology of the NSDAP: The Question of Working Class Membership', *Journal of Contemporary History*, vol. 15, no. 3, July 1980

Musil, Robert, *The Man Without Qualities* (2 vols.), trans. Eithne Wilkins and Ernst Kaiser (London, 1979)

Otruba, Gustav, *Österreichs Wirtschaft im 20. Jahrhundert* (Vienna, 1968)

Pauley, Bruce F., *Hahnenschwanz und Hakenkreuz* trans. Peter Aschner (Vienna, 1972)

——, *Hitler and the Forgotten Nazis: A History of Austrian National Socialism* (London, 1981).

Pelinka, A., 'Kommunalpolitik als Gegenmacht: Das "rote Wien" als Beispiel gesellschaftsverändernder Reformpolitik', in K.H. Naßmacher (ed.), *Kommunalpolitik und Sozialdemokratie: Der Beitrag des demokratischen Sozialismus zur Kommunalen Selbstverwaltung* (Bonn, 1977), pp. 63–77

Pfabigan, Alfred (ed.), *Vision und Wirklichkeit. Ein Lesebuch zur Austromarxismus* (Vienna, 1989)

——, and Norbert Leser (eds.), *Max Adler: Ausgewählte Schriften* (Vienna, 1981)

Pferschy, Gerhard, 'Steiermark', in Weinzierl and Skalnik (eds.), *Österreich 1918–38. Geschichte der Ersten Republik* (Vienna, 1983), vol. 2, pp. 939–60

Philippovich, Eugen von, 'Wiener Wohnungsverhältnisse', *Archiv fur soziale Gesetzgebung und Statistik*, vol. 7, 1894

Pirchegger, Hans and Rudolf, Töpfner, *Eisen Immerdar* (Graz, 1951)

Pollard, Sidney and Colin Holmes, *Documents in European Economic History, vol. 2. Industrial Power and National Rivalry* (London, 1972)

Rabinbach, Anson, 'Ernst Fischer and the Left Opposition in Austrian Social Democracy', (unpublished PhD thesis, Madison, Wisconsin, 1973)

——, 'Politics and Pedagogy: The Austrian Social Democratic Youth Movement 1931–32', *Journal of Contemporary History*, 13, no. 2, April 1978, pp. 337–56

Rabinbach, Anson, *The Crisis of Austrian Socialism: from Red Vienna to Civil War 1927–1934* (Chicago, 1983)

——, (ed.), *The Austrian Social Experiment: Social Democracy and Austromarxism, 1918–1934* (Boulder and London, 1985)

Reichl, Sepp, *Der große Aufstieg. Eine Geschichte der arbeitenden Menschen und der Arbeiterbewegung in der Steiermark* (Graz, 1966)

Reventlow, Rolf, *Zwischen Alliierten und Bolschewiken. Arbeiterräte in Österreich 1918–23* (Vienna, 1969)

Rintelen, Anton, *Erinnerungen an Österreichs Weg* (Munich, 1941)

Rosenfeld, Siegfried, 'Die Gesundheitsverhältnisse der industriellen Arbeiterschaft Österreichs während des Kriegs' in Ferdinand Hanusch and Emmanuel Adler (eds.), *Die Regelung der Arbeitsverhältnisse im Kriege* (Vienna, 1927), pp. 419–40

Rothschild, K.W., *Austria's Economic Development between the Two Wars* (London, 1947)

——, 'Wurzeln und Triebkräfte der Entwicklung der österreichischen Wirtschaftsstruktur', in W. Weber (ed.). *Österreichs Wirtschaftsstruktur gestern-heute-morgen, vol. 1.* (Berlin, 1961)

Schacherl, Michael, *Dreißig Jahre der steirischen Arbeiterbewegung, 1890 bis 1920* (Graz, 1931)

Schlicker, Wolfgang, 'Arbeitsdienstbestrebungen des deutschen Monopolkapitals in der Weimarer Republik (unter besonderer Berücksichtigung des Deutschen Instituts für technische Arbeitsschulung)', Jahrbuch für Wirtschaftsgeschichte, 1971/III, pp. 95–101

Schmidlechner, Karin, 'Die Situation der steirischen Industriearbeiter zwischen 1918–1934' (manuscript of social conditions in Styria for the exhibition, 'Für Freiheit, Arbeit und Recht – Die Steirische Arbeiterbewegung zwischen Revolution und Faschismus (1918–38)', coordinator, Robert Hinteregger, February 1984)

Schorske, Carl E., *Fin-de-Siècle Vienna* (London, 1980)

Schwimmer, Walter and Ewald Klinger, *Die Christlichen Gewerkschaften in Österreich* (Vienna, 1975)

Seliger, Maren, 'Zur Politik des "Roten Wien"' in *Traum und Wirklichkeit – Wien 1870–1913* (catalogue of an exhibition by the Historical Museum of the City of Vienna held in the Künstlerhaus, October 1985) (Vienna, 1985) pp. 640–44

Spender, Stephen, '*Vienna*' (London, 1935)

Stadler, Karl, *Austria* (London 1971)

Starhemberg, Ernst Rüdiger, *Between Hitler and Mussolini* (London, 1942)

Stein, Viktor, 'Die Lage der österreichischen Metallarbeiter im Kriege', in Ferdinand Hanusch and Emmanuel Adler et al. (eds.), *Die Regelung der Arbeitsverhältnisse im Kriege* (Vienna, 1927), pp. 222–62

Steiner, Herbert, *Die Arbeiterbewegung Österreichs 1867–1889* (Vienna, 1964)

Stiefel, Dieter, *Arbeitslosigkeit. Soziale, politische und wirtschaftliche Auswirkungen am Beispiel Österreichs, 1918–1933* (Berlin, 1978)

Stone, Katherine, 'The Origins of Job Structure in the Steel Industry,' *Review of Radical Economics*, vol. 6, no. 2, 1974, pp. 61–97

Strakele, Heinz, *Die Österreichische Alpine Montan-Gesellschaft* (Vienna, 1946)

Streeruwitz, Ernst von, *Springflut über Österreich* (Vienna, 1937)

Strong, David F., *Austria (October 1918–March 1919): Transition from Empire to Republic* (New York, 1974)

Turner, Henry Ashby Jr, 'Big Business and the Rise of Hitler', *American Historical Review*, 1969, pp. 56–78

Vlcek, Christine, 'Der Republikanische Schutzbund in Österreich. Geschichte, Aufbau und Organisation' (unpublished PhD thesis, Vienna, 1971)

Bibliography

Wallisch, Paula, *Ein Held stirbt* (Graz, 1946)

Wandruszka, Adam, 'Das "nationale Lager"', in Weinzierl and Skalnik (eds.), *Österreich, 1918–38*, 2 vols. (Vienna, 1983)

Weidenholzer, Josef, *Auf dem Weg zum 'Neuen Menschen' Bildungs- und Kulturarbeit der SDAP in der Ersten Republik* (Vienna, 1981)

Weigl, Karl, 'Die Organisationskrise bei den Wiener Straßenbahnern', *Der Kampf* (XVI) 1923, pp. 220–2

Weihsmann, Helmut, *Das Rote Wien* (Vienna, 1985)

Weinzierl, Erika and Kurt Skalnik (eds.), *Österreich 1918–38. Geschichte der Ersten Republik*, 2 vols. (Vienna, 1983)

Whiteside, Andrew, *The Socialism of Fools: Georg Ritter von Schönerer and Austrian Pan Germanism* (Berkeley, California, 1975)

Index

Index